LIBRARY

D0488165

The Ethnography of Political Violence

Cynthia Keppley Mahmood, Series Editor

A complete list of books in the series is available from the publisher.

Unraveling Somalia

Race, Violence, and the Legacy of Slavery

Catherine Besteman

PENN

University of Pennsylvania Press

Philadelphia

Printed in the United States of America on acid-free paper

10 9 8 7 6 5 4 3 2 1

Published by
University of Pennsylvania Press
Philadelphia, Pennsylvania 19104-4011

Library of Congress Cataloging-in-Publication Data
Besteman, Catherine Lowe.
Unraveling Somalia : race, violence, and the legacy of slavery / Catherine Besteman.
p. cm. — (Ethnography of political violence)
Includes bibliographical references and index.
ISBN 0-8122-3488-X (alk. paper). — ISBN 0-8122-1688-1 (pkb. : alk. paper)
1. Qossoldoor (Somalia)—Politics and government—19th century. 2. Qossoldoor (Somalia)—Politics and government—20th century. 3. Qossoldoor (Somalia)—Ethnic relations—History—19th century. 4. Qossoldoor (Somalia)—Ethnic relations—History—20th century. 5. Gosha (African people)—Somalia—Qossoldoor—19th century. 6. Gosha (African people)—Somalia—Qossoldoor—History—20th century. 7. Slavery—Somalia—Qossoldoor—History—19th century. 8. Slavery—Somalia—Qossoldoor—History—20th century. I. Title. II. Series.
DT409.Q27B47 1999
967.73—dc21 98-33372
CIP

For Jorge, Gabriela, and Darien

Contents

Acknowledgments

Writing this book has shown me how much I still do not know about Somalia and the middle Jubba valley. I've become uncomfortably aware of how many things I overlooked or ignored while in Somalia, of how many questions I forgot to ask or left unpursued, of how many issues I put off for a later time which never came. But for the things I did learn or come to understand—and about which I can confidently write—I am indebted to a great number of people.

I must first thank the Land Tenure Center of the University of Wisconsin, who hired me to study the effects of land registration in Somalia. They paid for my year-long field research and generously continued my salary through the initial period of writing. I was very lucky indeed to be able to work for John Bruce and Michael Roth, whose support, encouragement, and high expectations set a standard for professional research.

I remain deeply indebted to my teachers and mentors at the University of Arizona. The late Robert McC. Netting provided a stellar model of professionalism, scholarly integrity, deep dedication, and good humor which will guide me the rest of my life. Ellen Basso, Dick Henderson, Helen Henderson, and Tad Park taught me the rigors of anthropological theory, research methodology, fieldwork pitfalls and successes, and the value of enduring friendships. Thanks also to Glenn Stone, who pointed me toward fieldwork in Somalia and dissertation support in New Mexico.

In Somalia, I was fortunate to enter a community of dedicated researchers and fieldworkers, who provided support, encouragement, and welcome mats in Mogadishu. Thanks to James and Nancy Merryman, Kathryn Craven, Gus and Marie Tillman, Ian Deshmuck, and Kenneth Menkhaus. I am enduringly grateful for the companionship and assistance my husband and I received from Annie Hellstrom and the Swedish Church Relief in the middle valley. Francesca Declich helped guide me through colonial archives in Italy. I have also benefited greatly from the scholarly activities and expectations of the international community of Somalist scholars. In particular, I have been much inspired by Lee

Cassanelli's prodigious and creative intellectual energies. He read the entire book manuscript, offered trenchant criticisms which forced me into rewrite after rewrite, and provided a model of enthusiasm for debate, critique, and learning. Several other colleagues read portions of this book and provided thoughtful, insightful criticism which encouraged me to rethink or better articulate significant points. In particular, I want to thank David Nugent, James Webb, Roger Sanjek, Ali Jimale Ahmed, Ken Menkhaus and an anonymous reviewer. I'd also like to acknowledge how important a collegial department is for one's scholarship: I have been lucky to work in such departments at both Queens College (CUNY) and Colby College.

The farmers and herders of the middle Jubba valley who taught me about their lives and histories also gave their friendship, trust, endless patience, courage, and poetry. While I owe thanks to hundreds of mid-valley dwellers, I would particularly like to acknowledge Xassan Isaaq Towoqal and his family, Macallin Caddow Nasib, Sheikh Axmed Nur, Iido Rooble, Jimcale Matan Gosar, Cali Osman Iido, Adan Kabirow Boore, Xeffow Yusuf Cali, Binti Dhoore Baraki, Matan Garad Garas, Maxamed Muxumed Maxamed, and Hassan Ibrahim Diriye. I also thank Sheikh Biyoy, Haji Farxaan Abshir, Axmeey Cabdi Xaadle, and Deerow Xassan Dhogor. Cali Ibrahim Axmed, Cabdi Axmed, Maxamed Maxamed Raghe, and Sadiiq Cabdiraxmon Axmed worked tirelessly with me in Loc on all aspects of the research. I am profoundly grateful to them for their substantial contributions to this study.

The research for this book was funded by a variety of institutions, in addition to the Land Tenure Center: a Jacob Javits Fellowship supported my graduate work; the School of American Research supported my dissertation writing with a Weatherhead Fellowship; Sigma Xi, the American Philosophical Society, the National Endowment for the Humanities, PSC-CUNY Research Foundation, and Colby College supported archival and comparative bibliographic work; and Wenner-Gren provided sabbatical support with a Richard Carley Hunt Fellowship. I am extremely grateful to these institutions for their generous funding.

Funding is critical, but so is time to write. I'd like to acknowledge the support I received from my department chair at Queens College, Frank Spencer. Colby College's policy of providing a pre-tenure sabbatical allowed me the time to finish the manuscript. Laurie Besteman and Jack Lauderbaugh provided a warm home for an extended family, companionship, good humor, and great wine for part of my sabbatical. Colby supported excellent summer research assistants who helped with library work: thanks to Karen Fried, Jill Kooyoomjian, Brian Schwegler, Andrew Rice, Pia Rice, and Jenny McElhinney. I am grateful to Suzanne Jones for her technical assistance. Many thanks also to the series editor, Cynthia Mahmood, and to Penn's wonderful editor, Patricia Smith.

It is impossible to express my deep gratitude to my family: my husband and children, and my parents and siblings. My parents taught me a love of learning and inquisitiveness. My children still love books despite the amount of time their mother devoted to this one. My husband, Jorge Acero, shared the fieldwork, took the photographs which grace this book, and encouraged me through every stage of the research and writing; its completion owes as much to his patience and encouragement as to my efforts.

Part I
Introduction

Chapter 1
Somalia from the Margins: An Alternative Approach

A letter arrives, telling me that every child under the age of five was now dead in the Jubba valley village in southern Somalia where I had lived several years previously. The collapse of the Somali state in 1991 ended these young lives in starvation and warfare, opening yet another violent chapter in the short history of the Jubba valley. In just the past 150 years, the people of this valley—most of whom were considered racial minorities within the Somali nation-state—had endured a series of violent encounters that shaped their relationship to the state and to regional Somali society. Such encounters—including enslavement, forced labor on colonial plantations, periodic pastoralist raids, kidnapping by the state military, and forceful land dispossession in the biggest political landgrab in Somali history—presaged their vulnerability in the violence of civil war. When the Somali state collapsed, the people of the Jubba valley disproportionately faced genocidal assault, banditry, and widespread rape. Although the valley's population has been massively reduced through starvation, murder, and flight since 1991, the valley remains one of the most contested areas in the militia wars that continue to plague southern Somalia.

How does a place become so violent? In 1991, journalists, pundits, politicians, and academics groped for metaphors that could simply and concisely explain the warfare. The most persistent and pervasive explanation knit together popular perceptions of "tribalist" Africa with models derived from anthropological descriptions of northern Somali social groups to claim that "ancestral clan hatreds" played out in warfare both caused Somalia's collapse and hindered future state-building efforts. Since I. M. Lewis's (1961) classic book on northern Somali pastoralist social organization first appeared, Somali society has usually been described in academic and popular literature as an egalitarian and ethnically homogenous population of nomadic pastoralists who shared an overarching genealogical system and a common language, culture, and religion. Lewis described Somali society as consisting of six patrilineal clan-families formed by the descendants of mythical Arabic ancestors who arrived in Somalia twenty-five to thirty generations ago. His pioneering work on Somalia explained that each clan-family encompassed a set of patrilineally related clans, subclans, sub-subclans, and lineages. Historically, political activity usually occurred at the level of lineages or groups of lineages tied together by social contracts who collectively paid *diya*, or blood compensation, for wrongs committed by any group member. While clan-families rarely acted as a unit, diya-paying groups and lineages could join forces at higher levels against other groups of lineages for warfare and payment of diya.

Drawing upon this model (called a segmentary lineage structure by specialists), the American media and some academic accounts of Somalia's collapse presented Somalia's destruction as having been almost inevitable. The model of the tensions inherent to this kind of genealogically based system provided an explanation of built-in conflict, making Somali social structure appear fundamentally divisive and resistant to state-building efforts. Journalists' reports portrayed Somalis as continuing to act out Stone Age ancestral clan rivalries, but with Star Wars military technology. Media reports were filled with evocations of ancestral violence: "The clans of Somalia have regularly battled one another into a state of anarchy" (*Time* 1992); "ancient clan enmity pursued with the modern weapons that are so abundant in Somalia is at the root of the country's conflict" (*Washington Post* 1993); "Instead of fighting with traditional spears and shields, the clans have more recently conducted their feuds with mortars and machine guns" (*New York Times* 1992); "the crisis in Somalia has been caused by intense clan rivalries, a problem common in Africa, but here carried out with such violence, there is nothing left of civil society, only anarchy and the rule of the gun" (CNN 1992).[1] In refashioning academic terminology to present a portrait of Somalia's collapse, Somalis became cartoon-like images of primordial man: unable to break out of their destructive spiral of ancient clan rivalries, loyalties, and bloodshed.

This book challenges the prevailing explanation that the violent breakdown of Somali civil and political society was the result of deep clan-based hatreds and ethnic loyalties. Most specifically, it argues that this explanation is inadequate for understanding the most violent areas of contemporary Somalia, such as the Jubba River valley. Taking the Jubba valley as my focus, I suggest that the dissolution of the Somali nation-state can be understood only by analyzing the turbulent history of race, class, and regional dynamics over the past century and a half—processes which produced a deeply stratified and fragmented society.

Over the past several generations a social order emerged in Somalia that was rooted in principles other than just a simple segmentary lineage organization—a social order stratified on the basis of racialized status, regional identities, and control of valuable resources and markets. To understand the 1990s breakdown of the Somali nation-state—and the particular victimization of agricultural southerners during and after dissolution—one must acknowledge the basis and significance of these alternative forms of stratification.

By focusing on one particular community on the margins of Somali society and the Somali nation-state—the people of the Gosha area of the middle Jubba River valley—this book probes the tensions produced by these alternative forms of stratification. I will be looking beyond the fantasy of an ethnically and linguistically homogenous culture to illuminate some of the other critical fracturing points of Somali society. Such fracturing points—of race, class, and region, as well as status, occupation, and language—become clearer when we turn our focus away from the urban elite politics of the center that have dominated both media coverage and scholarly analyses. Scrutinizing the history of the margins can magnify the primary processes shaping the center; looking at state disintegration from the margins of the Jubba valley reveals the dynamism of Somali society (which is left uncaptured in the segmentary lineage model) in general, and illuminates the tense dynamics of racialized identities and stratification, in particular, which were central to state formation in Somalia and which patterned much of the violence of disintegration.

While aiming to illuminate some critical aspects of the state, this book is not an ethnography of the state, of state-building, or of state-collapse; rather it is an ethnography of the local, situated at the margins of the state. Nevertheless, one of my goals is to use the view from the margins to apprehend the institutions, discourses, and forces of the state as well as the tensions and frictions which contributed to the state's collapse. As Michael J. Watts has argued, localities "are always political and struggled over," a fact which allows us to see "locality as a fundamental part of national identity and hence a repository of various rights and memberships that are regularly spoilt and fought over" (1992:121).[2] Looking at the expression of the state on the margins and the way people on the margins experience and imagine the state can, I believe, illuminate its structures of domination, its technologies of power, the effectiveness of its discourses, the nature of its hegemonic representations, and the extent of its popular support. As James Scott has noted, referring to analyses of state collapses: "And whenever . . . the ship of state runs aground on such reefs, attention is usually directed to the shipwreck itself and not to the vast aggregation of petty acts that made it possible" (1985:36).

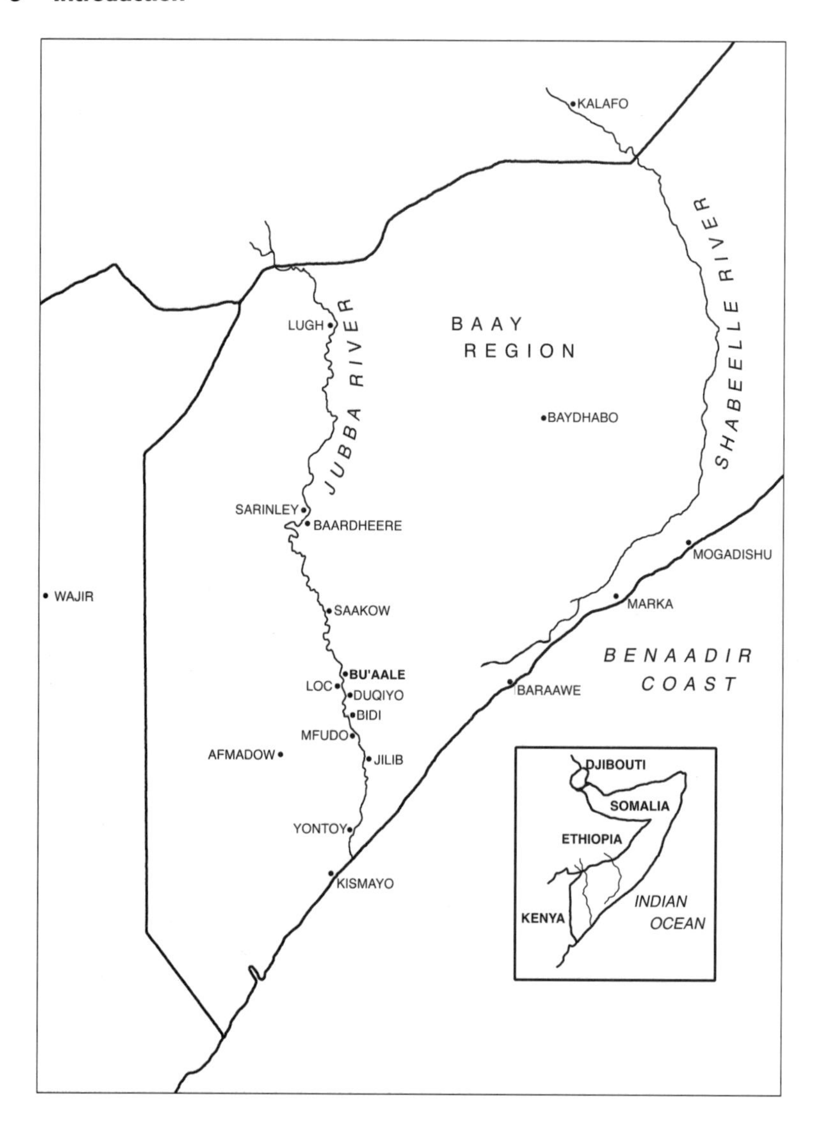

Map 1. The Jubba valley of southern Somalia.

Focusing on the local—where we can perhaps best see the vast aggregation of petty acts—is still, I believe, what anthropologists do best, and what we do better than any other discipline: we can use these strengths of local-level ethnography to analyze and theorize the state.

Some of the major processes that have shaped Somali society and defined its power dynamics are inscribed in the marginal space of the Jubba valley and in the historical experiences of the people who live there. Over the past 150 years, the Jubba valley (Map 1) has been imaginatively constructed and ecologically utilized in a variety of ways by the people who live there, by the Somali national community, by the state, and by foreign authorities and donors. The valley has alternatively been viewed as a refuge, as a frontier, as a dangerous place of magic and sorcery, as a place of fantastic agricultural potential, as a desolate backwater, as a national ecological resource, and, most recently, as one of the premier "shatter zones" *and* valuable prizes in Somalia's civil war. The Jubba valley in the mid-1990s has been the site of massacres, of famine, of years of militia wars, and of a disproportionate outpouring of the surviving local farmers into refugee camps; many of the faces shown on television screens depicting Somalia's tragedy belong to people from the valley. The valley has now emerged as one of the most significant areas of contention, ending a century (or beginning a new century) of land occupation, expropriation, and development plans carried out by colonial governments, by the Somali state, and by international donor agencies.

The people of the Gosha have participated in, been subjected to, supported, and struggled with the significant cultural, political, and economic changes sweeping through the Horn of Africa in the past century. Their ancestors, taken from the area stretching between contemporary Kenya to Mozambique, arrived in Somalia in the nineteenth century as slaves to work on Somali-owned plantations producing cash crops for export. After escaping as fugitives or being manumitted as Muslim converts, these former slaves settled the uninhabited forests of the Jubba River valley. Twentieth-century Gosha history reflects key elements of the national experience: Gosha communities had their land taken over by colonial plantations and their bodies claimed for colonial forced-labor schemes, they lost complete rights to their land through socialist-inspired nationalization laws after independence, experienced the speculatory effects of a 1980s capitalist-inspired commodification of land, and suffered from phenomenal Cold War–linked state militarization. Although discriminated against as a racial minority on the basis of their "Bantu" heritage since their arrival in Somalia, Gosha people have throughout this tumultuous history continuously struggled to define their identity and a legitimate place within Somali society, using Islam, kinship, and economic relations as their tools.

The historical experience of the people living in the Gosha brings into relief the critical significance of racial and growing class distinctions in Somali society during the twentieth century. Because their status as racial minorities took precedence over their lineage and clan affiliations, the Gosha peoples' history offers a window into the ways that

Somali society was stratified by constructions other than clan. Their increasing economic marginalization reveals the basis of emerging class stratification in southern Somali society during this century. By tracing historically the creation of "the Gosha" as a large, subordinate (and disparate) group in southern Somalia, this study highlights the problematic and contingent nature of "ethnic consciousness," identity politics, and class formation. Trying to understand the brutal victimization of Gosha farmers since 1991 highlights the tragic cultural logic informing race, class, and regional dynamics in contemporary Somalia.[3]

Despite its often chaotic appearance, violence is never simply anarchic, but rather is informed by a particular logic and a sense of purpose. "For analysts of specific cultures and places," suggests Kay Warren, "the imperative is to dispel the view that violence is inherently chaotic and irrational by tracing the implications of particular forms of domination, resistance, and violence" (1993a:3). Also invoking culture and history—and thereby challenging anthropologists—Fernando Coronil and Julie Skurski (1991) argue that political violence can be understood only by attending to the specific historical context of social relations, cultural forms, and memory in violent places.[4] While we may lack the ability to "explain" the ruthlessness of violence, people participating in violence often do have at least a momentary sense of what they're doing. What appears senseless is often informed by a particular sensibility that emerges in particular historically conditioned moments and is shaped by particular cultural practices and ideologies. While the act of violence may remain ultimately unapprehendable, we can seek to understand the historical and cultural tensions that surround that act and provide it with meaning. Although this book is not an ethnography of Somalia's disintegration, taking a good look at some of the heretofore relatively masked aspects of cultural and social stratification in Somalia will, I hope, take us part of the way toward a better understanding of the historically produced social relations that have patterned much of the postcollapse violence in southern Somalia.

* * *

This book also examines the thorny problem of how to understand the widely experienced simultaneity of domination and resistance, subjugation and collusion. Analyzing Gosha peoples' historical experiences illuminates the position of subjugated peoples living within structures of domination which define the hegemonic terrain of morality, social identity, and appropriation. This book attempts to interrogate history in order to understand how an ideology of hierarchy which assigned a denigrated, subordinate status for Gosha peoples was constructed and symbolically represented, morally legitimized, and materially enacted in Somali culture and society. Apprehending the structures of domination also means recognizing the contours of collusion: how people in the Gosha simultaneously resisted the ideological basis of denigration—which subjugated them as "slaves," "Bantus," and low status farmers—while accepting as legitimate the hegemonic Somali social order based on kinship.

As I will argue below, despite their denigrated position within Somali society most Gosha people did not view themselves as any kind of recognizable ethnic group set on a course of resistance against the society that denigrated them. To the contrary, rather than fostering a group sense of cultural distinctiveness and subjugation, most Gosha villagers oriented their cultural practices and identity politics toward dominant Somali patterns. A central question of this book is how to understand Gosha peoples' choices to participate within and actively seek incorporation into a society which subjugated them, and how to understand their creative ability to manage the juxtaposition of domination and accommodation.

Gosha peoples' historical experiences firmly situated them at the intersection of racial hierarchies, class stratification, the hegemonic Somali kinship system, and state politics—a tension-filled space within which they negotiated a personal politics of identity, culture, and social relations. Understanding this space, which will occupy us in Part III, reveals the mutually constitutive dimensions of culture, identity, and politics. Seeing in Gosha experiences the processes of nation-building and state dissolution in Somalia, we can probe the critical links between cultural struggle, identity politics, class, and the state that exists throughout Africa.

For decades, anthropologists have grappled with the concept of identity, as we have argued over how to define it, how to identify it, where to locate it (assuming it is a single entity, which we cannot). Responses to these questions have variably addressed the political and cultural dimensions of identity, usually reformulated as ethnicity. The 1970s and 1980s marked a turn in our disciplinary approach to studying ethnicity/identity, when anthropologists began rejecting earlier assumptions of cultural/ethnic primordialism/essentialism to emphasize instead the fluid and situational aspects of ethnic identity, where people made choices about their ethnic identities in different sociopolitical contexts.[5] While transformative for the understanding of identity formation, this situational or constructionist approach often lacked sufficient attention to the role of political struggle and state-formation in setting constraints, delimiting options, or defining the possible in the shaping of identity.[6]

The rise of a political economy focus in anthropology in the late 1970s and early 1980s, together with a growing postcolonial acknowledgment of colonialism's impact on our anthropological "subjects," spawned a view of contemporary ethnicity/tribalism as the result of the political economy of colonial rule[7]—a realization first suggested by an earlier generation of anthropologists.[8] Writing from a similar perspective influenced by political economy, others suggested contemporary forms of tribalism or ethnicity resulted from violent warfare in the context of European expansion.[9] Applying the lens of political economy has allowed some scholars to explain local forms of ethnicity as a creation of global capitalism played out in local contexts through labor relations,[10] or to emphasize how the semantics of primordial sentiments are situationally used to generate ethnic cohesion in the context of warfare, violent competition, and global capitalism.[11] Most recently, scholars have highlighted the role of the postcolonial state in directly fostering ethnic identities and ethno-nationalisms through authoritarian rule, unequal distributions of resources, and polarized competition for political power to explain rising ethnic tensions, violence, and aggressive new nationalisms in eastern Europe,[12] Africa,[13] and elsewhere. Again transformative in our understanding of ethnicity, tribalism, and identity because of their attention to the state and global capitalism, such approaches have been critiqued for their lack of attention to the role of (local) culture in identity formation.[14]

Another dimension of identity, racial constructions, has recently reemerged from hiding after a long period of prominence in anthropology. After ignoring the concept of race for decades because of our inability to define it, our discomfort with it, and perhaps because of its politicized close-to-home associations,[15] anthropologists are once again confronting the significance of racial constructions in identity politics and the complex dialectic of race and class.[16] The politicized and persistent recognition of racialized identities offers the strongest critique of the situational view of ethnicity (one cannot always situationally shift one's racial identity) and the most forceful evidence of the political dimensions of identity.

For me, this academic heritage has clarified that cultural identities and practices of the subaltern result from how people construct themselves as cultural beings within fields of power shaped and directed mostly by others—whether colonial, ethnic, class, or political others. The cultural content of these identities—how people define themselves and their history—is shaped in particular political moments, under particular historical conditions, as a result of particular historical experiences, and in the memory of particular historical nightmares (to borrow Karl Marx's [(1852) 1973:146] much borrowed image).[17] In order to apprehend how cultural identities take shape within historical and political moments, we need to study, in the words of William Roseberry and Jay O'Brien, "the *context* of inequality and contestation; the *process* of struggle and the place of naturalized and oppositional historical images within it; and the *production* of historical images themselves" (1991:12, italics in original). We need to focus on the intersection of identity, culture, and politics in the living of daily life and to recognize how historical experiences get reworked within this intersection in meaningful ways which shape cultural practices and beliefs, political struggles, and the ways groups of people represent themselves and are represented by others.

Identities take shape from cultural content within political fields of unequal power; culture affects and is affected by political struggles over signifying, representing, and providing meaning for identities. Groups of people incessantly shape and reshape their cultures and identities in dialogue with the state, the nation, and nation-state hegemonies.[18] Historical memories, historical consciousnesses, and historical knowledges saturate these mutually constituting processes. People in the Gosha lived every day in the midst of memories of particular historical nightmares; one goal of this book is to analyze the changing significance of these nightmares in shaping the confluence of identity, politics, and culture in their lives.

* * *

Before moving on to the central arguments of the book, in the remainder of this chapter I provide an overview of the past century of Somali political history.[19]

In the imperial era of the late nineteenth century, Britain, Italy, France, and Ethiopia subdivided the territory inhabited by Somalis—people self-identified as members of the Somali genealogy traced to common ancestors—among their governments. In the division of Somali territory, Britain claimed two areas of Somali-inhabited territory; the northern coast and inland area along the Gulf of Aden inhabited by pastoralist Somalis became British Somaliland and the area west of the Jubba River, also inhabited by pastoralist Somalis as well as by farmers on the west bank of the river, became part of the Northern Frontier District of British Kenya. Agricultural, agropastoral, and pastoralist southern Somalis from the east bank of the Jubba River to the boundary with British Somaliland found themselves living in Italian Somalia. In 1925 Britain ceded to Italy much of Somali-inhabited territory west of the Jubba, drawing a boundary between Italian Somalia and British Kenya's Somali-inhabited Northern Frontier District. A British military administration took over southern Somalia following Italy's defeat in World War II until 1950, when southern Somalia was returned to Italy (against much local opposition) as a United Nations trusteeship. Independence in 1960 united into one nation the southern Italian colony and northern British Somaliland, although the maintenance of colonial boundaries with French Djibouti, Kenya, and Ethiopia left much Somali-inhabited territory within these neighboring states. The colonial legacy of illegitimate boundaries took on enormous significance in a pastoral economy where family members were separated from each other and from critical grazing areas. Furthermore, different colonial histories, languages, and political systems contributed to continuing regional distinctions in the postcolonial era.

The decade following independence was marked by increasingly fragmented politics, as Somalis splintered into dozens of clan-based political parties that drew support from a patronage system well maintained by massive injections of foreign aid. In 1969, army officer Siyad Barre led a successful coup that overthrew the postcolonial parliamentary democracy, and established rule by the Barre-led Supreme Revolutionary Council under the banner of "scientific socialism," which Barre defined as a commitment to equality, economic independence, and economic growth.[20] The political intricacies of Barre's rule have been explored elsewhere;[21] a brief overview must suffice here. With substantial military aid from the Soviet Union through the mid-1970s, Barre embarked on a set of ambitious programs to foster nationalist sentiment and consolidate state power. One of Barre's earliest acts was to abolish "tribalism" through outlawing the recognition of clan distinctions, ethnic distinctions, patron-client relationships, and any other formal relationships based on social inequality. Siyad explained this drastic decree as a step toward nationalist unity that would nurture economic, political, and social "progress" through erasing social inequalities, clan conflicts, and loyalties built along clan or ethnic lines. Many Somalis initially welcomed this political ideology, probably in part because of their desire to move beyond the kind of clan politics that had characterized the post-independence parliamentary democracy of the 1960s.[22]

To ensure that the populace followed the law and gave their loyalty only to the state, Barre developed several branches of the government police and judiciary structure to oversee, adjudicate, and punish disloyalty or "treason" under the National Security Laws of 1970. The National Security Service (NSS) investigated all suspected security offenses, maintained its own detention centers, and became "the main agency supplying defendants for trial in the National Security Courts" (I. M. Lewis 1988:213). Lewis describes how the NSS and the National Security Courts "jointly dealt with a wide range of 'political' offences including nepotism and tribalism . . . as well as with such charges as 'lack of revolutionary zeal' and treason. Members of the National Security Service, under a Sandhurst and K.G.B.-trained commander, enjoyed arbitrary powers of arrest, sometimes following the denunciation of a suspect by his personal enemies. Members of the public services were kept under surveillance and N.S.S. reports played an important part in promotion and demotion" (1988:212).

The NSS and National Security Courts reported directly to the president, as did the police, the prisons, the military police (who also served as the presidential guard), the military intelligence service, and the militia-styled Victory Pioneers (civilians who were to maintain revolutionary fervor and who could arrest suspects for the NSS; Rakiya Omaar [1992:231] likened them to Haiti's Tontons Macoute).[23] Amnesty International summarized the "enormous powers" thus held by the president: "The President is in direct control of all facets of state power, including the security institutions and all branches of the judiciary, and the Constitution is so drafted that no provision obstructs his exercise of all decision-making should he wish it" (1990:9). In addition to these policies and institutions designed to oversee and maintain ideological control, Barre introduced a torrent of laws and policies to abolish local forms of authority and leadership—in control over land, water, health, marriage, inheritance, mediation, commerce, production, speech, political participation, and the media—and replace them with state control. Public executions of prominent secular and religious people who spoke out against the regime and its new policies sent unequivocal messages of the fate awaiting those who did not support the government, its ideological orientation, and its laws.

As part of his scientific socialist package, Barre inaugurated a variety of social programs to support his nationalist vision of an egalitarian country united behind his leadership. His 1973–75 literacy campaign established the first written script for Somali and sent students and civil servants throughout the countryside to teach Somali citizens to read. He targeted women's participation in nation-building by establishing a national organization for women that provided social programs and revolutionary teaching to women, by introducing new laws governing marriage, divorce, and inheritance which gave women greater individual rights backed by the state rather than their kin, and by outlawing the universal practice of female infibulation. He established "orientation centers" throughout the country where people could learn about the revolution, where marriages were to take place, and where rituals supporting his revolutionary aims could be staged. He mandated the participation of the citizenry in public displays of revolutionary fervor, including marches, dances, songs, and poems which proclaimed him the "Father" of the nation, associated him with great Somali leaders of the past who Barre claimed had fought against external enemies on behalf of the Somali nation, identified him as part of "the new holy trinity" of Marx, Lenin, and Barre (I. M. Lewis 1988:211), and praised his leadership by elaborating a "vigorous personality cult" (Omaar 1992:231) around his image as head of nation and state.

One of his greatest nationalist aspirations was to unite Somalis throughout the Horn into one expanded nation-state. Following the fall of Ethiopia's Emperor Haile Selassie, the Somali-inhabited Ogaadeen region claimed by Ethiopia became the focus of his most intensive irredentist effort. Somalia invaded the Ogaadeen in 1977 to reclaim Somali territory from Ethiopian control, but was forced to retreat when the Soviets (and Cubans) backed the new Marxist Ethiopian government with massive military support against the Somali incursion. Following Somalia's defeat and retreat in early 1978, Barre all but severed links with Moscow and distributed arms among the civilian population of the north for self-protection against Ethiopian incursion across the disputed border.[24]

Many observers see the loss of the Ogaadeen war as the beginning of Barre's declining popularity, loss of ideological vision, increasing manipulation of clan politics, and rising tactics of state repression. Nationalist spirit, at its height during the early months of the Ogaadeen war,[25] began to disintegrate in the face of economic crisis, political insecurity, state repression, and lack of ideological leadership. The Somali government had lost the military and economic support of its superpower patron and had drained state coffers for the war effort. Refugees poured into northern Somalia, making further demands on state resources exhausted by the war and creating tensions among northerners over access to land and water. Domestic politics dissolved into "blame and recriminations as to who lost the Ogaadeen" (Cassanelli 1993a:13). An unsuccessful coup against Barre led by military officers of the Majeerteen clan resulted in a purge of the military, the formation in exile of a Majeerteen clan-based anti-Barre guerrilla group, the tightening of domestic security, a reshuffling of government officials, and a consolidation of control over government institutions by Barre and his closest relatives.

Over the next decade, two significant trends came to dominate the political economy of Somalia: (1) a massive influx of foreign aid, and (2) a virtually complete disintegration of popular trust in the government as a result of flagrant human rights abuses, state-backed terror, unpredictable political appointments and demotions, and the increasing concentration of state power by a small circle of Barre's relatives and supporters.

In the aftermath of the breakdown in relations between Somalia and the Soviet Union, Barre sought support from the other global superpower, the United States. Cold War geopolitics provoked U.S. interest in Somalia, which was seen as strategic because of its proximity to the Middle East and the Persian Gulf.[26] The late 1970s saw the fall of the Shah of Iran, the humiliating takeover of the U.S. embassy in Iran by revolutionaries, and the U.S. perception of a growing Soviet influence in the Gulf area.[27] In order to maintain military bases in Somalia that could monitor affairs in the Gulf, the United States government provided $163.5 million in military technology and four times that much in economic aid during 1980–88.[28] By the late 1980s, Somalia was receiving 20 percent of U.S. aid to Africa.[29] The growing U.S. interest in Somalia accompanied large influxes of foreign funds from other donors to alleviate the refugee crisis and to welcome Somalia into the anticommunist fold. Throughout the 1980s donor funding to Somalia soared into the *billions* with contributions from Italy, Britain, Germany, and Saudi Arabia (as well as from China, who had provided economic support to Somalia since Barre's rise to power). The value of arms alone imported by Somalia during the two decades of Barre's rule totaled nearly two billion dollars.[30] The United Nations High Commission for Refugees (UNHCR) spent hundreds of millions of dollars to maintain refugee camps for those displaced by the Ogaadeen war.

In the context of huge foreign aid support, growing popular dissension against his government, domestic tensions in the wake of the war, and the influx of millions of refugees, Barre seemed to abandon his vision of socialist development, equality, and nationalist unity by increasingly utilizing terror and repression to retain personal power and personal control over state resources, including the distribution of foreign aid funds. By the early 1980s, the Somali state was one of the most militarized in Africa, having grown from 3,000 troops at independence to "a suffocating 120,000" by 1982 (Adam 1995:71). In Hussein Adam's words, "The army of liberation had been converted to a huge army of repression" (1995:71). In tandem with state militarization, Barre began to concentrate power in the hands of a small circle of supporters drawn largely from the clans of his father (Marehan), his mother (Ogaadeen), and his son-in-law, the head of the NSS (Dulbahante) (all part of the Darood clan-family). As head of state, he controlled most of the lucrative resources of his country (such as foreign aid, refugee relief, and land, as well as political appointments), and his redistribution of these resources to political supporters came to be popularly perceived as overtly clan-based rather than ideologically socialist. The prominence of Marehan, Ogaadeen, and Dulbahante clan members in his government was reflected in the "clandestine code name 'M.O.D.' given to the regime. . . . Although no-one could utter the secret symbol of General Siyad [Barre]'s power openly, the M.O.D. basis of his rule was public knowledge and discussed and criticized in private" (I. M. Lewis

1988:221–22). Ever the political strategist, however, Barre ensured that any perceived M.O.D. favoritism was offset by other political appointments and demotions which kept people uncertain about the requisites for success in the Somali government. As Lee Cassanelli explains,

> The President did not want to turn the struggle into one of his own Mareehan (with its Dulbahante and Ogaadeen allies) against a series of united clan opponents. From the beginning, and continuing even into the mid-1980s, the President sought to distribute favors to erstwhile representatives of every clan. Acknowledged (even by his avowed enemies) as a master manipulator of the country's byzantine internal politics, Siyad consistently managed to isolate influential individuals while wooing less prominent rivals from the same clan. He was able to coopt many with funds and contracts his regime was accumulating from the substantial foreign relief assistance and military operations in Somalia. Each individual who joined the President's fold was expected to bring the support of his lineage or sub-clan with him. (1993a:16)

Such political practices produced a "pattern of uncertain promotion and demotion as members of a rotating elite [became resigned to a] trajectory [which] extended from prison through ambassadorships to ministerial office" (I. M. Lewis 1988:250).

The perception of a highly unequal distribution of state resources based on clan favoritism, combined with the overall sense of personal insecurity generated by the pervasive security system and the unpredictable pattern of political appointments and imprisonments, began to have effects most clearly in the north, where state-backed Ogaadeen refugees were beginning to challenge Isaaq dominance.[31] By the late 1980s, Barre policies in the north following the loss of the Ogaadeen war had begun breeding revolt among the Isaaq, the largest northern clan-family, who felt excluded from politics and state resources.[32] Barre's efforts to wrest away control over livestock exports and *qat* (a popular narcotic) sales from Isaaq merchants and entrepreneurs,[33] and his resettlement of Ogaadeeni refugees in Isaaq-dominated territory, were seen in general as part of a continuing subversion of northern interests by a southern-dominated government,[34] and in particular as an attempt to undermine the economic and political strength of the Isaaq clan-family.[35] This "growing sense of Isaaqi alienation" (I. M. Lewis 1994:179) prompted Isaaqs and others in exile to form a resistance group, the Somali National Movement (SNM), against Barre's government.

Following his inability to fully control the lucrative northern commerce in qat and livestock and aware of growing Isaaq-led challenges to his authority, Barre embarked on a variety of harsher measures against Isaaqs in the north that contributed to further tensions between refugee Ogaadeenis and resident Isaaqs. The Somali government armed Ogaadeeni refugees, conscripted refugees into the military to be used as soldiers against Isaaqs, and encouraged Ogaadeeni refugees to claim the property of displaced Isaaqs.[36] The SNM's low-grade guerrilla war against the government culminated in several attacks on UNHCR refugee camps for Ogaadeenis and on government installations in the north in 1988. Barre responded in a series of "savage counterinsurgency tactics" (Human Rights Watch 1989:22), ordering the bombing and strafing of northern towns, villages, rural encampments, and even people fleeing on foot.[37] In its retaliatory attacks, the government killed tens of thousands of its own people; almost half a million northern Somalis fled from Barre's repression into Ethiopia, and over half a million were displaced within the north.[38]

By the final years of the 1980s when the Somali state began to wage open war against its own citizens, its international patrons could no longer ignore the fact that foreign aid supported Somalia's extreme militarization and state repression. Amnesty International's 1988 report documented "a persistent and long established pattern of gross violations of fundamental human rights" (Amnesty International 1988:2) in which detentions, summary trials, executions, and routine torture were normal state procedure.[39] That same year, Barre replaced the top officials "of all the ministries where there was money to be made" with Marehan clan members (Rawson 1994:157), further (and flagrantly) consolidating control over state resources and information in the hands of his closest relatives and supporters. By the late 1980s, Barre's personal control of information (through his well-developed security system), state resources, political appointments, and the military/judiciary allowed him to become "a tyrant" (Adam 1995:71), or in the words of another analyst, a modern day sultan—"a ruler who makes no attempt to restrain from the abuse of force" (Compagnon 1992:8).

By 1989 the series of reports from international human rights organizations documenting the regime's massacres, human rights abuses, and torture practices finally forced the United States to sharply reduce aid to Somalia, a decision made easier by the American "victory" in the Cold War. During the next two years, the insurrection begun by the SNM in the north spread south, as the anti-Barre United Somali Congress (USC) of the central area, formed in 1989, joined the fight to overthrow the Siyad regime. Although these resistance groups are usually identified as representing particular clans, they were formed in exile—the USC in Rome and the SNM in London[40]—pointing to the connection between colonial history and regional identity. Nevertheless, the explicit clan basis of many of the resistance movements of the 1990s helped to establish the primacy of a kinship-based explanation of Somalia's disintegration.

Siyad Barre's regime fell in 1991. Following Barre's 1991 flight south from Mogadishu, southern Somalia degenerated into a war between resistance leaders and their followers over power and between dozens of factions over food, water, and political alliances, which seemed to shift daily. The intensified fighting during the final period of Barre's regime, combined with drought conditions, and the scorched-earth campaign undertaken by Barre to prevent pursuit as he fled the capital, led to the immediate displacement of farmers from their lands and undercut food production in the agriculturally important area between the Jubba and Shabeelle rivers.[41] Eyewitness reports of the warfare in southern Somalia following Barre's flight describe the massive and brutal victimization of the Jubba valley farmers. They were among the earliest victims of warfare, looting, and famine;[42] a report from July 1991 explained that "The Gosha have been hit harder by looting than any other social group in the area; only recently have they also been the targets of widespread physical violence" (Menkhaus 1991). For the next several years, the people of the agriculturally productive Jubba valley were "repeatedly victimized by the scorched-earth tactics of the . . . militias as their forces looted livestock, seeds, tools, and grain, destroyed water sources, raped the women and killed the men" (Prendergast 1994a). As in Bosnia, widespread rape emerged as a powerfully violent and brutally denigrating form of violence against thousands of Jubba valley villagers.[43] Warfare between competing militias raged back and forth across the interriverine "triangle of death," forcing farmers off the land because of widespread and constant looting of farming villages.[44] "With each advance or retreat, marauding armies and their thousands of armed camp followers looted and pillaged without restraint. . . . Destruction was systematic, with wells, ponds, grain stores, seeds and livestock consumed, carried off, killed, or destroyed" (Shields 1993:39). Mortality rates from fighting and famine in the Jubba valley soared during 1991–92, prompting an Oxfam official to describe the middle valley as "one big graveyard" (quoted in Prendergast 1994b:12). By the middle of 1992, most of the valley population had died or had fled to refugee camps within Somalia or in Kenya. Many became "boat people," setting out in overloaded boats to seek asylum on the Kenyan coast—or to drown. A World Concern survey in mid-1993 suggested that the ratio of children under the age of five in the middle valley was as low as 8 percent.

In 1992 the United Nations stepped in and began negotiations between warring factions, and the United States sent in troops in a highly publicized effort to secure food supplies for starving refugees. The north had seceded along the earlier boundary of British colonial rule to form its own independent country. Food relief became a significant commodity in the war-torn south. The "warlords" were able to maintain their power grip through their control of large stocks of weapons, which were used to acquire food.[45] After using their arms to cut off the food supply and to undermine the ability of people to produce their own food in areas they wished to bring under their sphere of influence, the warlords turned to looting food relief as a strategy to finance the extensive patronage system on which they relied.[46] "Bantu" refugees—the Gosha peoples of the Jubba valley—again became targets, as warlords and their militias looted their food relief, just as they had earlier looted their homes, their underground silos, their maturing crops, and their villages.[47]

By the mid-1990s, tens of thousands of people from the Jubba valley had died in the fighting or from starvation, tens of thousands still inhabited refugee camps within Somalia or in Kenya, thousands were seeking asylum in Tanzania, and many were trying to return to their devastated villages, avoiding land mines on the way, to reclaim their land from occupying militia forces. They had become a massively displaced population.

* * *

This trajectory of events, well-documented by the media as an outsider's coherent narrative view of Somalia's political history, established the predominance of a clan-based explanation of state dissolution. Siyad Barre's manipulation of clan relations, the clan basis of the guerrilla groups, and the appeal to clan sentiment for recruitment by "warlords" or militia leaders contributed to the perception that clan loyalties had brought down the Somali nation-state. The emphasis on the power of kinship and the solidarity of lineages captures an important reality in Somali society. No one will deny the existence of lineages in Somali society, nor their importance to personal identity. To be sure, people living under the terror of a collapsing state sought refuge in social networks with great emotional bonds—ties of kinship—and some killings were clan-oriented revenge killings. It is true that much of the recent fighting between the so-called warlords has taken place between groups pulled together on the basis of clan affiliations. Using the sentiment of clan (in addition to the promise of booty and food) to rally support has apparently been a useful strategy for Somalia's warring factions. The various larger militias claimed to be representing clan interests, and many Somalis living in exile are quite divided by clan affiliations.

However, a unitary focus on clan rivalry as the destructive force fueling genocidal conflict and state disintegration in Somalia overlooks the many other aspects of Somali society, politics, and history that informed people's daily lives prior to 1991. It also fails to explain why clan tensions should suddenly erupt on so grand a scale and with such brutal devastation, apparently for the first time in history.[48] The academic literature on precollapse southern Somali society offers a plethora of examples of other aspects of Somali social life that are ignored in the focus on "primordialist" clan sentiment; let us briefly review some of them.

First, while lineages have long been part of Somali society, they have never been rigidly inflexible or primordial. Rather, Somalis historically used this system to ensure flexibility in times of stress. In spite of the implication of primordial clan/lineage identities, Somali clan membership is not irrevocably ascribed at birth. Movement between Somali clans was not only possible, but was particularly widespread in the populous southern interriverine area (the area between the Jubba and Shabeelle river valleys). People switched clan affiliation for protection, for marriage, for grazing or land rights, for labor, for political reasons, or for other personal reasons. Some clans, especially those in the south, had more members who were adopted than members who were descended from the purported founding ancestor! (Helander 1996, 1988, I. M. Lewis 1971). These facts indicate an enormous flexibility in the Somali clan system, especially in southern Somalia. In short, there was nothing necessarily primordial about clan membership. Explaining conflict in Somalia as a result of ancient and deep clan hostilities overlooks the significance of the well-documented flexibility and situational mobility in the Somali kinship system. We will see how ex-slaves and their descendants used this flexibility to claim membership in Somali society.

Furthermore, revisionist ethnographic studies of such lineage classics as the Nuer and the Tallensi (see Kuper 1982, Southall 1986, Verdon 1982) suggest that the anthropological vision of a segmentary lineage structure has ignored the important role of people related by marriage in addition to those related through the male blood line, and of neighborhood and village ties in addition to kinship, for mobilization and action. Certainly, the segmentary lineage model when applied to Somalia cannot take account of the importance of the variety of kinship ties (see Barnes 1994, Helander 1988 for examples of these ties), nor the role of neighborhood and village ties in limiting clan solidarity in the daily practice of social life. Rural agricultural and agropastoral villages typically contained people from a number of clans; decisions about land and water use were made by village committees, not clan councils. Further undermining the claim of primordial clan sentiment and rivalries is the fact that, historically, kinship-based political activity was conducted at the local—not national—level among small territorial and kinship-based networks. Recall that lineages or groups of lineages tied together by social contracts have historically been responsible for political activity, primarily by mediating disputes and alliances through managing the collective payment and receipt of compensation, called *diya.* In southern Somalia, one's primary political affinities were held at the village and diya-group level—villages could function as diya-paying groups, even if villagers were members of different kinship-based diya groups—not at the clan or clan-family level. The recent civil war marks the first time that Somalis have experienced conflict on the clan-family level throughout the nation, indicating that, far from repeating an age-old pattern of clan conflict, something entirely new was happening.

Third, significant numbers of Somali citizens were not members of any clan: people of Arab-Persian heritage had lived in the coastal cities for centuries, Islamic Somali-speaking people of slavery heritage (the focus of this book) had lived in the river valleys for generations, and Islamic Somali-speaking people of non-Somali ancestry lived (most recently as clients to Somali lineages) along the Shabeelle River valley for centuries. Somali society also contained "out-caste" groups identified by their ancestry and/or occupation, only some of which were associated with particular clans, while others lived outside the clan system altogether. The existence of these social groups adds greater complexity to Somali society than that suggested by a segmentary lineage model. Their role in Somali society, in the Somali state, and in the state's collapse is left unacknowledged in the focus on segmentary lineages, and yet these groups were some of the most victimized in the violence of disintegration.

Status differences based on perceptions of racial heritage and occupation also divided Somali society. Such status differences marked those of slavery heritage (considered "Bantu") in particular, as we shall see in the following chapters, but they also marked regional differences as well. Those Somalis who held a racial identity of "Bantu," whether clan members or not, were historically discriminated against socially and marginalized politically. Within Somali clans, adopted members of "Bantu" ancestry held a lower status; among clans, the clans of the south that absorbed (or were believed to have absorbed) large numbers of "Bantus" or Oromos were considered lower status in the national arena. Compounding the implications for status of "impure" ancestry is the fact that a substantial population of southerners practice agriculture—considered by many Somalis an occupation inferior to nomadic pastoralism—and speak a distinct dialect of Somali, *Af-maay-maay*, which was ignored when "standard" Somali became the official language of the state. The combined factors of language, racial constructions, and occupation served as regional distinctions which divided the Somali "nation." The segmentary lineage model ignores these distinctions.

Moving away from ethnographic particulars, analyzing the Somali conflict speaks to more general theoretical concerns about defining and understanding "tribal"/ethnic warfare. Recent arguments over the roots of tribal warfare demand that we acknowledge the impact of the global political economy, trade, capitalism, class stratification, and state formation on what appears to be ethnically motivated strife among "tribal" peoples.[49] These arguments suggest that tribal warfare—from Africa to Amazonia—emerges in the context of expanding states. Such a formulation begs the question of situations where tribal warfare appears to occur in the context of shattering states, such as in Somalia. As Anna Simons has argued, making sense of Somalia's dissolution should be part of the greater anthropological concern with, on the one hand, theorizing the global disintegration of nation-states and, on the other, intervening on behalf of segments that are being wiped out by the violence of dissolution, "segments of society and cultures we purport to care so much about" (1994:822).

An additional problem with the segmentary lineage model is its inability to explain why so much of the destruction, the militia wars, the looting, and the killings have occurred in the farming regions of the south. The analytical focus on urban-based clan politics—the careful academic scrutiny of political appointments and relationships among urban elite individuals and groups—has shifted attention away from the rural areas of the country whose resources and inhabitants bore the brunt of the violence of disintegration. In this book I am calling for a fuller recognition of the actual resources involved in the struggles for state power, the relationships defining rights over resources, and the central role of land as a state resource. In so doing I will be arguing against the view that the warfare that raged across the southern "triangle of death" was a simple "war over resources" in which clans fought to claim land. Instead, I suggest that this scenario resulted from a much more complex set of relationships and power hierarchies that defined rights to land, access to agricultural technology, and control of production, and that affected (and will continue to affect) Somalia's ability to meet its food needs.[50] Looking carefully at struggles over land resources reveals the inadequacy of viewing clan enmities as the single most important factor causing the collapse of the Somali state.

These are some of the immediately apparent shortcomings with explaining Somalia's destruction as a result of primordial clan hatreds finding violent expression through the divisions inherent to a segmentary lineage system. The following chapters, which focus explicitly on the middle Jubba valley, will further explore these alternative facets of Somali society (as well as others) in order to probe how the confluence of localized politics, nation-state policies, and international involvement have affected patterns of violence in southern Somalia. In so doing, the book argues that racialized status hierarchies, global geopolitics, and late twentieth-century political economic transformations contributed far more to southern Somalia's destruction than "ancestral clan tensions."

* * *

Following Chapter 2, which describes my fieldwork, Part II integrates colonial archival materials with oral histories I collected in the valley to build a picture of nineteenth- and early twentieth-century slavery, kinship organization, stratification, and identity politics in southern Somalia. This historical narrative details the settling of the Jubba valley and the construction of Gosha communities within Somali society. In addition to providing necessary background information for the remainder of the book, I also aim in Chapters 3 and 4 to contribute to our expanding historical knowledge of the Jubba valley and the people who live there.

These two chapters introduce several primary themes that will be revisited and developed from different angles throughout the book. The first theme is the transformation of space caused by the entry of ex-slaves into the Jubba valley. In claiming the Jubba valley as their refuge and establishing the valley as a place of agricultural productivity, ex-slaves initiated a significant historical transformation in which the valley became, in turn, a target of colonial empire-building, of capitalist foreign development interest, and of nation-state consolidation. These two chapters introduce this theme by reconstructing in straightforward fashion the pragmatic transformation of space: how immigrants made farmland out of forest, established communities, and built support networks for survival. Later chapters develop this theme by analyzing the cultural struggles and political economy of spatial transformation. The Jubba valley was a place where the hierarchies of state and empire, the stratifications produced by unequal power, and the creative logic of capitalism have claimed central stage.

The second theme introduced here is the historically contingent and dynamic nature of social identity in Somalia. We will see how most ex-slaves and their descendants utilized flexibility in the Somali kinship system to claim membership in Somali clans. In so doing, they were trying to bend and shape established Somali practices of adoption, affiliation, and clientship to their benefit, while at the same time continuing to recognize and utilize non-Somali aspects of personal identity in face-to-face encounters within and between Gosha villages. In later chapters, we will see how their recognition of these dynamic and historically shifting identities became useful for Gosha villagers in their challenge of larger structures of domination that categorized them as a racially distinct, homogenous, and subordinate group within the Somali nation-state.

Recognizing the historical agency of Jubba valley dwellers is the third theme, one that speaks to the debate within slavery studies about whether ex-slaves assimilated to the host society or transformed it following abolition. We will see—especially in Part III—that although most ex-slaves in the Gosha became "Somalized," they were not simply assimilating, but rather were pursuing a subtle transformative agenda of the structural constraints that defined Somali society and their place within it. Their presence in Somalia, far from representing simply an insignificant minority population on the fringes, indirectly and directly affected the dreams of empire held by colonial Italy, the technologies of state developed by the postcolonial government, the conceit of "development" peddled by Western powers, and the patterning of violence by the poststate militias. In tracing this theme throughout the book, we will be continually evaluating how local agency variably and simultaneously challenged, accommodated, and/or mediated the semiotics of systemic power in Somalia.

The chapters in Part II lay the groundwork for developing these themes in later chapters. The goal of these two chapters is to describe the general contours of slavery, of valley settlement, of spatial transformation, of social identities, and of localized "common knowledge" history in order to establish a point of departure for analyzing the contradictions and complexities of historical consciousness, agency, domination, cultural struggles, and inequalities that have permeated the Jubba valley for the past century, and which, I will argue, provide a window into Somali nation-state formation and disintegration. A further goal in this brief exploration of historical dynamism is to challenge and work toward dismantling the persistent stereotype of Somali homogeneity, traditionalism, and primordialism.

Part III begins by discussing the shaping of Gosha identities within Somali society during the colonial and postcolonial periods, analyzing the integration of colonial racial constructions, Somali kinship, Islamic ideologies, and socialist state rhetoric. In discussing the varying roles of state policy, nationalist sentiment, colonial intervention, and Islamic influences on the cultural construction of Gosha identities, this section analyzes Gosha villagers' understandings of subordination, highlighting conflicting and contrasting knowledges and understandings of local and national identity politics. In detailing Gosha peoples' confrontations with Somali ideologies of denigration and the technologies of power of the Somali state, this section probes the complex web of resistance and collusion that characterized people's lives in the Gosha prior to Somalia's collapse. The goal of this section is to highlight the confluence of race-making and state-building, and to address the position of subaltern groups in resisting the hierarchizing tendencies of nationalism and state-building while at the same time accepting as legitimate many precepts of nation and state.

Part IV, on violence and the state, focuses on the confluence of class stratification and racialized identities in structuring the violence of fragmentation. These chapters detail the political economy of stratification in the Jubba valley, describing the vital struggles over land that have punctuated its history throughout the twentieth century and have given material reality to the symbolic forms of denigration described in Part III. The chapters deconstruct the dialectic of internal stratification and external interventions (Cold War geopolitics, donor funding, military technology) to demonstrate the late twentieth-century transformations in the nature of state power, Somali identities, and the definitions of space that were pivotal in the Jubba valley's destruction in the midst of state collapse.

Chapter 2
Fieldwork, Surprises, and Historical Anthropology

When I arrived in Somalia in 1987 to begin my year of fieldwork, I had no intention of studying politics, kinship, race, class, or conflict directly. I had been hired by the Land Tenure Center of the University of Wisconsin to study the effects of a ten-year-old land reform law on Somalia's farmers in the Jubba valley. I was to evaluate the success of the statute, which outlawed previous landholding practices (customary tenure) and enacted a "modern" system of land registration, in increasing security of land rights and raising agricultural productivity. Beyond meeting these requirements for the Land Tenure Center, I was free to pursue whatever research interested me. I chose to situate my fieldwork in the middle valley, rather than the more accessible lower or upper reaches of the valley, specifically because I wanted to find a place that offered the opportunity to make a clear comparison between customary tenure and state tenure; that is, a place where the new land law had not entirely taken effect. Relatively easily accessible by paved road from Mogadishu, the lower valley consisted of a patchwork of large-scale state farms, private plantations of cash crops, and smallholder plots of subsistence crops, and had been subjected to a significant degree of colonial penetration and postcolonial land speculation. The upper valley was characterized by higher aridity, dispersed settlement, refugee camps, and a mixture of pastoralism, agropastoralism, and agriculture. The middle part of the valley appeared best to meet my requirement: its remoteness, isolation, and reputation as a "backward" place of subsistence agriculture unpenetrated by markets, state policy, "development," capitalistic social relations, or other modern aspects of the world system seemed to fit the bill of what I was looking for. Although I had read Eric Wolf (1982) before arriving in Somalia, I suppose I still clung to earlier notions of "ethnographic subjects" living in isolation from the world system. (Of course, I was quite wrong.)

The initial impression of the middle valley supported its reputation as an isolated backwater of subsistence agriculture unpenetrated by modern life. To get to the middle valley (the area centered on Bu'aale stretching from Jilib to Baardheere: see Map 1), one drove from Mogadishu along a deeply pot-holed paved road to the lower valley town of Jilib, turning north on a graded gravel road that followed the east bank of the river for a few kilometers to the Fanoole barrage. From Fanoole, one wound through the bush on dirt tracks to the middle Jubba valley regional capital of Bu'aale, but only during the dry seasons, as the heavy black cotton soils became impassable by car during the rains. During the main dry season of *jilaal* (mid-December until mid-March) this route was trustworthy although very rough, but was unpredictable during both the *xagaa*, a dry season with intermittent rains (mid-June through mid-September), and the light rainy season of *dayr* (mid-September through mid-December). It was generally impassable during the *gu* season of heavy rains from mid-March through mid-June. During the rains, the better route into the middle valley from Mogadishu was from the north, although this route could also become impassable for several weeks or months during the gu season. The northern route left Mogadishu for the interriverine town of Baydhabo on a paved highway, continuing on a graded gravel road to the upper middle valley town of Baardheere. From Baardheere, one again traversed dirt tracks through the bush south along the river, reaching the town of Saakow first, and then continuing on through heavier and less navigable soils to Bu'aale. During the jilaal the entire Mogadishu-Bu'aale trip (about six hundred kilometers) could be made in two days by car. If one had to walk through the middle part of the valley on foot during the rainy season (from Bu'aale to Fanoole or from Bu'aale to Saakow), however, the trip could take several days longer.

Although Bu'aale was the regional capital, it was much smaller than any of the other significant middle Jubba valley region towns (Jilib, Saakow, Baardheere). It sported one deeply rutted main dirt road through the center of town lined by less than a dozen (mostly unoccupied) small cement buildings constructed as federal, regional, and district offices. Townspeople joked that one would never know Bu'aale was the regional capital because most of the regional officials posted there rarely visited, preferring the comforts of Jilib or Mogadishu to the rigors of life in Bu'aale. Many officials considered the middle Jubba a "punishment post," assigned to civil servants who had in some way annoyed a superior. A high-ranking official in the regional Ministry of Agriculture office, for example, recalled to me his (in his words) "hard luck story" of how he came to serve in the middle Jubba: at his previous (more prestigious) post he had lodged a formal complaint against his fellow ministry employees because they had commandeered for their personal use all the state-supplied inputs and machinery that were to be distributed to the area's smallholders and cooperatives. Identified as insubordinate, he was immediately reassigned to the middle Jubba.

The bulk of Bu'aale's population lived in thatched mud huts, which formed neighborhoods behind the main street. The central pump in town provided drinking water, although many people hauled buckets of Jubba River water for their domestic needs. A town generator occasionally provided intermittent electricity to a few offices and homes, although lack of diesel fuel made this an increasingly rare occurrence during my stay.

A paved open pavilion at one end of town overlooking the river served as the market, although it was rarely visited by vendors or buyers. Sometimes women would bring a few baskets of tomatoes, a couple of onions, some corn or beans, a bucket of lemons, mangoes, or bananas, and sometimes a pastoralist would sell a camel, cow, or a few sheep, but in general market activity remained at a minimum. A few shops to one side of the pavilion sold imported goods like cloth, sugar, rice, pasta, matches, soap, and other household basics. A Swedish nurse and her Somali medical counterparts staffed the Swedish Church Relief's small primary health care clinic in Bu'aale; they also carried out primary health care projects like latrine building and pump installation in some of the middle valley villages.

One of Bu'aale's attractions was the fact that one of the few bridges across the Jubba River was located there, making it a prime area for pastoralist crossings and for the transport of black market goods from Kenya. Since regional officials suggested to me that the west bank of the middle valley had experienced less land speculation and remained further out of reach of state officials than east bank villages, I too crossed the bridge to look for a west bank village in which to live and study for the year. I decided to settle in Loc,[1] a relatively large village perched on the bank of the river within twenty kilometers of the Bu'aale bridge. Loc appealed to me for a variety of reasons: with over five hundred people (about eighty households) it was larger than most west bank mid-valley villages, some of which consisted of only large extended families of under one hundred people; every family supported itself by subsistence farming; it was close enough to Bu'aale that I could walk there—especially during the rainy season—to get food, medical assistance, or when I wanted to interview regional officials; some land registration under the new law had taken place there; but not too much (or so I thought); and it was pretty.[2] The village was divided into two parts by a large central grassy plain overlooking the river, where pastoralists brought their animals to drink and where Loc women stood to dip their pole and bucket

1. Main Street, Loc. Photo by Jorge Acero.

mechanisms into the river to draw household water. Several full, large trees spread shade throughout the village, which consisted of scores of circular and rectangular thatched mud huts. A decorated cement structure that stood at one side of the central grassy plain turned out to be the tomb of the locally revered Sheikh Nasibow, who had resided in Loc prior to his death. Loc's farmland, crisscrossed by numerous footpaths, spread along the river to the north and south and encompassed several large *dhasheegs,* inland ponds fed by springs or river floods. I thought that Loc's (relatively) large size would provide an insight into diverse tenure strategies, that the presence of pastoralists would afford me the opportunity to learn about pastoral-agricultural tenure issues, and that the presence of registered farmers would allow me to make a comparative study of registered and nonregistered agricultural practices. While these predictions were accurate, I also learned a great deal about subjects I did not initially expect, for various reasons, to be able to pursue in detail: state corruption and repression; ethnicity, racialized identity, clientship, and clanship; stratification, inequality, and class dynamics; domination, resistance, and violence. Land tenure dynamics became a window into these issues, which in turn became the central questions in my research.

Anthropological Surprises

In the 1980s, Somalia was a place of opulent decadence and quiet terror. Upper-echelon government officials lived in lavish villas, drove expensive cars, and dined in fancy restaurants. Lower-level government employees scrambled to access as many funds of money as they could find. Rural people—farmers, pastoralists—tried to evade state control and to keep from being arrested, while working to meet their subsistence needs from a dwindling productive base. Arbitrary arrests and detentions, unpredictable official promotions and demotions, and torture of prisoners in Somalia's jails lent an aura of uncertainty and fear which extended outside of urban areas to small rural villages hundreds of kilometers from Mogadishu. The highly trained and pervasive National Security Service infiltrated all corners of the country, inhibiting open speech and fostering tensions and suspicions of neighbors, acquaintances, and even friends and relatives. A militarized state meant a proliferation of weapons, a persistent threat of armed force, and a knowledge that disobeying the will of state representatives could bring about violent retribution.

For many, these were terrible conditions to live under. A generalized atmosphere of fear and uncertainty in a context of massive weaponry, state repression, and economic collapse translated into a quiet violence of corruption, threats, subterfuges, mistrust, and desperation as the fare of daily life. I arrived in Somalia in May 1987 only dimly aware of this state of affairs, and I am even now still coming to understand both my position as an anthropologist under these circumstances and some of the ways these circumstances shaped my work. Hearing about other researchers who were declared persona non grata or who had been denied entry visas because of state objections to their work encouraged me to be very careful about who I spoke with and what I said. Yet I quickly discovered that learning about and discussing illegal topics and activities was, of course, unavoidable. My education on state repression and corruption began during my first weeks in Somalia in the form of personal experiences typical of the widespread forms of corruption, graft, and state molestation that plagued nearly everyone's life.

After navigating the webs of competing claims that surrounded foreign-funded research contracts in Mogadishu (which included, among other things, having my car commandeered for the personal use of a high-ranking military officer, having the battery from my rented car stolen by the regional police chief, and being threatened with arrest for hiring a field assistant who was not related to one of the ministry officials involved with my project), my first days in the Jubba valley reflected the pervasive government practice of surveillance and bodily control. On our way to the middle Jubba for the first time, my husband and I stopped in the upper middle Jubba valley town of Baardheere for the night. Almost immediately upon our arrival, we were taken into police custody for stepping out onto the bridge over the river to admire the view: the policemen explained that "permits" were required to use the bridge. The next night—our first in Bu'aale—we were arrested and had our film confiscated after taking a picture outside of a teashop at the request of a local policeman. The two local official NSS agents followed our every move in Bu'aale, and continued to do so whenever we visited the town during our year of residence in Loc: they followed us as we bought tomatoes, rice, and soap in the little market, as we drank tea with our friends in local teashops, as we filled jerry cans with water from the town pump, as we dropped off our laundry at the home of one of the town's washermen. Their personal surveillance was highly localized, however; for some reason they made no attempt to follow us to Loc. Perhaps our generally domestic activities were simply boring to them, perhaps the idea of leaving town life for a bush village was anathema, or perhaps Loc village affairs warranted little official interest. Nevertheless, such experiences contributed early on to my education, ensuring that I could not remain ignorant of state techniques of surveillance and control.

Although the degree of state surveillance and control over our actions diminished considerably when we were physically in Loc, our residence there brought an enormous burden of state presence on our host, the village head. We first went to Loc with the mayor of Bu'aale to ask (or so we thought) if we could live in the village and learn about land tenure. Despite my anthropological preconceptions of what the "first meeting" would be like, I became but a spectator during our initial interview with the village elders. The meeting consisted of the Bu'aale mayor speaking forcefully for a very long time to the assembled villagers, who sat quietly unresponsive. At the conclusion of the speech, of which I understood very little, the mayor told us we could take up residence in the compound of the village head in a week's time, after a new cooking shed was constructed for us. He also told us that the villagers were happy to have us, a sentiment belied by their countenances. It was only much later that I learned the substance of the mayor's speech and the circumstances under which we were welcomed to Loc the following week.

From the beginning of our stay in Loc, it was clear that the village head, Xassan, had many concerns about our presence and was nervous about our actions. My husband and I occupied two huts in his ring of eight huts around a central firepit, which housed himself, his two wives (prior to his divorce of the younger one), his married son, daughter-in-law, and granddaughter, and his unmarried two sons, daughter, granddaughter, and stepson. During our first several weeks, he warned me about certain villagers, he asked me to stem the tide of constant visitors from the village to my dwelling, he asked me to leave word where I was at all times, and he insisted that I employ his daughter for help with domestic chores because he could not allow someone from outside his family into my house. He and his eldest wife rarely left the compound, which was strange for a farming family. In turn, I understood that my visitors were entering his family space and so tried to visit with friends and neighbors outside the compound, in keeping with his wishes I initially employed his daughter (until she married), and I tried to calm his obvious anxieties by spending as much time as possible visiting with his family in the early weeks of my residence. Gradually I began to realize that something else besides discomfort with my foreignness and uncertainty about my purpose was at issue.

One day, while returning with my field assistants, Cali Ibrahim Axmed and Cabdi Axmed, from some farming areas to the north of Loc, we came face to face with a lion who stepped out from the tall corn into our path. We momentarily froze in terror, and then slowly began walking toward the village as the lion turned and sauntered away in another direction. As we got closer to Loc, we met some villagers in their fields and excitedly told them of our adventure; my moment of terror had become an absurdly naive pride at having walked away from an encounter with a lion. By the time we reached Loc, Xassan had already learned of our confrontation and was beside himself; he forbade me to leave the village to visit the farm fields any more. I was speechless until he explained to me the mayor's charge to him in that introductory meeting months before: the mayor had told Xassan that he would be held *personally* responsible by the government if *anything* happened to me while I lived under his care in Loc. I thought back to how upset Xassan had been when we took the unstable village canoe across the river to visit another village, remembering how he had asked us to drive around via the bridge at Bu'aale rather than take the canoe in the future. I thought of the mornings when we awoke to find his son sleeping in our doorway because crocodiles had been climbing the riverbank into the village during the night. I thought about the two-week period of fear and sleeplessness when bandits were attacking villages in the area and travelers on the road outside of Loc, and how we had refused to leave the village when a representative from the Bu'aale mayor had suggested we come to town for a week or so until the bandits moved on. I began to realize the enormity of the mayor's charge to Xassan—to ensure the safety of two foreigners in an area where every year people are killed and mauled by wild animals, where the village canoe is overturned into the crocodile-filled river by surfacing hippos, where bandits attack villages, shooting and looting before disappearing into the bush, where deaths from malaria, tuberculosis, fevers, and accidents claim far more lives than does old age. My presence ensured an indirect state interest in Loc, an onerous burden of state intervention personally shouldered by the village head. I had come to Loc to study the effects of state intervention (in the specific form of land tenure), and yet I myself embodied a highly visible and generalized reminder of the state's presence. Anthropologists have only recently begun to acknowledge the dangers we face in doing fieldwork; but we also sometimes neglect to realize (as I did) that we put others in danger by our very presence.

While I had imagined that I could study state intervention without becoming a part of it, I had also imagined that it would be impossible to talk about ethnicity, heritage, status, clientship, clan, or lineages because acknowledgment of these kinds of social groupings had been outlawed. Under Barre, any reference—formal or informal, verbal or written—to clan, lineage, or ethnic affiliation was strictly forbidden, and offenders, if caught, could be imprisoned. I. M. Lewis described how "effigies representing 'tribalism, corruption, nepotism and misrule' were symbolically burnt or buried in the Republic's main centres . . . [T]he word comrade (*jaalle*: friend, chum) [was] launched into general currency with official blessing to replace the traditional polite term of address 'cousin' (*inaʿadeer*), which was now considered undesirable because of its tribalistic, kinship connotations" (1988:209–10).

I had told myself that I could study land tenure and valley agricultural history without needing to use kinship, ethnic, or status terms, and I promised myself I would never knowingly request information about such groupings. If I was oblivious to the state presence I brought to Loc, I was acutely afraid of endangering someone by talking about illegal matters. Yet I soon found that kinship, ethnicity, and status were the currency of life in the middle valley and that people talked about these relationships all the time. In other words, talking about clan, lineage, ethnicity, heritage, and status was unavoidable: heritage (slave ancestry) defined villagers' place in Somali society, clan affiliations were a central aspect of local history, status distinctions marked the terms of villagers' daily lives. Only once did the law become an issue during my conversations with valley dwellers. I was talking with Khadija, who at close to ninety years old was the oldest person in the village and the only daughter of Loc's founder, about her father's early years in the area. She was explaining his choice to affiliate with a lineage of the Ogaadeen clan when several village boys interrupted her narrative to say she was going to be arrested for talking about clans. She retorted, "Let them imprison me if they want! Let them take me if they want! Maybe they'll put me among other Ogaadeens! Who wants me now that I look like this?" The boys laughed and walked away as she continued with her story. This incident, which occurred toward the end of my stay, jolted me into remembering that much of the substance of my interviews and conversations throughout the middle valley had been illegal.

Regardless of what the law said, status, race, ethnicity, clanship and clientship were central aspects of life, meaningful history, identity, and local politics. People talked about what was important to them and used terms that were meaningful to them, and I often found myself sorting out family, lineage, and clan affiliations—with the aid of pages full of kinship charts—with groups of men and women who were my guides to village relations. But embedded within these comfortable public discussions of kinship and clanship were less discussable knowledges of ethnic heritage, slave ancestry, and bitter historical memories. As these (unofficial and illegal) knowledges began emerging in private conversations and narratives, as well as in more formal discussions, the substance of my conversations and interviews became more sensitive, more subtle, and many times, more awkward. Martin Klein (1989) has written about the sometimes insurmountable difficulties of researching the history of "those who would rather forget": people whose ancestors were enslaved. Talking with people of slave heritage about their histories is a very delicate process indeed, as recalling such personal and parental histories may be embarrassing, painful, or simply impossible. This fact obliges me to describe some of the interview contexts within which I learned bits about the more private personal and collective histories of middle valley farmers.

Doing Anthropological History Among People Who Would Rather Forget

Aside from my assigned project on land tenure, my initial historical goals were relatively modest and rather ill formed. I basically wanted to uncover what really happened in the Gosha history: to chronicle where the people living in the Gosha came from, how they came to live there, and something of what they had experienced in the process. Part of this interest stemmed from my desire to reconstruct land use patterns in the area, which required a history of village settlement, population growth, and social organization; part of this interest grew out of a desire to chronicle the history of a marginal area inhabited by people who had been ignored in most studies of Somali politics, culture, and history. Most of the major works on Somalia relegated the history of "Bantu minorities" to a footnote, a passing acknowledgment, a brief mention of servile or even uncertain origins. I sought to add a factual basis to the speculative nature of "Bantu minority" history in Somalia. But as I gathered "facts," I also discovered the inseparability of the history of *facts* ("this is what really happened") from the *meaning* of history (as it is, or is not, remembered, used, altered, contested, debated, revitalized, or rejected in the present). The inseparability of "fact" and "meaning"—the mutually constitutive nature of remembering and interpreting historical events, experiences, and eras—made clear the false dichotomy (what Krech [1991:352] called "the tired old creed") of "objective" and "subjective" history. Middle valley farmers may not have been full of historical "facts," but they knew a great deal about the ongoing meaning of history.

In my initial search for "facts," I began by trying to learn the common parameters of local historical knowledge: important dates, events, and so on. In solid graduate school fashion and for lack of any better ideas, my first undertaking was a household census on which I wrote everyone's name (including nonresident children), birthplace, age, the date of their arrival in Loc, their parents' names and birthplaces, and previous residences.[3] While marriages, divorces, births, deaths, and child fostering made Loc households dynamic—30 percent of the housholds had a different composition of adults at the conclusion of my field research from what I had recorded a year earlier—the census at least helped me learn names, introduce myself, and get a sense of population changes over time. I also began my year in Loc by creating a chronological event history—that much used, much maligned form of history as seen through a progression of significant moments. In order to get a grasp of the event-filled march of history, I met repeatedly with groups of elders to develop a sense of village foundings, village movements, land clearings and abandonments, specific colonial encounters, epic happenings (remembered floods, droughts, famines, epidemics). My aim was methodological rather than born of a desire to generate a "highlights" of middle Jubba history: people in Loc talked about their history by making reference to such remembered highlights. Valley villagers tracked historical time in seven-year intervals, identifying each year by the day on which it began (according the Muslim calendar): Tuesday Year, Wednesday Year, and so forth. Years in which special or memorable events occurred were identified by those events as well: the Tuesday Year of Smallpox; the big drought of Arbaca Shahi, the Wednesday Year of Tea; the Thursday Year of Cholera. People recalled significant events in their own lives by reference to these kinds of commonly recognized dates: "My son was born in the year after Jimco Basto [the Friday Year of Pasta]," or, simply, "My mother died five Axads ago [five Sunday years ago]."

To fill out the "event history," I worked with villagers poring over aerial photographs and walking throughout Loc's farmland to piece together a detailed picture of Loc's settlement and land use patterns, which I could match with household censuses and land tenure questionnaires to generate a fairly clear picture of Loc population growth and land tenure history. I repeated this line of inquiry, in much more general fashion, in villages throughout the middle Jubba by meeting with village elders to ask when the first person had settled their village, how it had grown since that time, what significant events had affected their lives (they usually named droughts, floods, epidemics, famines, and colonial activity). The villagers would debate among themselves to produce specific dates, events, and names of historical figures. Generating a time-line of chronological historical events in the valley of village settlement, population movements, and land use patterns proved to be a relatively straightforward unraveling of the dense tapestry of local history because of the area's shallow time depth.

Because its settlement history spanned only a century, the middle Jubba valley stands in contrast to other parts of Africa where elaborate historical myths surrounding the occupation of land and its devolution through the generations have developed.[4] Figuring out how villagers were related through deceased ancestors, charting the devolution of land parcels through inheritance, marriages, and out-migrations, and tracing family connections through marriages of the previous generation were essential to joining—at least minimally—the world of basic, collective local historical knowledge. This kind of history was open to all and was relatively uncontested; it was the history of common knowledge by which marriages were made, favors were requested, land was divided, events were remembered. Beyond this kind of placing names and dates in a village chronology, however, things became much more opaque.

Moving into the terrain of where people had come from before entering the valley and of the texture (rather than the events) of their lives within the valley during the past decades introduced uncertainty, reticence, silences, and sometimes formalized narratives into our conversations. Discussions of slavery heritage and ancestral slavery experiences began tentatively during my initial months in Loc—an elderly man visiting me in my house telling me, quietly, that everyone in Loc was descended from slaves; a neighbor privately mentioning that another man with whom I'd been talking was descended from captives caught by the famous slave trader "Tippu Tup" (whether this was meant figuratively or in reality). These privately shared pieces of information were relayed in a regional atmosphere of denigration, as I will describe in Chapter 5, where villagers suffered the ignominy of being called "slaves" in public. Villagers could not avoid recognizing their heritage of slavery, but they also rarely discussed it among themselves, in public at least. Because I did not want to embarrass people, to ask people to talk about things which they preferred not to, or to press for information on subjects which made people uncomfortable, I followed the rule of self-selection. My conversations about slavery heritages began late in my fieldwork when Iidow, an elderly man descended from Boran pastoral slaves who was the most widely recognized local historian in the area, offered to talk with me about local history. We began meeting for an afternoon every couple of weeks. The issue of slavery first came up during our third meeting when Iidow was explaining to me the origin of the valley's settlers: some were Boran pastoralists and some were escaped slaves brought to Baraawe by the Arabs "from Mombasa." I asked if anyone in Loc was descended from these slaves, and he answered, "Yes, but they'd be offended if you asked them." In our next meeting he described what he knew of the personal histories of several Loc families, descendants of people who had been imported into Somalia as slaves by a prominent Arab merchant in Baraawe. About his own history he was more circumspect, saying only that his Boran father used to "look after the cattle" of a Somali pastoralist whose clan affiliation, language, and religion he assumed, because back then "they used to slap people who identified themselves as Boran." This was our last meeting, as he fell ill and died within a month; with his death the village lost its most knowledgeable historian.

Following Iidow's death, further stories, explanations, and viewpoints about mid-valley slavery heritages emerged in a series of conversations and interviews with several elderly men from Loc and other mid-valley villages who offered to continue my education in the area's history. Since I had only a few months remaining before the gu rainy season and my planned departure from Loc, I began concentrating on collecting extensive oral histories from these men, and briefer personal histories from others who were willing to share them. Additionally, I held several lengthy and directed conversations on area history with men from three local pastoralist groups whom I had come to know over the course of the preceding year. These men and I individually scheduled our meetings in advance, which took place over coffee or tea in my home or theirs, and with their permission I tape-recorded most of our conversations. Although many of these private discussions focused on the speakers' personal histories, the men also talked about more general aspects of mid-valley history, such as the impact of colonialism, relationships between pastoralists and farmers, clientship, or the effects of changing agricultural policies. Unfortunately, I was not very successful in eliciting historical information from women. Women did not seem to feel the same sense of entitlement to a legitimate historical memory as men did, and because of this often were not willing to attempt discussion on historical matters.

My field assistant and translator Cali Ibrahim Axmed accompanied me to all the interviews. Cali's presence was significant in a number of ways. Somali oratory is rich in metaphor, poetry, and allegory, much of which I would have missed without Cali's careful assistance. He transcribed the tapes and we translated them together, often discussing our impressions of the interviews, our questions about why different people had provided different versions of a particular experience or event, and mulling over particular terms, phrases, or expressions. Cali was not from a Gosha village; rather he was a Somali from the Ogaadeen who had fled into Somalia as a refugee during the Somali-Ethiopian war over the Ogaadeen. After living for less than a year in a refugee camp, he was hired by the Swedish Church Relief as a translator/health care worker, eventually resettling in Bu'aale. When I met him, he had been working for ten years in middle valley villages with the Swedish Church Relief, had a good knowledge of the area and its people, and had a very comfortable and non-threatening interview style. When his work with the Swedish Church Relief ended, I offered him a job as my assistant. He moved to Loc, bringing his brother, Cabdi, who had been living in a refugee camp, and we worked together for the next nine months. Cali's sensitivity and obvious interest in village life endeared him to Loc residents, while at the same time his status as an "ethnic" Somali elicited revealing comments about the "we-they" distinction between Gosha villagers and other Somalis that affected so much of Gosha life.[5]

These scheduled conversations were intense and focused. In light of the obvious ongoing significance of slavery heritage, in these conversations I was seeking to understand my interlocutors' views of their histories. What aspects of their histories continued to be meaningful for them? How did they explain/understand the circumstances of their ancestors? What historical knowledge did they call upon to define their present circumstances? What were the points of disagreement, the points of unity, the points of uncertainty? I showed up to our scheduled meetings with a list of questions, not always followed, which guided our discussions. Occasionally the local historian would begin a specific narrative, recounting a piece of tradition, which I would record without interruption, but usually our discussions were interactive and dialogical as I tried to understand the speaker's view of things. Sometimes I would push an issue to a certain point by introducing events I knew about or by suggesting alternative viewpoints, which gave the speaker the opportunity to deviate from his version of history to ruminate and comment on another version.

Remembering history in the middle valley did not follow broader African patterns of oral traditions or formally structured "mythicohistories,"[6] which could be recorded and analyzed. Rather, historical remembering tended to be more personal, more private, more idiosyncratic, more fluid, less certain, less clear, less distilled into commonly recited narratives. Sometimes I spoke with people about things they may never have discussed before. Some aspects of historical experiences in the middle valley were more accessible to recall and retellings, such as experiences as forced laborers on colonial Italian plantations; other aspects of middle valley history were much more obscured and idiosyncratically remembered, such as pastoralist-farmer relations in the early years of settlement. Many aspects of personal histories were simply inaccessible to my interlocutors, such as, in some cases, knowledge about their grandparents' or parents' birthplaces, enslavement, freedom, or decision to settle in the valley. I learned a great deal about the symbolic weight and ongoing meaning of history through hearing what these knowledgeable men, widely respected for their historical knowledge, could and could not (whether through constraints on knowledge or desire) talk about.

Doing these sensitive and sometimes personal interviews toward the end of my field research meant that I could reflect these local historians' versions of historical experiences and eras against what other people had told me, what I had uncovered in colonial archives, and what I had witnessed in daily life in order to produce richer interpretations, a more nuanced view of the symbolic weight of history, and a deeper understanding of how different views of historical periods or events took shape.[7] The words of these men are recorded unchanged throughout this book and provided much of the basis for my understanding of the personal significance of having a slavery heritage.

In addition to these private, ongoing interviews, I held group interviews with village elders in eight other mid-valley villages. In contrast to the private meetings mentioned above, these meetings were public, attended by dozens of men, women, and youths (children were usually shooed away). These interviews were held in villages I had visited with my Loc neighbors, some frequently and some just a few times. Usually just one or two men spoke—those who wanted to describe their personal experience as a new immigrant to the valley looking for a place to settle, as a forced laborer on an Italian-owned farm, as a conscripted soldier in World War II—although other men and sometimes women occasionally interjected a comment. Somewhat to my initial surprise, the village discussions almost always came around to the fact of slavery heritage. In most of these village meetings, the local spokesperson would describe how their village was formed by explaining that the first settlers had been ex-slaves looking for a place of their own, escaping slavery, leaving their patrons after serving as clients, and so on. Perhaps people were willing to discuss such matters openly because of the less personalized and more general nature of these discussions (we were talking about *village* history, not about Ibrahim's history or Abshirow's history); perhaps the knowledge that I already knew about Loc's history facilitated the discussion of slavery. I also wondered if an important local dimension to these village discussions was the presence of dozens of young men, women, boys, and girls quietly listening on the outskirts of the circle.

Doing these interviews during the final months of my field research greatly helped in the fuzzy and difficult area of trust. By then, most villagers had a good understanding of what I was doing in Loc, had come to recognize that I was not going to steal land or bring harm to the village, and were clearly aware that I supported their claims to their land, production, and persons against those of state representatives and other "outsiders." Nevertheless, people in Loc and other mid-valley villages had a lot to hide, and what they were willing to tell me about themselves and their personal/ancestral histories was limited in ways I cannot know.[8]

Fitting It All Together, Sort Of

My questions about the past in conversations during fieldwork and my interpretations of the past presented in this book are, without question, filtered through the concerns of the present. I wanted to understand historical land tenure dynamics as a way to evaluate (and critique) the effects of land speculation in the present. I wanted to understand the history of enslavement, manumission, and postabolition social relations in order to grasp contemporary definitions of difference, status, hierarchy, and domination. I sought Gosha peoples' visions of their personal and ancestral history in order to uncover their view of and their historical response to domination and as a way to interpret such responses in the present. In such ways, what I witnessed in the present guided my research and molded my research questions about the past.

The continuing significance of historical "nightmares"—the ways in which the past weighed on and pervaded the present—was apparent in symbolic practice as well as in the unfolding material dimension of social relationships in the mid-valley. John and Jean Comaroff have recognized the importance of interpreting the past through the medium of symbolic practice in the present; of interpreting the sedimentation of history into meaningful and powerful symbols that guide, dominate, define, shape, or reflect social reality:

> This implicit dimension—the study of symbolic practice—is a crucial contribution of ethnography to history, since it brings a nuanced understanding of the role of meaning and motivation to social processes. . . . The "motivation" of social practice . . . always exists at two distinct, if related, levels: first, the (culturally configured) needs and desires of human beings; and, second, the pulse of collective forces that, empowered in complex ways, work through them. (Comaroff and Comaroff 1992:35–36)

In learning about local visions of history, historical experience, and the symbolism that pervaded everyday life, I began to get glimpses of "the collective forces" that originated outside of the narrow geographical confines of the Jubba valley but that found particular and sometimes dramatic expressions within the valley. In local symbolic and material expressions of such collective forces (national power dynamics, state-building processes, ideologies of nationalism), I began to see how intertwined local history was with regional history and national history.

In seeing the significant processes shaping regional and national history through the historical experiences of Gosha peoples, I had to view culture as political: as a set of symbolic and ideological practices and beliefs historically constituted in the face of power. Bernard Cohn and Nicholas Dirks (1988:228) have called for just such a view of culture, in which culture is part of our historicist analysis "not just as some abstract 'construction,' not just as something which is at some level arbitrary rather than natural, but a particular conglomerate of constructions set in motion by agents, operationalized through the agencies of the state, contested through institutional means that themselves have been naturalized through the very project of state formation." Similarly, Kay Warren has called for a political view of culture and a cultural view of politics, arguing that anthropologists should focus on "the ways in which meanings are in fact linked to political practice, how local culture is relevant to the understanding of national society, and how state politics can be brought into cultural analysis" (1993a:10). In other words, local cultural practices can be probed not just as local expressions of localized historical experiences, but also as evidence of the processes employed by the state to extend authority and technologies of control, to legitimize domination, and to shape compliance to state-building (and sometimes nation-forming) projects, *and* as a "constituting element of political action and identity" (Warren 1993a:17) by those engaged by, struggling with, and supporting state power.

Over the course of my fieldwork, and certainly in the years since 1988, I have come to see very clearly that local, regional, national, and global history were part of the same package, affected by the same kinds of power dynamics and social forces. But tracing these linkages has been a processual undertaking: I had not gone to the middle valley armed with a theory which would make clear to me how the local could be easily seen to articulate with or be a part of the global. I generated notebooks filled with pieces of historically related information: on slavery, forced labor, identity, ethnic ancestry, neighborhoods, families, clans, lineages, diya-paying groups; on power dynamics, inequality, stratification, repression, fear; on "development," land tenure, economics, state politics, foreign aid policy. In tracing through local experiences the history of the valley's engagement with wider arenas of interaction (colonial empires, postcolonial nation-state[s], Cold War geopolitics) and the resulting contestations over local factors of production and redefinitions of labor, I caught glimpses of the historical agency of how local people worked through these structures to maintain their control over land, labor, and production. While trying to see the contours of domination and agency, structure and practice, as they unfolded in the Jubba valley, I remained focused on the *cultural* logics of these processes (looking for how domination was symbolized, explained, understood, resisted, accommodated), and it was in interpreting the cultural that the larger structures of interaction, domination, and compliance, which bound village, region, nation, and state, became visible. While I did not go to the Jubba valley to find colonialism, state-making, nation-building, race-creating, ethnicity-conjuring, class formation, or terror, these are exactly the things—among others—about which I learned there. As it unfolded locally (and as I apprehended it through everyday symbolic and material practice in 1987–88), the history of the Jubba valley very much turned out to be a regional history, a national history, and a global history.

Understanding these connections has taken a long time. The Comaroffs observed this dimension of writing historical ethnography when they asked: "*How,* then, do we connect parts to 'totalities'? How do we make intelligible the idiosyncratic acts, lives, and representations of others? How do we locate them within 'a historically determinate environment'?" (1992:17). The fragmentary nature of historical evidence, of lived immediacies, of ethnographic knowledge does *not,* despite the claims of postmodernists, mean that there are no "totalities." It means that understanding the way the parts fit together (imperfectly, incompletely, even awkwardly; in particular historical moments and in particular historically constituted spaces) may be difficult, may take time, may require (a lot of) work beyond the field research.

My own still developing, ever developing understanding of the "totality"—parts of which filled my notebooks, cassette tapes, and journals—began evolving during the course of my residence in Loc; in thousands of hours of conversation with farmers in the middle valley; in discussions with pastoralists, with regional officials; in months of poring over archival documents from the colonial era; in dozens of conversations with fellow Somalist academics from various disciplinary backgrounds. It grew over the three years after I left Loc as I watched Somalia disintegrate, and over the years following collapse as people from the Gosha began speaking (from Kenya, Canada, Tanzania, and Somalia) in new voices about new versions of history, new identities, new desires. What might once have been readily conceived of as the "totality" has disappeared since the events of 1991, and everyone implicated in the project of making sense of Somalia proceeds with only partial understandings of nontotalities.[9] My goal in writing this book is to show how *some* pieces of life, history, and experience in the Jubba valley fit together to illuminate certain aspects of the "totality" of the Somali nation-state and its demise. In attempting to say something about this "totality" through scrutinizing its localized parts—or to be more specific, by analyzing the *local* particulars of such things as how ideas of "race" were born in a particular historical moment, of how "ethnicities" gained and lost meaning, were created and refashioned under various historical conditions, of how stratification was produced out of historically determined regional and national political economies—I hope this book will contribute to the necessarily ongoing project of making sense of Somalia's disintegration.

Part II
The Historical Creation of the Gosha

Chapter 3
Slavery and the Jubba Valley Frontier

There has been debate in the literature about both the nature of slaveholding in African societies and the changes in social relations brought about by the ending of slavery in Africa. The transition from slaveholding to postslavery in Africa has been conceptualized by "traditionalists" as having been relatively smooth, where ex-slaves remained where they were and gradually assimilated (although never completely) to the host society.[1] Suzanne Miers and Igor Kopytoff (1977) describe "belonging" as the antithesis to slavery in Africa, where ex-slaves and their descendants pursued fuller incorporation into the host society through a variety of economic, political, and affective forms of social mobility. Conversely, "revisionists" (primarily Francophone and Marxist scholars) hold that abolition "resulted in a radical restructuring not only of the relations of production, but of family structure, kinship relations, and strategies for the accumulation of wealth" (Roberts and Miers 1988:31). In this view, "significant transformations of labor and issues of control and domination" (Cooper 1980:14) accompanied abolition. While cases documenting both viewpoints are available, in many societies the actual result was probably a combination of the two, where slaves both transformed societies *and* adapted within them.[2] This would seem to be especially the case where ex-slaves who left their owners at abolition were able to obtain independent access to land or other resources, forming what Sidney Mintz (1979b) has called a "reconstituted peasantry." Gosha villagers are an example of ex-slaves who claimed autonomous control over farmland and its products. Although perhaps agriculturally self-sufficient, however, such groupings formed by ex-slaves existed within a larger society, and thus were faced with reconstructing social relations and a social identity as freedmen.

To begin to unravel this process of social identity formation among Gosha villagers, this chapter and the next reconstruct the settlement of the Gosha landscape by ex-slaves, demonstrating the importance to Gosha settlers of maintaining multiple facets of identity. Together, these two chapters offer a contribution to the sketchy historical record of the Jubba valley, providing a sense of the regional historical context, the contours of slavery experienced by Jubba valley settlers, their varied backgrounds, their shifting strategies of settlement, their dynamic creation of new communities in the valley, and their role in the shaping of a regional society after the turn of the century.

Some may wonder at my choice to present these two chapters in the form of a historical narrative. It has become fashionable to disavow coherence, totalizing "master" narratives, and unitary historical trajectories in our ethnographic/anthropological accounts in favor of evoking the fragmentary nature of social life, the competing versions of "reality" held by members of a community, and the multiplicity of senses, sensibilities, and imaginings within groups once identified as "cultures." In these two chapters I flagrantly resist this trend by offering a single story of Jubba valley history pulled together from various sources (oral histories, oral traditions, colonial accounts, travelers' accounts, secondary analyses). History is not just an assortment of shifting, competing fragmentary imaginings of the present: things of import *have* happened in the past, although they may be recounted differently by different people in different eras. I am unwilling to focus solely on the present imaginings of the past because I think it is important to recognize certain realities about the Somali past: the magnitude of slavery and its different forms, the productivity and resilience of early Jubba valley farming villages, the impact of colonial labor policies. As we will see in later chapters, many aspects of Jubba valley history are indeed contested; but some aspects are not, and it is these latter which provide the basis of my historical narrative in these two chapters. In this age of reflexivity and self-critique, I realize that I am claiming a voice of authority over other peoples' histories. Nevertheless, while people in the Gosha may not need me to tell their story(ies), I can offer this account—what they taught me in the knowledge that I was going to write a book about them—in the hope that it can serve to further dialogue about, interest in, and critiques of historical accounts (including this one) of southern Somalia.

Using secondary sources and colonial documents, in this chapter I provide a broad background overview of slavery in Somalia and the early settlement of the valley by fugitive slaves. I begin by explaining the development of slavery in the south and its economic implications for the region. I then turn to the focus of this study by examining the importance of the valley as a frontier refuge for ex-slaves and sketching the initial settlement of the lower valley.

Slavery in Southern Somalia

The story of the Jubba valley begins with the entry of slaves into Somalia in the nineteenth century.[3] A reconstruction of the scope of slavery in Somalia is, of course, limited by the evidence currently available, which is particularly scant for pre-nineteenth-century Somalia. For the period up to 1800, we have only a few descriptions from early Islamic and Portuguese travelers of conditions in the coastal towns, although some coastal families have recently made their closely guarded historical family documents available to foreign researchers.[4] For the interior, we must rely primarily on oral traditions and narratives. Patterns of slavery in the nineteenth century—when slaveholding in southern Somalia dramatically increased—are much more accessible through eyewitness accounts, written accounts and colonial sources, and oral histories. In general, these sources reveal that Somalis acquired slaves for a variety of purposes during different historical periods: urban coastal families had used slaves in the Benaadir textile industry for hundreds of years; rural families obtained slaves for tending livestock, as concubines, and in increasingly large numbers for agricultural labor during the commercial boom of the nineteenth century.

Slaves arriving into southern Somalia in the nineteenth century entered a dynamic society in the midst of large-scale political and economic transformations, shifting demographic patterns, and newly emerging social identities.[5] Town and rural elites, foreigners and locals, nomads and urban dwellers vied for political and economic supremacy over the coastal ports, while in the southern interior wars, migrations, and economic changes were transforming the social topography. A brief overview of the shifting nature of commercial enterprise, political control, and social identities prior to and especially during the nineteenth century gives a sense of the society slaves encountered upon their arrival in Somalia in the mid to latter half of the nineteenth century.

The ports of Somalia's Benaadir Coast through which many slaves passed—including Baraawe, Marka, and Mogadishu—had long been a part of the Indian Ocean trade network. Virginia Luling (1971:17), I. M. Lewis (1988:21–22), and M. Kassim (1993) suggest that immigrants from the Arabian peninsula and the Persian Gulf settled the Benaadir ports by the tenth century, intermarrying with Somalis to produce commercially oriented "Arab-Somali" towns within a few generations. From the tenth century on, Lewis argues, these ports provided the conduit for Arab trade and became "the foundation for Muslim expansion in North East Africa" (1988:22).

Initially exporting raw materials such as ivory, ambergris, dark woods, and incense, the coastal towns began producing and exporting cloth by the fourteenth century when Ibn Battuta recorded impressions of his visit. Evidence from Portuguese travelers from the sixteenth century indicates that urban families used slaves in the textile industry,[6] and probably also in domestic service. These slaves were most likely Abyssinian,[7] as European visitors in the mid-nineteenth century noted the trade in Abyssinian slaves from Harar, Ethiopia.[8] During the 1600s and 1700s, a gradual process of nomadic involvement in town economic, social, and political life produced regional systems of interaction between town elite and nomadic pastoralists in trade, marriage, and politics,[9] firmly linking the fortunes of town and country and establishing political control over the towns by Somali clans of the interior.[10]

On the basis of eyewitness accounts, Edward Alpers (1983) describes Mogadishu in the mid-nineteenth century as being on the verge of collapse, a place of extraordinary tension and conflict that had become "a shadow of its former splendid self" (Alpers 1983:442). Following possible Portuguese disruption of Arab trade in the sixteenth and seventeenth centuries—which Robert Hess claims turned the Benaadir Coast into a "backwater" (1966:7)[11]—Mogadishu suffered from internal rivalries between elite families, a plague combined with drought and famine, and the disruption of the important internal ivory trade to the coast by Islamic militants from the interior that cumulatively resulted in "considerable trauma for the community as a whole" during the 1830s and 1840s (Alpers 1983:445–46). Struggles for political supremacy galvanized rival town factions, affected relations between town and country, and involved leaders from the hinterland of Mogadishu (such as the sultan of Geledi) as well as the sultan of Zanzibar.[12]

Indeed, the entire region was experiencing economic and political transformation. This time period witnessed the dramatic growth of Zanzibar as an international trade emporium, visited by American, European, and Asian merchants. Ships and Arab dhows carrying trade items regularly visited the Somali ports, which were steadily integrated "into the economic orbit of Omani Zanzibar through the medium of Indian merchant capital" in the form of several Indian merchant houses located in the Benaadir ports (Alpers 1983:448). An extensive system of caravan trade, manned exclusively by Somalis and primarily carrying ivory, supplied coastal ports with goods from the interior desired by foreign merchants.[13] The Benaadir ports, integrated into regional nomadic systems of trade and resource use in the interior, were thus also closely tied into the world outside Somalia through the commercial activities of the Indian merchant houses,[14] which drew substantial Arab trade to the coast.

One important commodity being transported by the Arab dhows to Somalia was slaves from other parts of East Africa. During the nineteenth century, the East African slave trade grew enormously due to demands by Arabs, Portuguese, and French. Slave traders and raiders moved throughout eastern and central Africa to meet the rising demand for enslaved men, women, and children. Somalia did not supply slaves—as part of the Islamic world Somalis were at least nominally protected by the religious tenet that free Muslims cannot be enslaved—but Arab dhows loaded with human cargo continually visited Somali ports.[15]

The cheap availability of slaves through the Indian Ocean trade coincided with several other factors to transform Somalia's Benaadir Coast into a commodity-producing region based on slave labor. First, the Benaadir involvement in the Zanzibar-based Indian Ocean trade brought slaves to Somalia and reestablished significant regional trading links between East Africa and Arabia. Participation in regional trade and access to slave labor encouraged coastal Somalis to develop a plantation economy in the Shabeelle River valley, which paralleled the Benaadir Coast for two hundred miles, at some places lying less than six miles inland.[16] Agricultural products from the Shabeelle were easily accessible to urban coastal populations and merchants, and the apparently large demand for grain and oil in Arabia as well as for competitively priced domestic cotton fueled the rise of commodity production in the fertile Shabeelle valley, where there was abundant land.[17] Unwilling to engage in manual agricultural labor themselves, which Somalis considered demeaning, inferior, and demanding, Somali pastoralists whose clan areas included parts of the Shabeelle began acquiring slaves as agricultural laborers in order to produce sorghum, sesame, orchella (a lichen used to produce dye), and cotton for the market.[18] By the time of his visit in 1843, Lieutenant W. Christopher called the Benaadir "the grain coast for the supply of Southern Arabia" (1844:87). Dozens of East African ethnic groups supplied slaves for Somalia, especially Zegua, Yao, Nyasa, Makua, Ngindu, and Nyika. Europeans also noted the large number of "Swahili" slaves brought to Somalia,[19] although it is possible that these writers used "Swahili" as a generic term for people originating anywhere in East Africa south of Somalia.

With the growth of the plantation sector, pastoralists could convert part of their wealth in livestock to wealth in slaves, produce for a market, and earn a cash income to reinvest in the pastoral sector.[20] The contemporary sedentary lifestyle of several of the Somali clans of the Benaadir can be traced to their nineteenth-century involvement in plantation agriculture. As Luling explains for the Geledi of the Afgoye area, "The Geledi Nobles (pastoralists) settled down not to farm, but to letting their slaves farm" (1971:108).

This development of an export-oriented plantation economy along the Shabeelle marked the growing involvement of Somalis with the outside world—both in terms of producing for an external market, and in terms of importing large numbers of foreigners of very different backgrounds into Somali territory and Somali society. While slaves arrived in Somalia as part of a political, economic, and moral transformation of productive activity centered on the Shabeelle, they were entering a dynamic society experiencing change in other sectors as well. In addition to the struggles for economic and political supremacy along the Benaadir Coast and the influx of rural Somalis to the coast as a result of increased commercial activity,[21] widespread population movements characterized the southern Somali interior in the mid-nineteenth century. The continuing fluid Somali-Oromo region of interaction along the Jubba River valley (discussed below), religious warfare in the interriverine zone, and ongoing conflicts in Somali-inhabited territory claimed by Ethiopia resulted in population migrations for political, economic, and religious reasons, which brought about shifting kinship alliances, new hierarchies of status and dominance, and new tensions and conflicts over access to resources throughout the south.[22] The commercial transformation to a slave-based plantation economy was but one aspect of a continual shifting of power and authority throughout the south, and slaves arriving in Somalia both fueled this process and were themselves transformed by it.

The arrival of an enslaved labor force as part of the "commercial agricultural revolution"[23] held particular significance for one set of relationships along the Shabeelle. Slaves imported in the nineteenth century were not the first to cultivate the Shabeelle River valley. Villages of non-Somali African farmers were already settled in parts of the valley as full-time agriculturalists. Their origins are obscure. They may represent a remnant group of pre-Cushitic Bantu-speaking farmers who had been overwhelmed by Somali migrations across the Shabeelle (a point discussed further below), perhaps now mixed with Somalis who settled down among them to farm, and they may also represent descendants of slaves acquired by Somalis centuries ago, who established riverine farming villages as freedmen prior to the nineteenth century. Oral traditions offer little help: some insist these farming populations originated in slavery; others are more vague, saying they settled the country together with Somalis.[24] Whatever their origins, their physical features and occupations distinguished them from Somalis and placed them in an inferior sociopolitical position in Somali cosmology.[25]

Somalis considered these populations *habash*, a derogatory term of Arabic derivation which was used to mean "Abyssinian slave" (Luling 1971:44 n. 2). Other terms used by Somalis to connote the Shabeelle valley cultivators were equally or more derogatory: *ooji*, *addoon*, and *boon*. *Ooji* and *addoon* translate as "slave"; *boon* is the same word traditionally used by Somalis to designate the "lower" occupational castes in Somali society. These terms suggest how Somali society absorbed the riverine cultivators into its status hierarchy.

Prior to the widespread purchase of slaves, Somali pastoralists and some Shabeelle valley cultivator groups had formed alliances based on a division of labor. Shabeelle valley cultivators (Somali-speakers) attached themselves as corporate groups to (or were forced into submission by) Somali pastoral clans, creating what Cassanelli (1982:163–65, 1988:314) calls client relationships.[26] The "client-cultivator" groups (1982; 1988) retained separate and clear rights to the land they worked, were represented in clan councils by elders in the pastoral clans to which they gave allegiance, participated in Somali warfare, and were entitled to a certain portion of blood compensation. Despite their economic autonomy, however, "client-cultivator" groups "could not easily renounce their 'client' status, since it rested on a position of perceived social as well as political inferiority. . . . The division of labor (between client-cultivators and pastoralists) was reinforced by an ideology of social superiority/inferiority and sanctioned by the language of corporate kinship" (Cassanelli 1988:314).

The transition to a slave-based plantation economy represented a departure from the pattern of corporate relationships and responsibilities based on notions of kinship and clientship that had characterized the dynamic between Somali pastoralists and Shabeelle valley cultivators. Slaves were the embodiment of kinless beings, divorced from the responsibilities that relations of kinship entail. Their production was not for tribute or trade; it was exclusively for the financial benefit of their owners. Thus slavery as a productive system transcended the relationships required to maintain kinship-based production by offering an alternative source of accumulation. At the same time, however, Cassanelli (1982) argues that such accumulation did not produce a wealthy class of slaveholding elite, because slaves were fairly evenly distributed among Shabeelle-based Somali families and because any accumulated profit was redistributed throughout kinship networks. In contrast, Alpers (1983:452) argues that slavery-based agricultural production along the Shabeelle resulted in a class alliance between town and country. Whatever class stratification slavery produced among Somalis waned with abolition, but the institution of slavery certainly contributed to the ongoing dynamism of Somali identities in the south through the introduction of large numbers of alien, unattached people to southern Somalia. Estimating the numbers involved provides a sense of the significance of slave imports to southern Somalia. While not as informative as one might like, the observations of nineteenth-century European travelers and colonial authorities and the reminiscences both of those who were masters and of those who were slaves can be pieced together to obtain a general idea of the scope of slavery in southern Somalia.

Numbers

It is clear that the seaborne trade in East African slaves to Somalia grew dramatically over the course of the early nineteenth century. In tracing the history of the trade to Somalia of East Africans, Cassanelli found "the earliest dates that can be isolated with any certainty fall around 1800, when Zigua slaves from the Mrima Coast were brought to the Bajuni Islands, and perhaps to Baraawe" (1982:169). The British naval captain W. F. W. Owens, reporting in 1833 on his voyages along the east coast of Africa, noted that Mogadishu imported slaves.[27] By the 1830s and 1840s, Arab dhows were bringing African slaves to the Somali coast in growing numbers.[28] Lieutenant Christopher, who explored the Somali coast for the Royal Geographical Society in 1843, reported consistently seeing slaves working the fields in the immediate hinterland of Baraawe, Marka, and Mogadishu. In one area of farmland five miles inland from Marka he observed "many thousands" of slaves working (1844:85).

The slave trade was carried on to this point largely by sea. With the British suppression of the slave trade and the stationing of British naval patrol boats (or "dhow-chasers") on the Indian Ocean in the 1860s, slave traders increasingly began driving slaves overland, across the Jubba to the Benaadir, from where some were exported by dhow to Arabia.[29] In 1875, the British consul in Zanzibar, John Kirk, was told in Marka that slaves were being brought in great numbers by land, destined not for the coastal towns but for the "extensive cultivated lands that lie one day's journey westward on the banks of a certain river" (the Shabeelle) (Nwulia 1975:141–42). On the basis of information he collected in Marka and Zanzibar, Kirk estimated that at least ten thousand slaves were being taken across the Jubba annually for the Somali plantations and for export to Arabia.[30] Reports from European travelers confirm Kirk's information that large numbers of slaves were being marched overland. Cassanelli (1982:169) reports that "in 1866, Brenner counted six slave caravans in four days passing through Baraawe." The German explorer Carl Claus von der Decken's expedition up the Jubba valley described a chain of black slaves they encountered as "unfortunate, half starved and totally exhausted" (Kersten 1871:291). Crauford, in his travels in Jubaland in 1895, learned of an inlet just north of Kismayu called Bunder El Khadam (which may translate from the Arabic as "slave inlet"), where Somalis would bring slaves from the interior. The port was perfect for picking up and letting off slaves by dhow, as it was concealed from view from the sea. Crauford wrote, "I am inclined to believe that at one time the Somalis made great use of this bunder in slave trading operations" (ASMAI 1896:5).

Transport of slaves on the high seas continued as well, although the stakes were higher. Letters sent between British colonial administrators and the sultan of Zanzibar, who agreed to a ban on the slave trade in 1875, reveal the frustrations felt by all parties in the effort to suppress the slave trade.[31] In the preceding decade, British reports discuss the recapture of hundreds of slaves by antislavery patrol boats, but are clear that such recaptures represented only a fraction of the total number of slaves taken by dhow from east Africa.[32]

Despite the Brussels conference of 1890 where the colonial administrative powers (Britain, France, and Italy) abolished the legal status of slavery in the colonies, the slave trade between other parts of East Africa and Somalia continued unabated. The Italian administrators in Somalia at the turn of the century did nothing to discourage slavery; in fact, several Italian administrators, including the royal commissioner, purchased female slaves as concubines.[33] A census conducted in the trading town of Lugh in the 1890s showed two and a half times as many slaves lived in the town as free citizens.[34] A newspaper campaign in 1902 in Italy, coupled with the actions of the Anti-Slavery Society of Italy, brought the issue of slavery to national attention. An independent report ordered by the Italian government in 1903 revealed that slavery was flourishing; slaves were still entering the Benaadir, being openly bought and sold with the sanction of the local Italian authorities, who were also returning runaway slaves to friendly clans.[35] Another report described Baardheere and Lugh as "two veritable slave markets" (quoted in Hess 1966:77). The resulting scandal forced the government to accept direct control and responsibility for the administration of southern Somalia, which for ten years had been in the hands of chartered companies.[36]

From 1903 to 1904 the Italian colonial government issued three ordinances outlawing the slave trade.[37] The major thrust for the suppression of slavery, however, was directed at a transition to domestic servitude. The coastal towns were the focus of this transition, as Italian colonial authority remained limited to the coast until 1908. A 1903 household census of Benaadir towns found that slaves constituted one-third of the Mogadishu population of 6,700, 830 of the 3,000 inhabitants of Baraawe, and 720 of the 5,000 inhabitants of Marka. These urban slaves were textile workers, operators of sesame presses, domestic servants, and port and dock workers.[38] From 1905 to 1908, the government negotiated the freedom of 1,300 slaves from Mogadishu, 850 from Marka, and 150 from Baraawe.[39] The ex-slaves were told to remain in their masters' homes as servants (Hess [1966:100] calls them "bond-servants"), exchanging domestic service for room and board, or, more rarely, paying a daily tribute earned from wage labor (opportunities for which were quite limited) as rent.[40]

Italian authorities favored the continued servitude of emancipated slaves as economically less disruptive and as a way to avoid what many viewed as the high potential for lawlessness, prostitution, and thievery by unassimilated, unemployed former slaves.[41] Transition to domestic servitude was also a way to placate Somali clans incensed over Italian efforts to suppress slavery (namely the Biimaal and Wacdan).[42] Racist ideas held by colonial authorities played a role as well. The colonial governor Carletti, in commenting on the gradualist policy of encouraging a transition from slavery to domestic servitude, wrote in 1907 that there are "some races destined to be servants" (cited in Hess 1966:98). The resident of Afgoye in 1910, Casali, wrote that "Swahili" slaves were so mentally inferior that they were resigned to their fate almost with joy.[43]

In rural areas of plantation agriculture, the transition to domestic servitude was not effected so neatly or easily. With the suppression of the slave trade, evidence suggests that plantation owners resorted to harsher forms of restraint to limit the freedom of their slaves, and therefore the possibility of escape. Tales of slaves being kept in leg irons or chains or suffering severe beatings for escape attempts are not uncommon.[44] Italians did not take control of the hinterland of the coast until 1908, and it was 1914 before they could claim control over the interriverine zone. Once they had established control, authorities were "very cautious" about applying the emancipation decrees in the interior, primarily to avoid rebellion by Somali slave owners and the creation of a potentially rebellious, independent landless class of ex-slaves (Cassanelli 1988:319). Consequently the figure of 4,300 slaves reported liberated by the Italian government from 1900 to 1914 must primarily represent those from coastal towns.[45]

It is clear that the number of slaves in the interior was much larger than on the coast. Cassanelli (1988:313) estimates that the riverine areas absorbed somewhere around 50,000 slaves from 1800 to 1890. By 1911, the Italian governor of Somalia, Cerrina-Ferroni, estimated the total number of slaves in southern Somalia at 25–30,000 in a population of 300,000.[46] The figures given by Cassanelli and Cerrina-Ferroni, in turn, must primarily represent slaves working for plantation owners in the Shabeelle River valley. In reconstructing slave-based plantation production along the Shabeelle, Cassanelli (1982:173) suggests an average farm size per family would have been five to ten hectares, which would require five to eight slaves.[47] Taking Cerrina-Ferroni's lower estimate of 25,000 (to account for urban slaves), these figures suggest there were about 3,800 families owning slaves in southern Somalia (in a total estimated population of 300,000) in the early twentieth century. Using six members as the average household size,[48] and deducting the population of the urban areas, these figures result in an estimation that about one-thirteenth of the rural households in southern Somalia had slaves. Assuming that Cassanelli is correct in his statement that "slaves were fairly evenly distributed among landholders" (1982:173 n. 71), the numbers proposed by Cerrina-Ferroni and Cassanelli must only account for the population of the clans in the Shabeelle area.[49] These figures, therefore, must not include slaves of a very different origin, used in the interior for very different purposes—for pastoralism. While accurate statistics are not available, oral histories and British colonial documents suggest the acquisition of slaves by nomads for purposes of herding and warfare was widespread throughout southern Somali clans. Internal (obtained locally as opposed to imported from elsewhere in East Africa) acquisition of slaves has not been well addressed in the literature, and yet was probably the primary method for acquiring slaves in southern Somalia for pastoral purposes.

"Hidden Slavery": The Pastoralists

The internal source of slaves were the Oromo. The great Somali migrations of the past three hundred years pushed the Oromo to their present location in northeastern Kenya and southwestern Ethiopia, where raiding and warfare between the two groups continues to this day.[50] Referred to in much of the colonial literature as the Galla, this group calls itself the Oromo. This term, as used here, covers the closely related Orma of the Tana River area and Boran of northern Kenya.[51] The Oromo inhabited the areas west of the Jubba River into the second half of the nineteenth century, when they were finally expelled by Somali Darood pastoralists. As late as 1865, when the ill-fated German explorer von der Decken made his journey up the Jubba, only "Galla" inhabited the west bank of the river.[52] Many of the contemporary village and place names along the west bank of the Jubba River are Boran words, adopted into Somali by the conquerors of the area. Local lore tells of many great battles in the late nineteenth century between Somali and Oromo west of the Jubba—battles that were finally halted by British involvement in the area at the turn of the century.

British colonial authorities were very concerned about Somali expansionist tendencies and Somali-Oromo wars, and carefully documented population movements and social relationships between the two groups. According to British documents from the Kenya National Archives and I. M. Lewis's (1988) reconstruction of events, Somali Darood pastoralists began crossing the Jubba River in small numbers as clients and allies of the Orma in the 1800s. Gradually, the number of Darood living under

Orma leadership increased to the point that they were able to take advantage of a smallpox epidemic among the Orma in 1865, attacking their former overlords. The Darood insurgency was so strong that most of the surviving Orma fled beyond the Tana River, leaving the Jubba-Tana area in Somali hands.[53] The Orma conquered by the Somali in some cases remained as clients and in others as slaves. Hilarie Kelly (1983) found that clientship resulted when the Orma quickly acquiesced, whereas serfdom and slavery were the result of more violent confrontations, which tended to occur when the Orma had their backs to the Jubba or Tana River. Orma conquered by Somalis and made serfs or slaves were called Warday, a term Kelly (1983:29) says is of Somali provenance.[54] While of Orma origin, Warday took on many aspects of Somali culture, including Somali as a first language. In 1988 Somalis still talked about how desirable Warday were as herder-slaves.

Further north, Somali Ajuraan were also crossing the river as clients to the Boran. According to one British colonial administrator, the Ajuraan increased their ranks by "admitting any Islamic tribe who wanted to join, with the ultimate aim of ousting the Boran" (KNA 1925). The Ajuraan attacked the Boran, but were subdued by the British, who had established military and administrative posts in the area in 1912. The Boran continued to be pushed north by the expanding Darood, and many Boran were captured and kept as slaves (or "clients") of Ajuraan, Darood, and other Somali groups.

The British self-image as gatekeepers against further Somali territorial expansion and protectors of Oromo and other groups perceived as threatened by Somalis is evident in a statement made by a colonial official in 1916 about the Darood in the Jubba-Tana area. The Darood, he wrote, are a

> continual menace to the peaceful tribes in the vicinity. The Wagalla, the Wapokomo and the Korokoro had been driven from the left bank by murder and dacoity and there could be no doubt that the desire of the Somali was eventually to establish themselves in permanence on the river. Their record in the district was one long unbroken series of lawless act [*sic*]: they had burned down coastal hamlets and massacred the inhabitants, they attacked the German Mission at Ngao and only a fortunate chance prevented the murder of the European residents, their constant raiding parties in the Dodori forest had driven capital from the province, they dealt actively in slaves, collected poll tax from the Boni, and being in possession of modern rifles they were from every point of view a serious obstruction to development and good government. (KNA 1916)

In an effort to finalize the continuing "fluid" situation between Somalis and Oromos, and to ease the growing tension between the two groups in the Jubba-Tana area, a Somali-Orma agreement was conceived in 1919.[55] The agreement stated that Oromo living on the left (east) bank of the Tana in subservience to their Somali conquerors could choose either to accept a formal position as serfs or to move across the Tana to join free Oromo kinsmen, previously resettled by the British. Those who chose to move, however, had to forfeit half their livestock to their Somali masters as a condition of gaining their freedom. As I. M. Lewis says, "Under these conditions, it is perhaps not surprising that few of the Warday Galla moved" (1988:31).

The next seventeen years were characterized by a series of Oromo attempts to gain their freedom while retaining their livestock. The British consistently intervened to maintain the stipulations of the 1919 agreement,[56] supporting a fervid Somali campaign to force their Warday slaves to remain in servitude. British documents mention the "use (of) all tactics" (KNA 1932c), including "threats and cajolery" (KNA 1932b) and appeals to "fear and superstition" (KNA 1932d), by Somalis to keep their Warday slaves. Despite their official actions, the British clearly recognized that the position of the Oromo living among the Somalis amounted to slavery. Summarizing the situation of "Galla" living under Somalis in 1930 and showing particular concern for the "exploitation of children," the district commissioner of Garissa District, H. B. Sharpe, wrote that "every Galla living with the Somalis is virtually a slave. . . . Children born of Galla girls among Somalis are virtually slaves and therefore exploitable" (KNA 1930).

The agreement ended in 1936,[57] when the British declared that the Warday had ceased to exist as an ethnic entity, having been fully assimilated as Somalis.[58] This was not the case, and Warday continued to live—and may still live today—in bondage to Somali masters. Regional knowledge of personal ancestries maintained these ethnic and status distinctions, and Somali pastoralists living in the middle Jubba in 1988 identified to me several local pastoralist Warday families.

Somali pastoralists in southern Somalia (including the Jubba-Tana area) clearly had control over substantial numbers of pastoral slaves or serfs by the turn of the century. These slaves were primarily, if not entirely, of Boran and Oromo (Warday) origin. While numbers are never provided, and indeed may have been impossible to obtain, British colonial documents report Somalis "were said to hold a considerable number of slaves" in the Northern Frontier District (GBCO 1909–10) and that "all Somalis have living among them purely slave clans" (KNA 1932e). On his 1896 march through the Somali Ogaadeen-dominated territory west of the Jubba River, Crauford noted the prevalence of Galla and Boran slaves held by local pastoralists (ASMAI 1896). While an estimation of the number of pastoral slaves living under Somali overlordship is impossible, it is safe to say that they numbered in the thousands at any one time during the second half of the nineteenth century. Based on the statistics available from urban censuses, from Cerrina-Ferroni's and Cassanelli's estimates, and from British observations of pastoral slavery, I believe slaves may have constituted as much as one-fifth of the southern Somali population in the decades around 1900.

* * *

Whether arriving by sea through Benaadir ports, on foot in long forced overland marches, or through capture by Somali raiders, slaves entering Somalia in the nineteenth century were part of a radically transformative period of economic and political change, and were themselves agents of change by virtue of their foreignness and their numbers. They joined a society characterized by fluidity, where Somali lineages were migrating and adopting new statuses along the way, where political turnover as a result of population migration was occurring in several areas, and where points of ethnic interaction were marked by flux and shifting identities—such as in the Somali-Oromo region; in relationships between Somalis and Shabeelle valley cultivator groups; and in coastal towns with the shifting influence of the Somali-Arab family lineages, Somali lineages with nomadic power bases, the power holders of the interior, and the sultan of Zanzibar's supporters. To borrow Cassanelli's (1982) apt image, southern Somali society was in the midst of a dynamic process of shaping itself, and slaves were a part of this process. Slaves entered southern Somalia outside of all kinship ties (although the situation was more complex with Oromo slaves), but there was precedent in Somali society for establishing a client basis of interaction with outsiders, for shifting identities, and for fluctuating forms of interaction. As we shall see in later chapters, within a half century ex-slaves and their descendants were drawing on a variety of such mechanisms to forge their place in Somali society.

After Slavery

Slaves in Somalia came from a variety of backgrounds and had experienced different forms of slavery, as urban domestics, agricultural laborers, and herders. Every year, some of these slaves escaped their enforced servitude and others were granted their freedom. Following slavery, their options were limited, especially for fugitive slaves. As Cassanelli (1988) notes, runaway ex-slaves or those who decided not to remain in their masters' homes as clients chose among three options: joining one of the already established villages of "client-cultivators" in the Shabeelle River valley; joining one of the religious brotherhoods which took in fugitives; or migrating into the Jubba valley to join villages formed by other fugitive slaves.

Since client-cultivators of the Shabeelle River valley maintained close ties with slave-owning Somali clans, intermarriage between clients and slaves working side by side on Somali-owned plantations augmented these client villages with ex-slaves. The significance of this option for ex-slaves remains unclear, however, due to the lack of evidence on the extent to which ex-slaves were absorbed by Shabeelle valley client-cultivator groups. Cassanelli suggests that "the assimilation of slaves into the client-cultivator population was certainly well advanced by the time colonial forces occupied the Shabelle Valley, which helps explain why early colonial observers found it difficult to distinguish between the two groups, calling them all *liberti*" (1988:316). Several factors contributed toward making this option perhaps the least desirable of the three. Joining a village of client-cultivators ensured a continuing relationship of dependence on and submission to Somali overlords, as well as a heightened likelihood of being conscripted into colonial work projects. The increasing brutality of Somali masters toward their slaves in the years between formal abolition (1903–4) and colonial enforcement (1908–14) in the interior region of the Shabeelle valley encouraged many ex-slaves to abandon the area rather than remain as part of client-cultivator groups.

Joining one of the many agriculturally based religious brotherhoods formed in southern Somalia between 1890 and the middle of the twentieth century emerged as an important alternative for many ex-slaves. Again, scant evidence precludes a firm assessment of the significance of these brotherhoods, but Cassanelli suggests that they may have absorbed somewhere between 15,000 and 30,000 ex-slaves by the 1940s.[59]

Many ex-slaves chose the third option of migrating to the Jubba valley. Claimed as a refuge by ex-slaves, the valley offered the promise of independence, autonomy from former Somali masters, and escape from the colonial conscripted work parties which were limited to the Benaadir until the 1920s.

The Jubba Valley

The ecology, geography, and demography of the Jubba valley provide important clues as to why the valley emerged as the preferred choice for many ex-slaves following manumission or escape. Fertile land bordering a perennial river offered the promise of agricultural sustainability, and forested riverbanks offered wild foods in times of shortage as well as protection from pastoralists. Furthermore, it appears that much of the riverbank land was uninhabited when fugitive slaves first arrived in the mid-nineteenth century. There is no clear evidence that agriculturalists lived in the valley prior to the arrival of fugitive slaves.[60] A hunter-gatherer population known as the Boni utilized the lower reaches of the valley.[61] Pastoral groups (the Oromo and Somali) utilized the mid-valley in the course of their seasonal movements, stopping at watering places on the river and in adjacent *dhasheegs* (inland, low-lying basins of water) for their livestock. These water sources were and are particularly crucial during the long, hot dry season of jilaal, an extremely difficult time for herder and beast alike. Judging from contemporary patterns and oral histories, however, the lower half of the valley was generally avoided by pastoralists except in times of great need, as it was dense forest, infested with tsetse flies (lethal to livestock) and malaria. The term coined by Somalis to signify the stretch of riverine jungle and inland ponds from present-day Yontoy to just below the mid-valley town of Saakow reveals a widespread perception of the area: *Gosha,* which glosses as "unhealthy forest."

Prior to the mid-nineteenth century, the mid to lower valley thus appears to have been a largely uninhabited area of "unhealthy" dense forest, partially utilized by hunter-gatherers, and seasonally utilized by pastoralists at certain optimal watering points. There is no evidence that a permanent farming population was living in the valley when the first groups of runaway slaves entered in the mid-nineteenth century. Many fugitive slaves escaping slavery chose this relatively uninhabited, isolated, agriculturally promising area as their refuge for freedom.

The People of the Forest

The Gosha Settlement Process, 1840–1895

Nineteenth-century travelers' accounts, oral tradition, and colonial documents provide a good understanding of how the lower Jubba valley was settled by fugitive slaves. Because several excellent secondary sources summarize this information in ethnographically rich historical reconstructions,[62] and because my focus in this book is the middle Jubba, a brief overview drawn from these secondary sources must suffice.

The first fugitive slaves to settle villages in the Jubba valley were Zegua (known in Somalia as Mushunguli) escaping from Benaadir plantations around 1840. These slaves, who probably knowingly and unknowingly had sold themselves into slavery to avoid starvation during the 1836 famine in their Tanzanian homeland, had escaped shortly after their arrival in Somalia and were intending to return home by foot.[63] Menkhaus describes this dramatic event:

> After a period of one or two years on the Somali plantations, the Mushunguli slaves plotted to return to East Africa by land. According to the account of Abdallah bin Simba [recorded in 1934 by the native treasury clerk for Handeni District], this escape was preceded by a meeting in which the Mushunguli discussed the dangers of traveling with children and women on a journey that would involve constant fighting, and decided to take everyone along despite the dangers. The next week, after a dance that lasted through the night, the Mushunguli escaped, having secretly made for themselves bows and arrows to protect themselves. After a number of encounters with Somali pastoralists, the group arrived at the forest of the Jubba valley, near present-day Jamaame, a distance of over three-hundred kilometers. (1989:108)

After an earthquake occurred one night during their travels, their leader, the prophetess Wanakooka, "had a vision in which she foresaw disaster if the group continued on to East Africa. She conveyed this dream to the Mushunguli, who then stayed and settled along the riverbanks" (Menkhaus 1989:109). The settlements they formed by 1840 in the lower Jubba were located just above the Somali settlements lining the river north of the mouth.

As the number of slaves imported to Somalia grew, and as knowledge of the refuge offered by the Jubba valley spread, a continual and growing stream of fugitive slaves made their way into the valley. In 1865, von der Decken estimated the fugitive slave population in the lower valley at around 4,000 living in a handful of villages.[64] By the 1890s, F. G. Dundas (1893) reported ex-slave settlements stretching from Yontoy to Mfudo (see Map 1), and Clifford Crauford (ASMAI 1896) estimated the total ex-slave population at 25–30,000. Perducchi's village census in 1901 suggests the population had reached 40,000.[65] The bulk of the population initially settled on the east bank,[66] probably because of the threat from Oromo in the early years of settlement, and fear of Ogaadeen Somalis by the turn of the century.

Based on these estimates, Kenneth Menkhaus (1989:110) believes, and I concur, that at least 20,000 slaves made their way into the valley from 1865 to 1895. While the vast majority of these settlers were escaping plantation slavery, their numbers were augmented by slaves released on shore by British antislavery naval patrols.[67]

Initially, fugitive slaves settled along the lines of their East African origin, the most numerous being Zegua, Yao, Nyasa, Makua, Ngindu, and Nyika.[68] Thus Europeans noted Zegua villages, Yao villages, and, occasionally, mixed villages.[69] Villages settled by one ethnic group were somewhat exclusive: von der Decken reported that the inhabitants of the Zegua village of Manamsunde "are very reluctant to adopt somebody who does not belong to them into their community; only if a refugee brings along gun and powder will they welcome him" (Kersten 1871:303).

Newly arrived slaves would thus search out communities formed by ex-slaves from their East African group of origin. In this way, villages formed prior to 1890 in the lower Jubba were separate "ethno-linguistic communities" (Menkhaus 1989), which retained their Bantu languages while apparently using Swahili as a lingua franca.

Cultural, ethnic, and linguistic distinctions were particularly strong among slaves who had been taken as adults for the slave trade. The most extreme example are the Mushunguli (Zegua originally from Tanzanian territory), who retained their Bantu language and sense of ethnic distinctiveness through the 1980s. The Mushunguli living in the lower Jubba in the 1980s held the strongest oral traditions of their group history: of their enslavement, slave experiences, escape from slavery (partially recounted above), and their settlement of the first Gosha villages.[70]

By 1875, villages from Yontoy to Mfudu had been settled, and the influx of runaways was still high. Runaways could either settle in a village of their ethnic background, or forge north into the forest to settle new villages of their own. The next two decades saw the rise of what Menkhaus (1989:127) calls an "independent Goshaland."[71] In the early 1870s, Gosha villagers were able to band together to defeat and subordinate the Boni to whom they had initially been forced to pay tribute, a victory achieved with the use of guns acquired from the sultan of Zanzibar in exchange for the promise of a share of ivory to the sultan. Following this victory, the growing prominence of several local leaders with spheres of influence outside their own villages and the forging of a political alliance with the sultan of Zanzibar further served to bring Gosha villages into a wider arena of joint political action.[72]

The most prominent remembered event of Goshaland history during this period (1875–95) was the Gosha peoples' ultimate defeat of the pastoral Ogaadeen Somalis around 1890, an event that was still recalled in oral tradition throughout the valley in the 1980s.[73] Gosha villages were constantly under threat from surrounding Ogaadeenis (who had pushed the Oromos away from the Jubba by the 1870s), and Europeans noted that many Gosha villages were fortified. Trade to this point had primarily been carried on between Ogaadeen and Gosha at a place called Regatta, a plain with wide visibility and little opportunity for subterfuge. Crauford (ASMAI 1896:4) mentions that Gosha villagers would not venture into Somali territory, and Somalis were afraid to enter Gosha villages. The relationship between Gosha villagers and Ogaadeen pastoralists during this period thus largely consisted of trading and raiding. The Gosha victory over local Ogaadeen pastoralists is primarily attributed to the leadership of a Yao ex-slave called Nassib Bundo. Nassib had achieved prominence in the Gosha-Boni skirmishes and, as the self-proclaimed "Sultan of the Gosha," his fame grew with his negotiations with prominent Somalis, the sultan of Zanzibar, the Egyptians, and, finally, with the British and Italian colonial authorities. Nassib has achieved superhuman proportions in some Gosha oral traditions as a man of astounding magical abilities who was able to crush Ogaadeen Somalis with his fighting power and his magical prowess. Colonial authorities treated him as the most prominent of the Gosha big men and written accounts portray the formation of a Gosha confederacy with Nassib as the leader.

Menkhaus (1989) provides a convincing alternative to this picture of a precolonial Gosha confederacy united under Nassib Bundo. He argues that Gosha villages retained a high degree of linguistic, cultural, and political independence and autonomy, with sometimes bitter rivalries existing between village or ethnic leaders. Intervillage affairs were marked as much by conflict as by cooperation (which occurred primarily in military affairs, such as the Gosha-Boni fights and the Gosha-Ogaadeen skirmishes). Menkhaus's portrayal accords well with (probably racist) European eyewitness accounts, such as Crauford's (ASMAI 1896:3) view of the Gosha population as having no unity: "owing to divided interests and impatience of discipline, no concerted movement is at all probable." Contemporary inhabitants of villages which formed in the middle Jubba at the turn of the century recount that they owed no allegiance to Nassib Bundo—his sphere of influence clearly did not extend upriver.

The picture that emerges of the initial settlement of the lower Jubba is thus one of groups of people with distinct languages and cultures settling together in villages on the basis of East African ethnic identity. These villages functioned independently and were socially exclusive, yet occasionally participated in military maneuvers against shared enemies: first the Boni and later the Ogaadeen Somali. The fervor and obvious relish with which accounts of Nassib Bundo's victories and powers are told in contemporary times are more indicative of the pride and social memory of the development of a Goshaland of independent villages unattached to Somali masters or patrons than of a Goshaland that was politically and socially unified. This fifty-year period (1840s–1890s) thus witnessed the creation of a new space in Somalia: an ecologically bounded physical and ideological space claimed by ex-slaves (and freed captives), whose hard work, struggles, and battles transformed the Jubba valley into a refuge for ex-slaves and an alien place for Somalis.

Their struggles to claim the Jubba valley as a place of freedom from slavery took place within the larger context of regional dynamism during the latter half of the nineteenth century. Not only was the lower valley in tumult, as ex-slaves battled Boni hunters and Ogaadeen Somalis for control of the riverbanks, but the plains surrounding the valley and the coastal towns which exported valley products were under dispute as well. Darood Somalis in increasing numbers pushed against the west bank Oromo pastoralists, resulting in the latter's virtual expulsion from the Jubba valley region (except, of course, for the Oromo slaves left behind). Along the coast and the lower plains, a new migration of Herti (Majeerteen) Somalis enticed by the commercial opportunities offered by the growing southern livestock export trade competed with the Maxamed Subeer (Ogaadeen) clan which had arrived several decades earlier, precipitating a regional struggle for power among Somali clans.[74] Arab merchants arrived in trading towns along the lower Jubba to deal in livestock products, ivory, and Gosha agricultural surplus, and to serve as moneylenders to the fledgling Gosha villages.[75] Thus a regional Jubba valley sphere of interaction was developing as a result of a variety of factors, including commercial forces created by Somalia's growing involvement in the global economy, which prompted waves of resettlement and reconfigurations of power in the Jubba region. Ex-slaves arriving in the valley during this time period contributed to this dynamism through their agricultural productivity,[76] their ambiguous but independent status, and, eventually, their sheer numbers. Their colonization of the valley established them as a critical force within a changing and emerging regional society.

Lower Jubba Settlement After 1895: The Emergence of a New Pattern

By the turn of the century, the place occupied by Gosha villagers in regional society had stabilized as conflicts between villages, between Gosha villagers and Boni hunter-gatherers, and between Gosha villagers and Somali pastoralists had evolved into accommodation. While the Gosha did defeat Ogaadeen Somalis in a prominent battle around 1890, equally important in the initiation of peaceful relations between Gosha and Somali in the years surrounding the turn of the century was the influx of large numbers of "Somalized" ex-slaves, the spread of Islam among the Gosha (attributed to the efforts of the revered Sheikh Murjan, among others), and the "pacification" of Ogaadeen Somalis by the newly arrived British colonial authorities.

The new arrivals to the Jubba valley during and after the 1890s introduced a new settlement pattern. Many of these ex-slaves had not maintained strong ties—cultural or linguistic—to their east African ethnic groups. Most likely, the majority of these slaves had been kidnapped as children. Unlike the Mushunguli, most groups interviewed by Menkhaus in the lower Jubba report their ancestors were stolen as children. According to the elders of one village: "(Our ancestors) were people stolen from the British territory (east Africa). There was a certain boat that went from Arab lands to British lands (*sic*), and the boat was at the British docks. All the children came around the boat and Arabs gave them dates to attract them, and then loaded the boats with these children. The boats left for Marka and the Arabs asked if anyone wanted to buy slaves" (Menkhaus 1989:99). Several of my informants in the middle Jubba reported their fathers had similarly been kidnapped.[77]

These reports find confirmation in British documents of the time. The British *Administration Report of Zanzibar for the Year 1864–65*, for example, complains that: "Kidnapping [of children for slavery] by Arabs has also been carried on to a great extent, and the Government of Zanzibar appears perfectly unable to put a stop to it" (ASMAI 1865). Other secondary sources also emphasize the importance of children in the slave trade, for reasons that are simple: children are easier to manage, make lighter cargo, and are more easily controlled and less likely to retain strong ties to their places of origin.[78] The ramifications of being enslaved as a child are great in terms of one's personal sense of place and identity, a point to which I shall return in Chapter 7.

These later runaways, who had largely been enslaved as children, were not easily accepted by already formed villages of ethnically united Yao or Zegua. As they held weak or no ties to a specific East African group, they used Somali clan affiliation as their template for settlement. By 1900, the villages settled north of Jilib had begun to identify themselves by Somali clan names (Eelay, Jiddu, Biimaal, Daafeed, Hawiye) rather than East African tribal names (Yao, Ngindu, Makua, Mushunguli). As described in the next chapter, this pattern marked the settlement of the entire mid-valley area.

In addition to their stronger affiliations with Somali clans, these newly arriving ex-slaves also brought a firm adherence to Islam and a lingua franca—the Af-maay-maay dialect of the Somali language. Islam spread rapidly throughout the valley around the turn of the century, partly as a result of the influence of arriving Muslim ex-slaves, partly as a result of the successful proselytizing efforts of great sheikhs who came into the valley to convert the villagers, and partly because of the numerous religious brotherhoods (*jamaacooyin*, sing. *jamaaca*) throughout the valley which accepted ex-slaves, offered religious instruction, and fed needy families from communal farms in times of shortage.[79] Furthermore, Somali served as the language of Islam in the lower Jubba, and thus language and religion became mutually reinforcing forces of Somalization among lower Gosha villagers. In addition to the impact of large numbers of arriving monolingual Maay-maay speaking ex-slaves into the valley and the use of Maay-maay by Somali sheikhs, Menkhaus (1989) speculates that the Maay-maay dialect of Somali replaced both Swahili and local Bantu languages as a lingua franca partly because of the increasing incidence of intermarriage among previously distinct ethnolinguistic communities (with the exception of the Mushunguli) and partly because of the need to communicate with surrounding Somali pastoralists for trading purposes. For whatever reason, Swahili rapidly died out as a lingua franca among Gosha villagers after the turn of the century.

Finally, British pacification campaigns against Ogaadeen Somalis lessened the need for fortified Gosha villages and arms in the lower Jubba. As the guns provided by the sultan of Zanzibar became obsolete, it appears the need for them became obsolete as well. No fortified villages are reported in the Gosha after the turn of the century, and while Menkhaus (1989:168) reports that some lower Gosha blacksmiths learned how to make guns, there is no evidence that this practice developed or spread up the valley to newly forming Gosha villages. The Loc local historian Iidow recalled to me how life changed "when the British captured the land and collected weapons from the Ogaadeen," allowing unarmed Gosha villagers to move freely to the west bank and to more exposed areas along the river. By 1990—almost a century later—the fact that Gosha villagers uniformly lacked guns directly contributed to their terrible victimization in the civil war.

Conclusions

These earliest Gosha villages shared many characteristics with New World maroon slave villages, which were also initially settled by newly arrived, unassimilated runaways (Price 1975). In both cases, maroon villages fiercely guarded their independence and autonomy, yet found it necessary to engage in trade relations with the dominant society. Furthermore, in both cases the earliest maroon villages were unaccommodating, unfriendly, or even hostile to later arrivals, many of whom were much more assimilated than the previous runaways.

Only toward the end of the century did a slight shift begin to occur in Somali-Gosha and intra-Gosha relations. Islamic conversion, the emergence of a lingua franca, and the shift in the basis of settlement from East African tribal identities to Somali clan identities marked the increasing Somalization of the Gosha people. The fiercely independent maroon character of the earliest settlements, founded by people who had only remained enslaved for a short time, gradually gave way to a pattern of increased accommodation to surrounding Somalis. For later arrivals, especially those after the turn of the century, Somali clan affiliation and unity in Islam emerged as the most important elements of village formation. As we shall see in the next chapter, later arrivals, more indoctrinated to Somali society through extended slavery experiences, brought a different character to the settlement of the upper Gosha.

We have seen how slaves in nineteenth-century Somalia were joining a society in flux, characterized by struggles for economic and political supremacy along the length of the Benaadir Coast, by a trade-based commercial transformation of the coastal hinterland (plantation agriculture) as well as of the interior (livestock, ivory), and by population movements throughout the south precipitated by a variety of forces. Slaves entering Somalia became another migrating group of diverse identities and statuses who contributed to the flux and dynamism of an emerging southern Somali society in general, and to the fluid context of the Jubba valley in particular. By the turn of the century, ex-slaves had created a new society and a new ecological space in the Jubba valley which would prove to be of central interest to the occupying Italian colonial authorities, to the postcoup Somali state in the 1980s, to the "development" agenda of Western aid agencies, and to the poststate militias in the 1990s.

Chapter 4
The Settlement of the Upper Gosha, 1895–1988

The Jubba valley at the turn of the century was a dynamic place, where newly free ex-slaves were felling trees, building families, and constructing communities. The new settlers were also grappling with more than the material demands of day-to-day life; they were struggling to forge a place for themselves in the fluctuating regional sphere of social relations that comprised southern Somali society. The experiences of slavery, escape, manumission, resettlement, movement up the valley, shifting Somali clan affiliations, and conflict with Somali pastoralists and European colonial authorities all informed and contributed to Gosha peoples' construction of their identity and history. Contemporary Gosha villagers continue to draw upon their understanding of these histories—these ancestral experiences—to define and create meaningful personal and collective identities. As noted in the previous chapter, a striking aspect of the Gosha settlement pattern as it evolved on the upper Gosha (middle Jubba valley) frontier was the extent to which new settlers utilized Somali clan affiliations as the backbone for social organization. In fashioning personal identities within Somali society, ex-slaves arriving in the Gosha after about 1895 subordinated their diverse ethnic ancestries to their newer Somali linguistic and clan affiliations. This chapter describes how the process of settling the upper Gosha reflected the hegemony of Somali social organization, but we shall also see how village ties, and, to a lesser extent, ancestry, shaped people's lives and conceptions of their social identity and place.[1] Later chapters delve into the lived experience of Somali clan affiliations for Gosha people.

Historical Sources

My discussion of the settlement of the lower Jubba was drawn almost entirely from contemporary secondary sources and European eyewitness accounts written in the nineteenth century. My data for the settlement of the middle Jubba (upper Gosha) come almost entirely from my fieldwork. The colonial documents I have examined rarely mentioned middle Jubba villages or inhabitants, probably largely due to the fact that there was very little colonial activity in this region. Until 1924, when Jubaland was ceded to Italy, Britain maintained posts in the lower valley and at Sarinley in the upper valley, but showed no interest in the middle valley area. Italian activity remained limited to the more accessible lower valley for agriculture and trade, and to the upper valley Baardheere region, which was an important locus of caravan trade and Somali pastoral activity and the site of numerous intra-Somali and Somali-colonial military skirmishes. Perhaps the concentration of colonial energy on agriculture in the lower valley and military maneuvers in the Baardheere region left few resources to devote to the more inaccessible and lightly populated middle Jubba.

Furthermore, while Italian documents are clear that the Gosha consisted of fugitive and liberated slaves, they provide varied accounts of the geographical boundaries of the Gosha, perhaps because of the constantly changing nature of valley settlements. Thus it is unclear what geographical area is being referred to in colonial documents which discuss the "Goscia." A 1906 traveler's report mentions the Gosha as the area between Margherita and Bidi in the lower valley,[2] a 1916 administrative report notes the ex-slaves known as "the Gosha" settled the area between mid-valley Dujuuma and Margherita,[3] a 1923 colonial map similarly locates the Gosha between Dujuuma and Margherita,[4] and Italian ethnographer Corrado Zoli's 1927 book defines the Gosha as the lower valley area between Jilib and the mouth of the river. Administratively, the Italians considered Bidi the northern boundary of the Gosha, perhaps because the area north of Bidi was believed to be sparsely populated, and perhaps because the area over which Nassib Bundo claimed control ended at Bidi. The valley south of Bidi experienced greater Italian penetration, control, and scrutiny than did the area populated by ex-slaves stretching from Bidi to above Bu'aale. For this reason, and because the immigrants to the valley above the Bidi-Jilib area share characteristics that differ from those of the ex-slaves who colonized the valley south of Jilib, I will refer to the mid-valley area stretching from Bidi-Jilib to above Bu'aale as the upper Gosha in order to differentiate it from the area below Jilib, which I call the lower Gosha (see Map 1). This differentiation between the upper and the lower Gosha (because the background of settlers in the two areas and the nature of the historical evidence for settlement is different) can perhaps be most accurately described as a continuum of settlement patterns, slavery experiences, and personal identity, where the continuum is shaped by strength of association with an identified East African "homeland," chronology of settlement, and productive economic background (plantation agricultural labor, agropastoralism, or pastoral labor). As always, the lived historical experience of identity is much more squishy than categorical.

Charting population growth in the Gosha from colonial documents is also problematic. Unfortunately, population records for the Jubba valley kept by British and Italian authorities during the first two decades of this century do not offer any clear picture of population growth. British population estimates vary by up to ten thousand from year to year in no consistent direction, and administrators continually note that they did not attempt regular forays into the upriver interior due to the harsh travel conditions.[5] One British colonial official wrote tellingly of his government's ignorance of the population he was there to oversee:

> At the same time with the possibility of the handing over of Jubaland [to the Italians] in view it will be necessary to know who is to be kept and who sent packing from the territory remaining under the Flag. So that a knowledge of the peoples on the possible border should be really made a study and policy now aimed at effecting a simple division when the time comes if it does. All should be cut and dried or else we must confess to our visitors our ignorance of the country that we have been responsible for for so many years. (KNA n.d.)

Population figures reported by Italians are equally problematic, as discussed by Mark Karp (1960), and the Italians Zoli (1927:83) and Leo Magnino (1933) note the difficulty of conducting a Gosha census due to the constant movement of people.

Finally, the historical data on the nature of slavery experiences of Gosha settlers and early life in the upper Gosha are not rich. Foreign documentation of slavery experiences are limited to a few reports, although these contain large amounts of information.[6] By the time of my fieldwork in the late 1980s, there were few villagers left in the Jubba valley who had direct knowledge of slavery, either from personal experience as children or from family history passed down from their parents. People of Boran heritage in Loc held a much clearer idea of the slavery experiences of their parents than descendants of plantation slaves, whose family histories were more fragmented or unknown. Many adult descendants of plantation or Baay area slaves living in Loc knew remarkably little about their parents' lives, having only a vague understanding of where their parents had lived and what they had done before settling in Loc. The reasons why this was the case are important for understanding the force of Somali clan identity, and we will ponder them in the upcoming chapters.

What follows is a collection of upper Gosha settlers' stories of slavery and settlement experiences pieced together from interviews. My aim is to pull together some of the fragments remembered by villagers to gain a sense of their understandings of their different pasts and the relevance of these memories in the collective construction of community in the upper Gosha. I also weave in some observations from the Italian ethnographer Enrico Cerulli (1959). Cerulli studied the slaveholding practices of two trans-Jubba Somali clans, the Majeerteen, who obtained slaves from East Africa for plantations, and the Marehan, who captured Oromos as slaves. Cerulli's observations offer a perspective on the different character of slavery among sedentary and pastoralist Somali groups and provide useful comparative material which probably reflects the experiences of upper Gosha settlers and their ancestors. Taken together, the available evidence suggests that the different slavery experiences of farming and pastoral slaves reflected contradictory Somali attitudes toward these categories of slaves. Agricultural slaves remained distinct aliens within Somali society, whereas pastoral and even agropastoral slaves participated more intimately in Somali family life. These contradictory attitudes produced distinct master-slave relationships and had implications for how ex-slaves created new communities in the upper Gosha.

Upper Gosha Settlers

Having noted the evidentiary shortcomings, we can argue that as a result of abolition, the number of ex-slaves filtering into the valley after the turn of the century must have at least equaled Menkhaus's estimate of twenty thousand for the 1865–95 period. Settlers to the upper Gosha came primarily from five backgrounds: (1) Benaadir plantation slaves who received their freedom as a direct result of Italian abolition efforts between 1900 and 1914; (2) agricultural and agropastoral ex-slaves and "clients" from the Baay Region; (3) pastoral slaves and serfs of Oromo heritage; (4) people of unknown but clearly non-Somali ancestry living as clients to Ajuraan Somalis on the upper Shabeelle around Kalafo, Ethiopia; and (5) Somali pastoralists who were settling to take up a life of farming. Each of these groups contributed to the changing constitution of Gosha society, fostering the development of dynamic and complex relationships within the Gosha population and between Gosha and Somalis. As this listing more or less represents the chronology of new arrivals to the middle Jubba, I will discuss each wave of settlers in turn.

Benaadir Plantation and Baay Region Ex-Slave Settlers

Despite the intention of the Italian authorities, it is clear that many plantation slaves chose not to remain in conditions of servitude with their former masters following abolition, especially after the cruel ways in which some slave owners handled their slaves in the early years of abolition. The report on slavery commissioned by the Italian government in 1904 found that "now nearly all slaves in the interior are chained by their legs."[7] The same report quotes runaway slaves arriving in Mogadishu as saying the riverine "people talk of nothing else" but the abolition decrees (Cassanelli 1988:316). Cassanelli (1988) makes the point that the knowledge of antislavery ordinance enforcement on the coast encouraged desertion by plantation slaves further inland in the first decade of the century, as there was less likelihood that Italian authorities would return runaways to their masters. Luling (1971:117) reports that after abolition many slaves even left Geledi, an area where slavery was "a relatively mild form of bondage" (119), rather than choosing to stay with their former masters.

Ex-slaves entering the valley following abolition found the lower Jubba already settled by fugitive slaves who retained strong cultural and linguistic identification with their East African communities of origin, as described in the previous chapter. The first settlers to make their way into the middle Jubba were the later arrivals to the lower Jubba. Many, if not most, of these earliest postabolition settlers had been enslaved as children for plantation work along the Shabeelle. The elders of one of the first villages (Jabbi) formed in the upper Gosha (around one hundred years ago) related the story of their parents, the village founders: "They were taken from Kenya when they were small. Arab men who had boats brought them to Marka. Their people who birthed them [i.e., parents] didn't know when they were stealing them. They put them on boats. . . . When we grew, our old fathers told us they were brought via Marka."[8]

This village identifies itself as Biimaal, the name of the powerful Somali clan living around Marka. The children were probably brought to Marka in the late 1870s, and made their way into the Jubba in the 1880s. They settled first in several different villages in the lower Jubba, continuing upriver to settle their own village at least by the turn of the century.

The identification of settlements with Somali clans (or, for the area first settled in the lower Jubba, by African preslavery ethnic identities) forced newcomers of different clan affiliation to search out places of their own to live and farm. Immigrants arriving around and after the turn of the century found land in the lower Jubba already claimed by the clans/ethnic groups that had arrived first. Cassanelli (1989) and Zoli (1927) provide evidence that village founders and their descendants in lower Jubba villages maintained a greater degree of control over land than newcomers. Newcomers thus met with difficulties in obtaining land and being accepted in these already formed villages. This argument finds support in an explanation given to me by an elder of a middle Jubba village about why his father continued moving from village to village until founding the village in which my informant was born and raised: "He came to Bidi [village name] because of land. The land in the areas they settled before [in the lower Jubba] was all owned by the people that already lived there. They came to this land for the sons of Bidi [meaning for their inheritance]. . . . That land [where they first tried to settle in the lower Jubba] was owned by Jiido, Garo, it was owned by those people, Daafed [Somali clans]. . . . Those people owned that land. Dabare [a Somali clan] was our settlement [in the lower Jubba], but that was not our land."

What he means by his last sentence is that initially ex-slaves claiming affiliation to Dabare settled together in the lower Jubba, but were unable to acquire land of their own. The frontier environment of the Gosha inhibited the development of extreme social stratification between founders and newcomers, however, because disgruntled villagers could pick up and continue north. Newcomers unable to acquire sufficient land or political clout of their own in established villages of the lower Jubba thus continued pushing the frontier up the valley. There was a constant forming and reforming of new villages throughout the Gosha, and the expansion of the frontier continued into the mid-valley area through the first decades of the twentieth century. Very little settlement of new villages occurred beyond the northernmost edge of the Gosha forest, probably because the forest provided protection and wild foods in times of stress, and because the inland ponds called *dhasheeg*, which are critical for flood recession agriculture, are limited to the forest area.

Although newcomers arriving in the valley in the years around the turn of the century were immigrating for the same kinds of reasons as had earlier arrivals—to escape slavery, to start a new life—many were also immigrating after having spent a period of time as clients to their former masters. In addition to plantation ex-slaves unable to acquire land in the lower Jubba, the wave of ex-slaves entering the valley and settling in the upper Gosha after the turn of the century included many agropastoral slaves from the Baay Region who had remained in patron-client relationships with their masters following abolition. Their closer ties to Somali families contrasts with the experiences of the plantation slaves who settled the lower valley after fleeing more abusive and/or less familial situations along the lower Shabeelle and the Benaadir Coast. Former clients entering the Gosha were situated differently vis-à-vis Somali society and personal ethnicity than earlier arrivals. They had lived within the paternalistic Somali social order for longer, often since birth, and had been absorbed into the system of protection offered by the

Somali clan structure. These newcomers colonized the upper Gosha forest north of Jilib, eventually reaching the upper limits of the Gosha, just below what is now Saakow.

A comparison of slavery experiences as described in colonial documents and recounted by slave descendants helps illuminate the differences in plantation and agropastoral master-slave relations and the reasons why the latter more readily adopted the clan affiliations of their masters following slavery. Cerulli and other colonial observers describe plantation slavery in terms that suggest master-slave relations on plantations were characterized more by distance than intimacy. Lieutenant Christopher's (1844:79–80) observations on a Shabeelle valley plantation are revealing:

> the hospitality of our [Somali] host produced excellent mutton boiled with rice; the only peculiarity being that the slaves, seated at some distance, were eager to receive the bones picked by their masters, which underwent a second, third, and fourth gnawing from successive hungry mouths before they were finally scattered as useless. . . . The slaves and their wives [are] the labourers, housed miserably in small half-roofed huts, their usual food parched Indian corn and fish from the river. . . . There were many thousands of men employed in cultivation here; their only shelter is formed by the loose stalks of the common millet piled up in a conical shape, and allowing three or four persons to sit together in the interior. They are thus screened from the sun, but exposed, of course, to the rain, and whole families thus pass their lives.

Although it is possible that slave families only inhabited the millet huts during peak agricultural seasons, Christopher's observations suggest that slaves lived relatively separately from their masters. This picture of a clear separation between plantation slaves and masters finds confirmation in Cerulli's research. Juridical and sexual practices regulating Somali master–East African slave relations reveal the kinds of mechanisms which ensured distance and separation. East African slaves purchased for plantation work were considered private property, whose blood compensation (*diya*) value was equal to their market value, which varied according to age and gender, but which was only a fraction of the diya value for a Somali man or woman. Cerulli (1959) explains that unions between Somali masters and slaves of East African origin were discouraged and considered dishonorable because Somalis considered East African slave women inferior and unattractive. A slave woman who bore a child by her master remained a slave, although her child was considered a free person. Freedom was often achieved by escape, rather than manumission, which was the usual Islamic practice. At abolition, despite efforts by colonialists to force ex-slaves to remain in positions of dependant clientship with their former masters, most freed East African plantation slaves headed south for the Jubba valley, for the reasons discussed in the previous chapter. After settling in the valley, a fugitive slave might identify himself or herself as a member of the master's clan or could choose to affiliate with another Somali clan.

Oral histories I collected in the middle Jubba suggest that marriage between plantation ex-slaves of East African descent often may not have occurred until after their entry into the Jubba valley. People escaped individually, making their way into the valley, where they would find a mate who may or may not have been enslaved to the same Somali clan. The earliest East African ex-slave settlers thus did not generally come into the middle valley as family units, lessening the strength of their identification as a family with the clan of their Somali master.

Slaves of Baay Region agropastoralists, however, seem to have been more fully integrated into their master's household than Christopher's description of plantation slaves suggests. Baay Region agropastoral Somalis tended not to own large plantations, using slave labor together with family labor for household production in agriculture and herding rather than for export. As such, agropastoral slaves lived with and worked side by side with their masters' families. This sharing of home and work contrasted with the experiences of plantation slaves, whose masters did not participate in agricultural work, which they considered low status. As with slaves from Benaadir plantations, Baay Region slaves escaped and came into the Jubba, but others remained in relations of clientship with former masters after receiving their freedom through manumission or abolition, and came into the Gosha later. These "client" ex-slaves called themselves by the Somali clan name of their former masters, and the villages formed by them in the southern part of the upper Gosha are identified, for example, as Laysan or Dabare, which are Somali clans from the Baay Region. Although a patron-client relationship might suggest a greater closeness and mutual identification than would a master-slave relationship, the distinction between slave and client was very unclear in Gosha peoples' memories. In 1988 villagers referred to all their ancestors who came from the Baay Region as having escaped slavery, even if those ancestors had remained for a time as clients. In contrast to the pastoralist ex-slave settlers discussed later in this chapter, the oral histories recounted by descendants of agropastoralist ex-slaves tended to emphasize the slave heritage of their ancestors rather than their postslavery client status. In describing the settlement of his village, one village headman whose parents were slaves and clients of Baay agropastoralists explained:

The people of this land, the origin of these people were people who were owned by *bilis* [ethnic Somalis]. People used to run away. They were owned, the people who came together there; that person from the bush was "attracted" to this place, and another man who is "attracted" comes here. That's how they came together. . . . They left [their former homes in Baay Region] because of slavery. People were owned by the soft hairs [*jileec*; ethnic Somalis] and some of the people were brought from Boran. The people who are in this land are the hard hairs [*jareer*; ex-slaves]. They were people who were beaten to this side [forced to come to this side from the west by the *bilis*]. They were beaten from Boran. When these people were brought they were bought by the *bilis*. Then they used to say, "This slave is mine." While he [the slave] is with you he runs away. This land was not settled. This settlement started in the lower Jubba. All this land was not settled. The people of Somalia who were in this land used to go in groups to capture slaves.[9]

In this passage, the speaker describes how the settlement of the middle Jubba began. He says the earliest settlers "attracted" later settlers, by which he means people with whom they had been slaves, or with whom they shared some kind of kinship bond. Ex-slaves coming into the upper Gosha settled in small groups of related people, whose bond was often the Somali clan to which they had been enslaved.

One village leader offered an interesting narrative about the settlement of the middle valley which parallels—with one important difference—a similar narrative recorded by Menkhaus (1989:116) in the lower valley. The elder described to me how ex-slaves entering the middle valley would go first to the village of Bidi, from where they would be sent to the mid-valley village settled by their fellow clan members:

When people left slavery, they came first to Bidi. People who were Geelil, people who were Laysan, people who were Garo, all the people met in Bidi. When they arrived in Bidi [the local clan, Dabare, told them where to go]. Geelil was told to settle Farbitow; Garo, you settle Hurufle; Dafeed was told to settle Mana; Jito was told to settle Kaskay; Eyle was told to settle Boha and Sombotarey. Eelay, go to Boho and Dacaarta. Laysan, you go to Shoonto. Qoomale, you go to Kafinge . . . Ajuraan go to Loc, Nyartar go to Duqiyo. All these people met each other in Bidi.

While I believe this story is apocryphal—I found no one who could confirm Bidi's role as a clearinghouse for arriving ex-slaves—the narrative is interesting because of its similarity to the lower Jubba narrative that describes how leading lower Gosha elders met decades earlier at the village of Bangeeni to determine how to organize settlement of ex-slaves in the lower valley. The difference is that in the Bangeeni narrative, the basis of division was not Somali clan affiliation, but rather Bantu ethnolinguistic background. Whether or not either narrative accurately describes historical circumstances, the middle Jubba narrative shifts the frame of reference by replacing African ancestry with Somali clan affiliation as the basis for settlement in the middle valley, thereby capturing the highly significant transformation in settlement patterns which occurred around the turn of the century.

Typically, histories recounted by upper Gosha villagers related how ex-slaves coming into the upper Gosha would go from village to village, asking after their relatives.[10] The elder of another village described how relatives "attracted" each other when settling his village around 1905:

> In those days the man who founded this land was called Yaaqub Welidi and he came from Baydhabo. A place called Abbab Gala was his permanent settlement. He was among those who were brought by spears and stolen. . . . His wife and his family [came with him]. . . . The reason why they came here was this land was not occupied, and when one came one just took land. This is how we used to settle near the river. When he came he settled here. There was a place he settled first called Xawall Maanyaw. He came this way, as if he were looking for a good place for the animals [like nomads do]. After that he came to this place, Buurfuule. It was a place which has a dhasheeg. . . . When he came he was followed by the sons of his uncle whom he has attracted; "Yaaqub Welidi attracted us, where did he settle?" "Buurfuule he settled." "He has attracted us." That's how the village was settled.

Although "relatives" often meant people who had been enslaved to the same Somali clan—people who had experienced slavery together, rather than blood relations—with time blood relations grew out of Somali clan affiliations. The large number of easily obtainable slaves, the widespread practice of manumission, and ex-slave oral histories suggest that Somalis were not interested in biologically reproducing the slave population (a point Claude Meillassoux [1983] discusses for Africa in general). As with plantation ex-slaves, generally marriage between agropastoral ex-slaves did not occur until after manumission or escape. Slaves marrying after receiving their freedom often obtained a wife or husband as a gift from their masters accompanying manumission. As the spouse offered as a gift was usually a fellow slave, both marriage partners would be affiliated to the same Somali clan, regardless of their own, perhaps distinct, African heritages. Through children, a new set of blood relations would thus be created, produced from a union created through Somali clan ties.

Because meaningful ties to East African groups of origin had been lost in the disruptive process of kidnapping, sale, and enslavement, formal or informal affiliation to a Somali clan provided a shared bond for settlers of the frontier needing mutual assistance and support in the early years of settlement. By necessity, the earliest ex-slaves in the upper Gosha had to negotiate relations with surrounding Somali pastoral groups for trade and to avoid recapture. Early settlers often formally or informally affiliated with local, powerful Somali clans as a way to ensure protection. Throughout Somalia the process of formal affiliation is called *sheegad.* (To be of *sheegad* status means one is not a true descendant of the original founder of the clan, but rather has affiliated with the clan in a formal ceremony.) An individual wishing to become affiliated with a clan made his intentions known and the clan elders determined conditions of acceptance, which usually consisted of payment of a fee, a gift of an animal, and fulfillment of a ceremony. Gosha farmers and local Somali pastoralists used another term to describe the former's relationship of affiliation with the latter: *ku tirsan,* which simply means "leaning on." To be *ku tirsan* to a Somali clan does not necessarily imply formal adoption, but rather implies a looser form of affiliation.[11] The way in which these terms were used by Gosha villagers in the 1980s to describe their association with Somali clans, however, is not as clear as these definitions might imply. Gosha villagers used the terms interchangeably, and did not seem to feel the distinction between *sheegad* and *ku tirsan* was very important. Their use of these terms reflects their perception that they could switch their clan affiliations with apparent ease. Furthermore, as we will see in Chapter 6, Gosha peoples' accounts of these historical affiliations are contested and conflicting.

Living alone or in small, highly dispersed clusters, early settlers were offered a modicum of protection against potential raiders by affiliating with a surrounding Somali clan. Later arrivals to the upper Gosha often chose to affiliate with the same clan as had their previously settled relatives. As one elder explained: "When all came to know each other, the man who was the strongest, they leaned on him. Nobody cares for the other clan (their former Somali clan). You can leave the other one and come and follow your brother and lean on the same strong clan as he is."

The ku tirsan relationship ensured protection from other Somali clans, but also implied a kind of debt owed by Gosha villages. Gosha villagers sometimes had to provide grain for nomads; nomads would come to the villages and expect gifts of grain from families who were "leaning on" them. Nomads would only take food from those who were "leaning on" them, and would protect their "clients" from being subjected to other nomad groups. While the full nature of this relationship is not clear from oral histories (a point discussed further in Chapter 6), it seems that it was limited to exchanging grain for protection in a kind of patron-client relationship. Local nomad and Gosha historians both agreed that the Gosha villages held full control over the land they lived on and farmed; in no sense were they considered squatters, tenants, or laborers for nomads on land held by nomads. Control over land and access to land was determined by the head or elders of each village for surrounding lands and was completely an internal matter.

The earliest upper Gosha settlements cooperated with labor sharing and assistance in times of need, but there were also social divisions which were important. These divisions were based on Somali clan affiliation and also on degree of conversion to Islam. Settlers who had experienced closer relationships with Somali masters had already converted by the time of their entry into the Gosha, whereas other ex-slaves (usually plantation slaves) had not yet become Muslims. Khadija, the very elderly descendant of Loc's founder, explained why her father moved from place to place in the upper Gosha before settling alone in an uninhabited area on the west bank: "The reason was he heard those *ooji* [non-Muslim slave] people eat children so he escaped with his children to this side. We were very small." These divisions did not last long, as Islamic conversion spread throughout most of the valley in the early twentieth century. (Nevertheless, upper Gosha villagers remarked in 1988 that the continuing use of pre-Islamic dance forms and rituals by some lower Gosha communities attested to their incomplete conversion.)[12]

In general, the slavery experiences of the earliest settlers to the upper Gosha fell along a continuum from the kind of extreme master-slave distance maintained on Shabeelle plantations to relations of greater intimacy resulting in periods of clientship following slavery in Baay Region agropastoral households. Despite these differing recollections of ancestral slavery, descendants of plantation slaves and agropastoral slave-clients in the upper Gosha similarly characterized their ancestors as slaves, not clients. Their personal sense of slave ancestry contrasted with the emphasis on ancestral client (as opposed to slave) status maintained in the recollections of Oromo slave descendants and settlers from the upper Shabeelle in Ethiopia.

Oromo Ex-Slave Settlers

While plantation and agropastoral ex-slaves entering the lower Jubba and moving up into the middle Jubba were almost entirely of East African origin, some of the earliest settlers to the middle Jubba during the first two decades of the twentieth century were Oromo Boran and Warday ex-slaves. Many Oromo settlers came into the Gosha from the north, coming down the river from Baardheere, and from the west, coming into the Gosha from Afmadow up to Wajir. As with immigrants from the Baay Region, the distinction between slave and client among Boran/Warday settlers was very unclear and the descendants of these settlers often simply said their fathers settled into the Gosha because they had lost all their animals. Most of my informants were insistent that all immigrants to the Gosha had a family history of enslavement, even though some experiences (such as those of the Warday) were "milder" than others. Nevertheless, it was the loss of animals and not their slave ancestry that Oromo descendants emphasized when recalling why their ancestors had settled in the upper Gosha.

Descriptions and recollections of the lives of pastoral slaves indicate significant differences from those of plantation and agropastoral slaves.[13] In the Somali raids on Oromo settlements during the nineteenth century, Oromo women and children were claimed as slaves, while men were usually killed. These women and children were taken into the family life of their abductors, while still, of course, remaining subjects. Abducted Oromo children became "children" of the master. Somalis took only very young children because they were easier to abduct and adopt. Oromo women, valued for their beauty, were kept as concubines or as domestic servants or were given in marriage to other slaves. After a concubine gave birth to her master's child, she (as well as the child) became free (in theory at least), considered of equal status to other Somali wives.[14] The sexual mores which characterized relations between male Somali masters and East African and Oromo slave women highlight the different Somali treatment of these two categories of slaves.

The differing motivations for enslaving Oromo women and East African women have been recognized for Africa in general by Meillassoux (1983), who categorizes African slaveholding societies as: (1) self-sustaining domestic societies where men taken prisoner are killed or integrated and women prisoners are made wives, (2) merchant societies which hold a productive class of slaves where women are valued for their labor and not for their reproductive capabilities, and (3) aristocratic societies where women are acquired solely because they are women (for sexual purposes). The first and second categories most usefully characterize Somali society, where the difference in the destiny of slave women was determined by their origin and ethnicity.[15]

According to Cerulli (1959), in contrast to East African slaves, the life of an Oromo slave could be measured by the same standard as the life of a Somali in the payment of blood money. One punishment for renegade Oromo slaves was to be sold to work the farm—clearly considered demeaning and undesirable work. Oromo slaves were never acquired for agricultural work directly; their abilities as pastoralists were recognized, as was their lack of agricultural knowledge.

Following manumission, pastoral slaves often remained in a patron-client type relationship with their former masters. Since pastoralists in the interior remained out of reach of colonial authorities until the second decade of the twentieth century, and in many ways remained out of reach throughout the colonial period, it is unlikely that herder slaves were subjected to the harsh treatment experienced by plantation slaves during abolition. Furthermore, without animals or grazing land, manumitted pastoral slaves may have felt they had no alternative to remaining attached to a former master. Herder slaves, upon manumission, were much more likely to remain in a relationship with their former masters, adopting the nomadic way of life with their small "inheritance" of livestock and continuing to live in the vicinity of the master's clan. One former slave explained to me how this might occur:

> If you are obedient, you may say, "I want my father Cali [a man's name], I won't go anywhere. I will be with you. The animals you gave me will breed, as I am your son. I might say I have heard that I was born from that tribe, didn't you set me free? Now I am the same with your children. They call me brother. I have worked for them. You brought me for slavery, because you didn't have children before you got married." When [the master's] children become mature enough, the master doesn't need you [the slave]. After that you will say to him, "Your children are enough for you. I leave this morning." You take your animals and you read *fataxaad* [an Islamic blessing] for each other.

Upon manumission, a master would frequently provide his male slave with a wife. Families entwined in relations of clientship or affective attachment were thus formed within Somali pastoralist society. In contrast to settlers of East African slave heritage, middle valley settlers of Oromo slave heritage often arrived in the middle valley as families, seeking other family members. Stronger ties to their Somali clans of affiliation were maintained through family linkages in this way. Oromo ex-slaves moved into the Gosha to join relatives in ex-slave communities when their herds died off from disease or drought.

Oromo ex-slaves settled in large numbers in the mid-valley area around Bu'aale, and their immigration has been continual since the earliest decades of the twentieth century. Many of the earliest Oromo settlers did not actually settle permanently, but went back and forth from agriculture to pastoralism. This was possible because of the abundance of land and the stronger ties that Oromo ex-slaves retained with Somali pastoralists. Movement between different forms of subsistence has not continued, and few Oromo descendants of the upper Gosha in 1988 were trying to build or maintain a herd of animals with the intention of returning to a pastoral lifestyle. Since Warday were not directly affected by abolition efforts, many Warday remained in conditions of servitude into the 1960s and 1970s, and some probably still do. Those Warday who were manumitted also trickled into Gosha villages throughout the century. The settlement process of pastoralist ex-slaves thus contrasts with the more concentrated arrival of early plantation ex-slaves and Baay Region ex-slaves.

Clearly, the slavery experience of Oromo pastoral slaves and East African agricultural slaves differed in important ways. Somalis bought adult and children East African slaves to farm; these slaves worked separately from and under the control of their masters, did undesirable work, and often lived separately as well. Sexually and juridically their bodies were devalued. Somali mores discouraged sexual unions between plantation slaves and Somali masters, thus enforcing the social distance maintained between master and slave. Plantation slaves often acquired their freedom through escape, marrying after their entry into the Gosha.

Herder slaves were involved in relations of greater intimacy with their masters. They were taken in as family members—as adopted children or legitimate (in Somali eyes) sexual partners—and they worked side by side with their masters. Freedom was obtained through manumission, which was often accompanied by the gift of livestock and a spouse. Herder slaves did not generally come immediately into the Gosha upon their release from slavery, but remained as pastoralists until losing their animals to drought or disease.

Different members of a Somali clan could have slaves of both Oromo heritage and East African heritage, used for different purposes. Once these slaves attained their freedom, they and their children could then be affiliated with the same Somali clan, despite their separate areas of origin. In this way, villages formed along Somali clan lines in the Jubba valley could contain people of both Oromo and East African heritage, who claimed affiliation to the same Somali clan. Within a village, while working together and cooperating on village matters, people of different ancestries often lived separately and married endogamously (due to a preference for parallel or cross-cousin marriage) in the late 1980s, although this was rapidly changing. I will return to these intravillage dynamics in Chapter 6.

Ajuraan Reer Shabeelle

Beginning in the late 1920s and continuing into the 1960s, groups of people began arriving from Ethiopia, fleeing bloody tribal wars in their homeland. These people, loosely called *reer* Shabeelle (the people of Shabeelle),[16] came from the area around Kalafo, on the Shabeelle River across the border in Ethiopia. Although they are physically characterized, along with descendants of plantation and agropastoral slaves in the Gosha, as "hard hairs," their history is obscure. I. M. Lewis (1955:34) says, "The Shabelle are a confederacy recognizing the authority of a lineage of Somali Ajuraan for the purpose of electing their chief."[17] About the area called Shabeelle inhabited by Ajuraan, Cerulli writes: "As the Adjuran are there proportionately few in number, the most part of the tribe being former slaves or freedmen, the Ogaden often call the group the Addon, viz. the slaves, who have been incorrectly considered by some ethnologists as a Bantu tribe or a Bantu-speaking people" (1957:143). Their language is Somali and their religion Islam. Villagers' views varied: a few were adamant that reer Shabeelle had once been slaves centuries ago, brought from East Africa via northern Somali ports (such as Berbera), while others were equally adamant that they had always lived freely, and some were unsure. It is clear, however, that reer Shabeelle, who were farmers with some livestock, lived in some kind of a dependent relationship with Somali Ajuraan on the Ethiopian Shabeelle.

The Ajuraan have a long and distinguished history in Somalia, which has been carefully reconstructed and convincingly presented by Cassanelli (1982). According to oral tradition and Cassanelli's historical reconstruction, an Ajuraan confederacy developed into a state which encompassed much of southern Somalia by the sixteenth century. The power of the state waned during the seventeenth century, and currently pockets of Ajuraan exist throughout southern Somalia: on the upper Shabeelle, on the lower Shabeelle, in the middle Jubba around Baardheere and Bu'aale, and across the border in the Northern Frontier District of Kenya.[18] The Ajuraan living between Baardheere and the middle Jubba are called reer Dooy Ajuraan (the geographical area is called Dooy) and are ethnically Somali pastoralists, as opposed to the reer Shabeelle Ajuraan, who are agriculturalists considered to be of non-Somali heritage.

Local Ajuraan oral tradition tells that the first Ajuraan man to establish a town in the middle Jubba around eighty years ago was a sheikh from Ethiopia who was instrumental in initiating peace between Gosha farmers and Somali pastoralists and in uniting reer Dooy Ajuraan and reer Shabeelle Ajuraan.[19] In the words of one locally prominent Ajuraan sheikh:

> Sheikh Cabdow Kheyr [an Ajuraan holy man who initiated Ajuraan settlement of the middle valley] came to this area from Ethiopia through prayer. Other sheikhs before him had visions about this place. A breakout of disease in the sheikh's homeland had killed off livestock and people. There were seven sheikhs, each of whom saw a vision of a thin, light sheikh coming to lead them. The seventh sheikh, Sheikh Cabdow Kheyr, decided to follow the vision, and, accompanied by fifty disciples, came here [to the middle Jubba]. They held extended prayer, which God accepted. After that, this area was settled. Anyone could settle. Those who settled included both soft and hard hairs. The jareer people [hard hairs] who had been owned, the sheikh told them to stay here. He told the other people to stay at their place. Freedom, peace, making a brotherhood of the people happened that day from here up to Nassib Bundo. Nassib Bundo

> was a man who used to catch the bilis ["noble" Somalis] to give to the crocodiles or to kill. The sheikh went and told Nassib Bundo to give peace to those people [the bilis] and they will give peace to your own people [the Gosha villagers].

In addition to giving the Ajuraan credit for founding the earliest settlements in the middle Jubba, for tempering Nassib Bundo's fiery temper, and for initiating peace between Gosha village "hard hairs" and surrounding "bilis" Somalis, local Ajuraan traditions describe in legendary terms how Sheikh Cabdow Kheyr drove the "Boran infidels" out of the area and undertook jihads into British Kenya in order to convert "black infidels" (*gaal maadow*) to Islam. These oral traditions, combined with those recounted below of the twentieth-century reer Shabeelle Ajuraan leader, Sooyan, clearly seek to establish the religious, political, and social significance of the Ajuraan—including the Ajuraan reer Shabeelle—presence in the middle Jubba.

As the origin of the reer Shabeelle people of the upper Shabeelle is unclear, they are not connected so overtly with a slave past. Nevertheless, their status as ethnically non-Somali (as *jareer*, discussed in the next chapter) is undeniable. Unlike other Gosha, however, reer Shabeelle have a very long history of participation within Somali society, as well as a well-known area of origin to which strong attachments are still held. Reer Shabeelle immigrants to the middle Jubba defined themselves as a group, tended to settle together in villages and change location as a group if it became necessary to move, and saw themselves as distinct from other Gosha villagers of East African or Oromo heritage. As one example, many of the adult men living in Loc in the 1980s who had grown up together in the reer Shabeelle middle Jubba village of Cabdow Yusuf continued to converse in their own "secret language," which was not understood by other, non–reer Shabeelle villagers.[20] The presence of the reer Shabeelle Ajuraan had a lasting impact on the social organization of the mid-valley area, as they were the first group to have no knowledge of a history apart from affiliation with a Somali clan.

Settlement Fluidity and Colonial Labor Policy

By the first decades of the twentieth century, there were scattered villages all along the banks of the middle Jubba, with new villages continually being formed. Somali clan affiliation had become an important aspect of village formation. Villages were autonomous, independent sociopolitical entities, which nevertheless cooperated in times of hardship and marriage. Settlement in this period was very fluid, as people moved from village to village, and moved villages from one area to another, searching for the best agricultural land, the fewest mosquitoes, and the fewest human competitors (other farmers and Somali pastoralists). Hunting, fishing, and gathering of wild plants were critical to the survival of these earliest settlers in the upper Gosha.

In addition to variances in the local environment, social conflicts, and problems with adjacent Somali pastoralists, occasionally events having to do with the colonial government caused movement of upper Gosha villagers. While the British and Italians made no effort to establish a permanent presence in the middle Jubba area early in the century, skirmishes between colonialists and Somalis resisting colonial rule sometimes affected the area. The most extreme case was the 1916 murder of Lieutenant Elliott (remembered by Somalis as "Elyan") at the British military outpost of Sarinley on the upper Jubba and the sacking of the town by Cawlyahan Somalis. The murder and the ensuing two years of warfare between British forces and Cawlyahan Somalis west of the Jubba are recalled vividly by Gosha villagers. Following the murder, the Cawlyahan went on a rampage against Gosha villages on the west bank, which were induced to supply the British with information on the whereabouts of Cawlyahan warriors. The west bank of the Jubba in the upper Gosha area was quickly abandoned as Gosha fled to the relative safety of the Italian controlled east bank. After the British subdued the Cawlyahan in 1918, the uprooted Gosha moved back.

Gosha villagers often used this ability to cross the river as a strategy to avoid unpleasantness. Until 1924, the British controlled the west bank of the river (then called Jubaland) and the Italians held the east bank. Villagers would frequently cross the river to avoid penalties, taxes, punishments, or to illegally sell ivory, a strategy recognized by colonial authorities.[21] As one villager explained, "If someone kills somebody on the other side of the river, he could cross to this side and be saved, and nobody could speak against him. 'You, donkey' he will say [to his pursuers], 'have you seen what I did to you?' " The low population density meant that land was still abundant, and moving around was not only a way to escape colonial authorities and Somali pastoralists, but also provided a way for Gosha settlers to become intimately familiar with their new environment.

When the colonial presence reached its peak during the years of Italian fascist colonial rule, village movements as a result of colonial activity greatly increased. After obtaining Jubaland from the British, the Italians gave concessions to Italian immigrants for the formation of large plantations on the lower Jubba to produce cash crops (especially bananas) for export to Italy.[22] Italian plantation owners desperately needed a source of labor for the plantations.[23] In the early days of the colony, Italian colonial administrators forced by their home government to pursue the abolition of slavery believed that ex-slaves would provide a ready supply of labor for the planned large-scale development of Italian-owned plantations. Colonial authorities had not counted on the existence of a frontier to absorb ex-slaves, who could make a decent living as free yeoman farmers. By 1935, when labor was not forthcoming for the plantations, the new fascist colonial authorities resorted to forced labor.

Their target was the ex-slave communities of the Gosha. Villagers stressed to me how the Italians definitionally separated the ex-slave population from the Somali population for purposes of conscripting laborers. One Gosha villager imitated the Italians: "I don't accept saying 'I am Mushunguli,' 'I am Bartire,' 'I am Shabeelle,' 'I am Cawlyahan,' 'I am Marexan.' It doesn't exist. You are all lying. You all are Mushunguli Mayasid [Bantu]. You have to participate [in the forced labor system]."

The Italians began relocating men and women from their villages to the Italian plantations by force in 1935. A village leader (*duq-taraf*) was paid to provide workers,[24] initially for permanent work (remembered as the *kolonya*) and later for work on a rotating basis, the "torno" (remembered as *teen*). Elderly survivors of the kolonya system hold bitter memories of the Italian plantation experience. One man poetically recounted his memories to me:

> There was a time they [Italians] used to catch people by force which was kolonya. People went, a woman and her husband, they were taken together. It is kolonya. People were made to work on the farms. . . . There's no youth who did not farm in the farms. . . . The Italians owned them [permanently]. Let them be there. Forget them [meaning do not plan to see them again]. We worked day and night on the farms. Even those who were born there worked there. . . . People were beaten and stepped on. A hundred strokes, fifty strokes, this is how people were beaten—one refuses to work, one is not able to finish his work because he is not strong, you know, and that is his strength [as much as he can do]. There are people who cannot farm. "Let him be beaten." One hundred strokes on the buttocks. He will be beaten. Then he suffers; when he suffers and goes into his house, there's no one who gives him food. If a man gets sick, he doesn't get food. If he's beaten he doesn't get food. He is "cut into pieces." Die or be alive, yes.

This man's sentiments were echoed throughout the villages of the lower Gosha and the southern part of the upper Gosha by those who had been subjected to the forced labor campaigns of the Italians.

The Ajuraan were a prominent clan in the mid-valley at this time. The local leader of the Ajuraan, a man named Sooyan, refused to send his people for kolonya, although he allowed them to serve as soldiers for the Italians in their campaign against Ethiopia. Sooyan was reer Shabeelle and had migrated to the area just after the turn of the century to settle among the nomadic reer Dooy Ajuraan. He was later chosen to be the head of the settled Ajuraan in the area, many of whom were also reer Shabeelle. When the system of forced labor began, he refused to allow the Italians to take anyone from the village of Duqiyo north, claiming they all came under his authority. As word spread of his refusal, reer Shabeelle and others living in the lower Gosha, and thus subject to forced labor, fled into the upper Gosha and affiliated with Ajuraan. Many reer Shabeelle also returned to Ethiopia to escape the kolonya. In the words of a reer Shabeelle Ajuraan, "It happened that we said 'Come close. For this country, we are birds. If you cause trouble, we will go back. . . . We can't be oppressed. Our country is broad. We will go back and even fight the Amhara [Ethiopians]. Otherwise leave us alone.' "

While it is clear that people did return to Ethiopia, it is also clear that the system of forced labor and Sooyan's refusal brought many people into the upper Gosha to affiliate with Ajuraan.[25] Before the Italians could take measures to curtail Sooyan's power and force his people to work, World War II had come to Africa.

The war introduced another kind of disruption for Gosha villagers, although one preferable to kolonya in their eyes. The Italians conscripted a few Gosha villagers into the army, and village elders in 1988 held humorous memories of the war. One man who was conscripted as a soldier described to me: "I didn't stay a soldier long. We were beaten quickly by the British. They captured us in one day, and then released us." By 1941 the war in Somalia was over, the British having crushed the Italians in southern Somalia in a matter of days. Gosha from the middle Jubba returned to their villages and their farms, and continued their lives relatively undisturbed by the changing colonial powers claiming control over their country until 1960.

Somali Settlers Since 1960

From the 1960s through the early 1980s, the majority of settlers in the Gosha were Somali nomads from the surrounding bush. Beginning during the droughts of the 1960s (1962–63, 1964–65) and the widely publicized *abaar daba dheere* (long-tailed drought) of 1974–75, Somali nomads who lost their livestock to drought or disease began settling into the Gosha communities, taking up farming, and, recently, even intermarrying. As a result of the 1974 drought, the Somali government attempted a massive resettlement of Somali pastoralists devastated by the drought into planned cooperative villages in the Jubba valley. Hundreds of thousands of Somalis were transported to these towns to live as farmers. The largest resettlement community was Dujuuma in the mid-valley just above Bu'aale, which received fifty-five thousand refugees. Conditions for agriculture in Dujuuma were very poor, and within a few years the vast majority of resettled pastoralists had abandoned the town, choosing to rebuild a life in the bush, to resettle on one of the large government projects in the lower Jubba as laborers, or to take up residence in one of the already formed Gosha villages with better agricultural land.

By the late 1980s the number of Somalis living in Gosha villages in the mid-valley were few, some villages having no ethnic Somalis living there at all. Settled Somalis tended to move back and forth to the bush, much as the Boran did in earlier decades, although families returning to the bush sometimes left a family member in the village to retain control of and farm the agricultural land the family had obtained during their residence.

Loc

A reconstruction of the history of Loc village settlement provides a localized sense of the people who settled the area, how they were drawn to the Gosha, and how they made a home and established a system of sustainable agriculture. In 1988, Loc was somewhat atypical of other middle Jubba villages because its population included people from different backgrounds affiliated with at least four different Somali clans. The area encompassed by Loc in 1988 was originally settled as five separate settlements, called, from north to south, Cabdow Yusuf, Gora, Loc, Loc Yare, and Bunbunle. In 1977 the government relocated these villages to the higher ground site of present-day Loc, creating an ethnically mixed community. As such, Loc provides a broad picture of the past, by incorporating the experiences of a wide variety of people in its history. Map 2 shows Loc's land base in 1988, including the previous locations of the five original villages and the names and approximate boundaries of different field areas to which I refer below when describing how immigrants settled the five villages and cleared agricultural land over the past century.

The first person to settle the area was an ex-slave called Isaaq who had come from the Baay Region. His relatives had exiled him from the Baay Region because of his propensity for troublemaking and fighting. According to his only two surviving children, Isaaq's body was covered in scars from fights and he was known for his violent temper, his pride, and his deep suspicion of neighbors. He settled first in several different villages along the east bank, but because of his difficult personality had continual clashes with other settlers. His wives and all his children but one died of malaria or other diseases in various villages, and finally, after the turn of the century, he found an uninhabited, open grassy spot on the west bank where he settled with his one surviving daughter, Khadija. He began farming in the nearby Dhasheeg Gora, after which his settlement was named, and married the woman who came to help him at harvest time from a Laysan Gosha village several miles to the south.

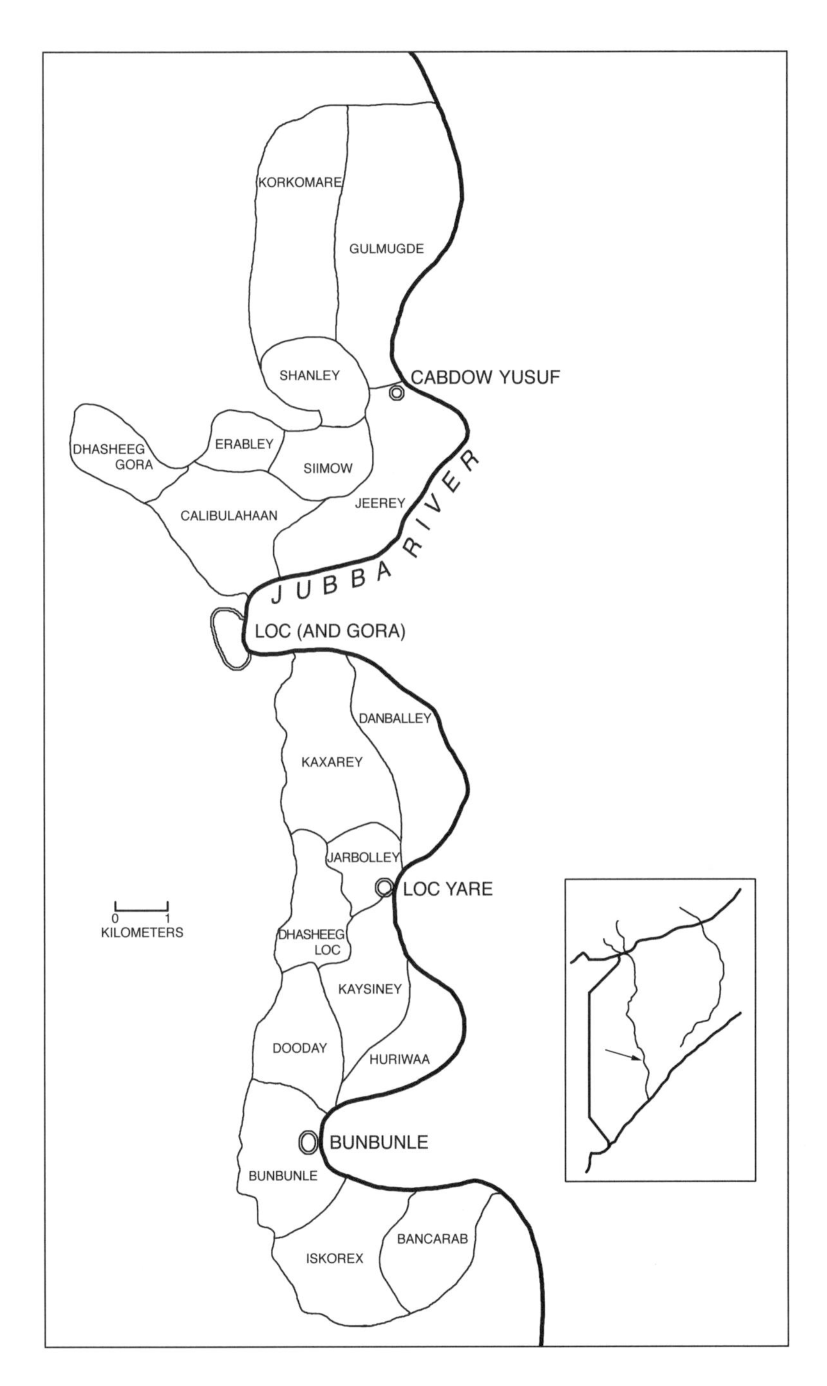

Map 2. Loc farmland.

As his son tells the story, after Isaaq worked side by side harvesting with the woman for two days he asked her if she was married. She replied that she was not, and Isaaq said, "Well, why don't we get married?" She agreed, and bore him a son but died from complications arising from childbirth. The child's elder half sister nursed the baby through his infancy, and he lived to serve as the Loc village headman during my stay.

Of Nyasa background and Laysan affiliation as a slave, Isaaq affiliated with a branch of the powerful Ogaadeen clan, Tolomoge, after settling Gora. It was clearly to his advantage. According to his daughter, when a Somali from another clan raided the family compound and carried off Isaaq's wife, ostensibly for slavery, Tolomoge Somalis intervened and returned the woman. Isaaq's part of the bargain was to take Tolomoge goats to the lower valley town of Alessandria for sale. While the daughter did not phrase the relationship in patron-client terms, this is the meaning I would attach. Interestingly, Isaaq's descendants still (quite adamantly) referred to themselves as Tolomoge in 1988, although everyone else called them Laysan.

In settling near Dhasheeg Gora, Isaaq followed a pattern established by thousands of settlers in the valley before him. The biggest agricultural attraction in the middle valley for arriving ex-slaves was the numerous dhasheegs—low-lying inland basins of fertile soil which are seasonally flooded by river channel overflows, rainfall, runoff, and underground water flow which percolates up through the soil. In-migrating ex-slaves and clients throughout the mid-valley located all of their settlements adjacent to dhasheegs, as they promised agricultural sustainability even during droughts. Dhasheegs, rather than riverbanks, were the focus of flood recession agriculture, as their heavy black soils (*caramaddow*) hold water and retain moisture for long periods of time and can yield up to twice as much as surrounding rainfed land (called *doonk*), including riverbank land. Water can remain in dhasheegs for weeks, months, or even years, as opposed to doonk and riverbank land, where floodwaters usually drain after a few days or, at most, weeks, and heavy rains run off within a day. When full, dhasheegs resemble shallow lakes, and are cultivated from the perimeter toward the center as the water evaporates.

In an area characterized by unpredictable water availability, dhasheegs proved to be critical for the survival of fledgling villages.[26] The local expression "there are no droughts on dhasheeg land" captures the local opinion of the sustained fertility and ability of dhasheeg soils to retain moisture for long periods of time. From the 1920s through the 1950s, dhasheeg agriculture in the lower reaches of the valley drew the attention of Italian colonialists, who used terms like "importantissimo" (Zoli 1927) to describe dhasheeg agriculture and its potential for exploitation.[27] Local farmers have long valued dhasheeg land for other reasons as well: labor inputs were lower, because flooding checked the regeneration of bush, so minimal land preparation was necessary prior to planting. Weeds were less of a problem than on doonk land. Planting, weeding, and harvesting continuously followed the receding water line, allowing farmers to avoid labor bottlenecks. Farmers began planting in dhasheegs only after the water from the rains or floods had started to recede, which meant they could be harvesting well into the dry season, a time when fresh produce was much welcomed.[28] Because dhasheegs were basins completely cleared of forest and bush, watching for animal pests was much easier (hippos, warthogs, monkeys, and cattle and camel herds of pastoral nomads were a primary source of crop damage), and neighbors could share guarding. Finally, when dhasheegs were full of water they provided abundant wild foods such as fish and starchy lily tubers (which were boiled or roasted), and they attracted animals which the farmers trapped. Isaaq certainly recognized the importance of Dhasheeg Gora when he claimed about six hectares of it—later considered a huge portion by local standards—for himself and his heirs.

Within a decade of Isaaq's homesteading of Gora, he was joined by a group of "brothers" and their close relatives from the Baay Region, all affiliated with Laysan. They cleared farms in the dhasheeg and intermarried with each other and with runaway Laysan slaves living in villages to the south.[29] The population of Gora never became large; starting with Isaaq and his daughter at the turn of the century, Gora grew to around ten inhabitants with the arrival of the group from the Baay Region after 1910. Two decades later these arrivals had found spouses (Isaaq gave his daughter in marriage to one of the Baay group; others married women from other Laysan villages) and had begun producing children, bringing the population to about forty. By the 1930s, the families living in Gora expanded their cultivation further into the dhasheeg as well as into the doonk area of Calibulahaan. By the 1950s, Gora had continued to grow and the villagers were farming larger areas of Calibulahaan, as Isaaq and his heirs continued to retain rights to much of Dhasheeg Gora.

Like Isaaq and the group from Baay who joined him, all the earliest settlers to the mid-valley acquired land on a first-come, first-served basis. While all early settlers began their valley farming careers on dhasheeg land, most early families also eventually cleared parcels of rainfed land which they farmed seasonally on a rotational basis. Villagers learned to farm doonk land during and after rains because the flood waters drained more quickly from the higher land, enabling earlier cultivation than in the dhasheegs and reducing the risk of disease-causing bacteria that sometimes came with water standing too long in dhasheegs after a heavy flood. On the down side, doonk land required more labor than dhasheeg land: following a season or a year or more of lying fallow, doonk land had to be cleared of bush growth, which was cut and burned, the soil had to be prepared by hoe, and maturing crops had to be weeded two or three times in the course of a growing season. Isaaq and the other immigrants from Baay thus utilized a flexible system of cultivation based on their access to both dhasheeg farms and doonk farms.

Shortly after Isaaq settled in Gora, an Ajuraan-affiliated Boran pastoralist family (reer Sabdow, or the Sabdow family) settled just across the grassy plain to the south, and began farming Dhasheeg Loc. They did not completely settle, and for several decades moved back and forth to the bush. At this same time, an Ajuraan ex-slave of East African origin called Baraki settled to the south of Dhasheeg Loc, in an area called Bunbunle. Baraki was one of the men imported and sold into slavery by Qaasin Baraawe, a well-known merchant and slave trader of Baraawe on the Benaadir Coast. Baraki and his children along with Sabdow and his family were the first to settle in the vicinity of Dhasheeg Loc, and their descendants have lived together for almost a century.

Reer Sabdow attracted dozens of their relatives over the next few decades. They lived in Loc (to the north of Dhasheeg Loc), or in Bunbunle, cultivating in the two dhasheegs and in the doonk area stretching from Dhasheeg Bunbunle to the riverbank. Additionally, several other individuals of Boran heritage who were affiliated with the Somali Gaaljecel clan found a home in Loc during the 1920s and 1930s, after years of searching. Some of these Boran families settled permanently, having lost all their livestock, but others continued with an agropastoral lifestyle until they were completely wiped out by the droughts of the 1960s and 1970s. In the late 1930s, the village of Loc was augmented by people escaping forced labor on Italian plantations, in addition to relatives of reer Sabdow continuing to arrive from the Dooy Region. Several families joined Loc village during this time. By the early 1940s, Loc was a combination of Ajuraan and Gaaljecel Boran who had either settled entirely or retained livestock in the bush, and Ajuraan and Gaaljecel ex-slaves of East African heritage.

By 1942, Loc village had about eight families and Bunbunle had about thirteen families. Families and individuals moved easily between the two settlements, often for marriage. In 1942 Loc village was abandoned. Loc men recalled that the move was necessitated by the proximity to Gora, which was a different clan, and the intrusions of colonial authorities who were interested in building a road up the valley which would pass through Loc. Older Loc villagers held unpleasant memories of these Italian colonialists; local poetry told of the behavior of Italians passing through Loc, demanding grain, livestock, and chickens, forcing villagers to serve as porters, and raping women. Some families fleeing Loc moved to a spot they called Loc Yare (little Loc) on the eastern edge of the dhasheeg between the dhasheeg and the river, one man moved his family to an area of mango trees (planted decades earlier with seed provided by the British) in Kaxarey, and the rest moved further south to Bunbunle. These areas were less accessible to colonialists, requiring a hike through the forest to reach from the dirt road. In the early 1940s, Loc Yare had about forty people, who cultivated Dhasheeg Loc, Jarbolley, and, more gradually, Danballey. Bunbunle had about forty inhabitants as well. By 1945, the inhabitants of Loc Yare determined that the area was too swampy, mosquito-ridden, and susceptible to floods, and about half left for the higher ground of Bunbunle. The newcomers to Bunbunle greatly expanded the area cultivated in the environs of the village, encompassing the entire Dhasheeg Bunbunle, much of Dooday, and the riverbank south of the village (Iskorex and Bancarab).

In 1945, a charismatic holy man named Sheikh Nasibow came from Jilib on the lower Jubba with a few relatives to settle on the spot where Loc had been located. He formed a small religious brotherhood, and several of the families remaining in Loc Yare (representing Ajuraan, Gaaljecel, and Ajuraan reer Shabeelle) joined him. Danballey had largely been abandoned, although the family living at Kaxarey continued to farm there. Several newcomers also settled with the brotherhood. Sheikh Nasibow's followers continued to expand cultivation in Dhasheeg Loc and Jarbolley. By the early 1960s, the population of Loc had grown to about fifty people.

Just a few years prior to Sheikh Nasibow's arrival in Loc, about ten reer Shabeelle families (about thirty people) founded the village of Cabdow Yusuf to the north of Gora on the edge of the swampy, dhasheeg-like area called Siimow, a name which indicates the presence of underground water near the surface. These families had left the Kalafo area of Ethiopia in the 1920s and 1930s, living in a number of villages in the valley before establishing the new settlement of Cabdow Yusuf in 1943. More families from Ethiopia as well as from the east bank continued to arrive during the 1940s, when the area under cultivation in Siimow reached its highest point. During the 1950s, Cabdow Yusuf farmers were forced to abandon the Siimow area for permanent cultivation, due to problems with unpredictable waterlogging causing crop losses. Most of these families moved continually between several reer Shabeelle villages in the area, clearing, farming, and abandoning pockets of land throughout the northern area of what is now Loc village lands, including portions of Gulmugde, Korkomare dhasheeg, Shanley, Jeerey, and Erabley on the edge of Dhasheeg Gora.

Bunbunle grew rapidly in the decades after 1940 as Ajuraan Boran ex-pastoralists continued arriving to join previously settled relatives. By the late 1940s arrivals from Dooy, from Loc Yare, and the birth of new

2. A Loc father and his sons cultivating maize in Dhasheeg Loc. Photo by Jorge Acero.

children brought the population to about one hundred people. A small continual stream of new arrivals from Dooy and Afmadow areas and new births increased the population to about 150 by the late 1950s, when all land in Bunbunle and Dhasheeg Loc was taken. A few men began clearing and farming Huriwaa (which one man told me means "no other choice") riverbank land to expand the land base and to let the previously cultivated farms rest.

In these early decades of settlement, villagers moved about the landscape, learning about the different soil types, productivity, seasonality, labor demands, pest problems, and other aspects of middle valley farming. Gradually a pattern of land ownership emerged of fragmented family holdings spread over different soil types, cultivated in different seasons and/or years with different crops and different distributions of labor. Generally, Loc farmers would begin preparing doonk and riverbank land in March, in anticipation of the gu season rains after the long hot dry jilaal. Shortly after the onset of the rains, farmers would begin planting maize, although sometimes they would intercrop sesame a month or so later if the rains were quite good. All farmers planted by hand using a short-handled hoe to make a small hole into which they dropped a few maize kernels or sesame seeds.

Farmers would wait to plant their dhasheeg farms until they were sure that any chance of a river flood had passed (although unanticipated flooding ruined maturing crops once every few years). Planting proceeded bit by bit as the accumulated water evaporated. Farmers could still be planting in their dhasheeg farms when harvesting their doonk or riverbank farms (ninety days after planting), and often found themselves harvesting from one end of a dhasheeg farm while still planting in the other end. With the onset of dayr season rains in September or October, farmers typically planted sesame on their doonk and riverbank farms, although they might forgo planting a dayr crop on doonk land if rains failed or if work was still proceeding on their dhasheeg farms. Because sesame was grown primarily as a cash crop, farmers reserved it for the riskier growing season, ensuring their food supply by planting maize in the more predictable gu season.

Following the dayr harvest, if there was one, farmers would leave their land fallow during jilaal, although work could still be going on in the dhasheegs. The jilaal brought pastoralists to the river, and farmers concentrated their attention on mediating the pastoralist use of their land. The end of jilaal brought the arduous land preparation tasks of cutting and burning, in anticipation of the gu season rains.

As we have seen, initial acquisition of land was based on the premise that land belonged to the man who cleared it and his heirs, even when it was left fallow, and even if the man had returned for a period of time to pastoralism. As villages formed in the area with rising population, villagers began delineating and recognizing boundaries between landholdings of adjacent villages. By the 1950s and 1960s, the earliest settlers or their descendants began to oversee the distribution of land to ensure that new arrivals did not try to claim and clear fallow land already claimed by earlier settlers. These men, who assumed the title of *nabadoon* (peace-bringer; pl. *nabadoono*) mediated land disputes and boundaries.[30] Oral histories suggested that the earliest settlers guarded their (often large) claims to dhasheeg land, and differential dhasheeg holdings remained one of the only indicators of inequality within Loc village through the 1980s (discussed further in Chapter 8). Later settlers claimed and farmed land further into the dhasheeg, which was less accessible and more prone to becoming waterlogged, or land on the edge of the dhasheegs, which, while still good quality, did not always receive enough water.

If newcomers did not have resident family to provide them with land, they approached the nabadoon of the village they wished to join, and he could direct them to unclaimed land. It is clear that some of the early nabadoono may not have been entirely altruistic: in 1988 one man still held bitter memories of how a nabadoon "stole" a parcel of land from his childless uncle to give to someone else decades ago. In general, the degree to which nabadoono abused their power seems to have been minor, as evidenced by the fact that I only heard one such story in the course of my fieldwork on historical land tenure, and the fact that this man held such an angry memory suggests that the usurping of land by a nabadoon was a rare, rather than a regular, occurrence. The practices of declaring one's intentions to the nabadoon and receiving clearance from him to begin farming a parcel helped minimize disputes over land ownership and protected the rights of previous claimants, but in no way indicated a village perception of nabadoon ownership or personal control over village lands.

Arrivals to Loc during the first three or four decades of this century claimed parcels of land for themselves which suited their needs. Arrivals over the next three decades, who were usually joining family members, often depended on their relatives while clearing new land for themselves under the guidance of the nabadoon. The story of Jimcale, an Ajuraan-affiliated pastoralist of Boran/Warday ancestry, provides an example of this process. He described to me his arrival in Loc in the early 1960s in terms that evoked the feeling of a homecoming. While living in Kenya, he had lost his animals to "thirst and disease" (although other villagers said he had been released from slavery) and made his way to Bu'aale, where his mother had settled with other Ajuraan former pastoralists. After a year, his mother advised him to move to Bunbunle (home of reer Sabdow and many other Ajuraan families), telling him that he wouldn't be able to acquire enough land for himself in Bu'aale:

> So I left for Bunbunle by my mother's *inshara* [will, vision]. All my relatives there were full of food. As soon as I arrived, they opened a *bakaar* [underground storage pit filled with maize] for me. They constructed a house. I settled. My uncles were there. My aunts were there too. All were my relatives, like Iidow [the local nabadoon]. I had no problems: I was settled well by those people. Iidow and another man, who is now dead, told me to clear a bush area. He told me, "You won't get a cleared farm." I got my first farm in that way, and I am still farming it. It's in Kaysiney. I was also the first to clear a farm in Danballey [after Danballey had been abandoned]. I named that area too. All the farms now called Danballey, I am their father! I cut down 250 *danbal* trees.

When I asked him how, as a lifelong pastoralist, he learned to farm, he laughed while he described his first attempts:

> A clever man can do what another man is doing. You just have to watch the man next to you. If you watch one time, your success will just depend on your

strength. Even with the seeds: without knowledge I used to put this much (a handful) in at once, and the plants all came up at once and died. Then I was told, "That's not the way to do it. Just put in this much, four or five seeds only. But don't put in that much!" Before I learned I used to put in ten, ten seeds in one hole. After I was told "Stop! No more than four!" I learned, and then I became a better farmer than other people.

Another pastoralist-turned-farmer, the nabadoon Iidow mentioned above by Jimcale, also giggled as he described his first attempts at farming, recalling how he and his family kept injuring themselves with the hoe—cutting their toes, feet, and shins in their initial awkwardness as farmers.

Many of the pastoralists who stayed in Loc, rather than returning permanently to nomadism, described how enjoyable they found the sedentary life. Jimcale praised life in Loc, justifying his decision to remain a farmer:

Young people don't want livestock now. They hate the thirst. The hardship of walking late at night, no water, nothing to cook with. They hate the hardship. They all came into the Gosha. All who live here now, from here to Kismayo, all who were pastoralists came into the *aziendo.* Life here is so much easier. As a pastoralist, your transportation might die. You walk around looking for water, but may not find it. Then the camel which you loaded this morning alive, he can die, and what will you do with the children? All your animals are dying of thirst. You have terrible thirst yourself. What to give to the children? How to carry them? It's a big hardship. Who wants that? All who are sick, you must leave them behind. If somebody dies, you can't bury them [properly]. The hardship is hated. Look at the luxury here [in Loc]. For the one with enough farms and labor here, only *qooq* [leisure, playing] will kill him. For the man who lives here, look at the bathing he has, look at the luxury. If you fill your stomach, do your planting, and rest, you are calm. I remember spending nights in lonely places, seeing nobody, eating nothing, looking for grazing. Nothing to eat, no water, no Muslims. If I die, who will take care of me? Will you be killed by a lion? Will you be killed by an elephant? Who wants the hardship of the bush? Look at this shade, at the cool breeze off the river, at this bathing, at this luxury. This is better.

Although my pastoralist-turned-villager interlocuters never mentioned it, I couldn't help wondering if life as an independent farmer with full control over one's life, labor, and land, rather than life as a client/serf/slave pastoralist, contributed to their sense of comfort and "calm" since settling in Loc. Certainly, their praise for the life of farming contrasted markedly with the typical Somali view of agriculture.

The position of nabadoon became more important as population and demand for land grew. By the 1960s, newcomers to the Loc-Bunbunle area were actually giving cash payments to local nabadoono in return for their help in choosing a piece of land. The decade of the 1960s brought many people into the Loc area because of the long *arbaca shahi*

(Wednesday Year of Tea) drought. During these droughts, the population of Gora grew to its highest point, probably around seventy people as people from other villages in the valley and the Baay Region were attracted to Loc because of its proximity to the dhasheeg. All of Calibulahaan was claimed by this period, although farmers did not cultivate their parcels every year. Following the droughts, some people left to return to their former villages and others died having never married or produced children. By the 1970s, the population was around sixty people (ten families), where it stayed until unification in 1977. While relatively insular vis-à-vis the other settlements in the immediate vicinity, Gora Laysan exchanged spouses with Laysan living in villages to the south of Bunbunle, maintaining special relations with these villages through the 1980s.

By the 1960s, following Sheikh Nasibow's death in Loc, several families of his followers remained and continued to farm in Dhasheeg Loc and a bit of Kaxarey. Many settlers had died childless, being unable to find wives, and no or very few newcomers arrived, so the population hovered around fifty until unification in 1977.

The population of Cabdow Yusuf grew steadily until the 1960s with new immigrants from Ethiopia, although settlement began to stabilize during the 1960s. By unification Cabdow Yusuf had a population of around one hundred, taking into account the continual movement of residents.

Bunbunle's stream of new settlers during the 1960s brought the population to around two hundred by the early 1970s. Bunbunle was large and crowded by this time, and Bunbunle's farmers were continuing to expand northward, claiming all of Huriwaa, Dooday, and Kaysiney, and were starting to reclear Danballey. Bunbunle differed from the other villages in its almost constant influx of settling Boran Ajuraan from the Dooy and Afmadow regions, augmented in the 1970s with several Somali pastoral families hit by the 1974–75 *abaar daba dheere.* Boran immigrants were following brothers, cousins, parents, and children to the Loc-Bu'aale area, which was growing as an area of settled Ajuraan. The story of one family, reer Sabdow, illustrates this process of families no longer able to survive as pastoralists following relatives to Loc. The story of Sabdow and his family, retold here, is quite similar to that of other families coming to Loc to join previously settled relatives as agriculturalists.

Sabdow's Story

Sabdow was a pastoralist who moved within the middle Jubba-Dooy area with his herds. His ancestry is considered Boran, although it is unclear whether just his mother or both parents were Boran. He had been visiting the Loc area his entire life, cultivating farms there since the first decade of this century. Sabdow did not settle permanently in Loc until the late 1940s; before that time he came and went depending on droughts and floods. He had several wives and many children who were born in the Dooy. His eldest living son, Ibrahim, age fifty-seven in 1988, similarly kept farms in Loc, had several wives, and lived an agropastoral lifestyle until losing his livestock to drought in the early 1960s. He divorced two of his wives, and settled in Loc permanently with one of his remaining wives. He kept another wife in Dooy with their children, finally bringing her and their children to Loc in 1981. Ibrahim's brother, Cali, age forty-three in 1988, followed Ibrahim to Loc in 1977, bringing his children but divorcing their mother and leaving her behind in Dooy. She came to Loc in 1982 to be near her children, eventually marrying a local man. A third brother and a sister also came to Loc from Dooy, each eventually marrying locally.

Sabdow had divorced the mother of these children, a woman named Caddey, and she remarried a man named Deerow, who lived an agropastoral lifestyle between Loc and the Dooy Region. Deerow's son by another wife, a man in his mid-fifties in 1988 named Xassan, similarly lived between Bunbunle and the bush. Xassan had married Sabdow's daughter Sumuney (his father's second wife's first husband's daughter), living an agropastoral life for several decades. Xassan lived permanently in Loc since at least 1970, but in 1988 was one of the only villagers to still own livestock in the bush, cared for by a relative. Caddey and Deerow followed their respective children to Bunbunle in the early 1960s, with their son, Cali, in his early thirties in 1988, who was brought up in Bunbunle as a farmer.

Another of Sabdow's sons, named Xeffow (now dead) married a Dooy woman named Xalima and they had a son Cabdiraxmon. Xeffow took a second wife, Xabiba. They lost all their livestock to disease and followed Xeffow's brothers to Loc around 1970, settling as farmers. Xalima had formerly been married to a man named Yusuf. Yusuf was the son of another of the earliest settlers of Bunbunle, a man named Cali Muuse. Cali Muuse had had three sons, one of whom lived in Bunbunle, the other two, including Yusuf, lived as pastoralists in the Dooy, which is where Yusuf married Xalima. After their divorce, Yusuf remained in the Dooy as an agropastoralist with his three children by Xalima until 1974, when he brought his children to settle in Bunbunle with their mother and his brothers. Their livestock had all succumbed to disease, and they followed their relatives to take up a life of farming. Their children, ages forty-three, thirty-three, and thirty-two years old in 1988, continued to live in Loc, one son (Weheliye) having married his mother's niece (mother's brother's daughter), a girl living in the Dooy Region, whom he brought to Loc.

This complicated story of names, relations, and movements continues with more of Sabdow's children from the Dooy, and Sabdow's wives' children by different husbands arriving to join brothers and cousins. As far as I have retold the story, twenty-seven people over several decades came to Loc from Dooy as a direct result of kinship relations with Sabdow, the first arrival. Their pattern of immigration and eventual settlement is quite typical of other Boran-derived families in Loc. People settling in Loc and Bunbunle often initially retained livestock in the Dooy in addition to acquiring farmland in the Loc area. Movement between village and bush ensured continuing communication between relatives. As various members of the quite extended family (extended by divorces and remarriages) lost livestock to disease or drought, they followed their relatives who had become successful farmers to the Loc area. Mothers followed children, brothers followed brothers, men and women followed aunts and uncles, and adult children followed elderly parents. The pull was due to ties of kinship by marriage and to the fact that other Boran Ajuraan ex-pastoralists were settling into the area (such as the extended families of Cali Muuse and Deerow).

Loc Village Dynamics Since the 1970s

The most recent settlers to come to Loc-Bunbunle were primarily Somali pastoralists of the Bartire clan. Bartire territory encompasses the bush area surrounding Loc, and there is much familiarity between Bartire pastoralists and Loc villagers due to relations of trade and exchange. Several Bartire men acquired farms in the Loc-Bunbunle area, eventually settling permanently with family members. Some intended to return to a pastoral life after rebuilding their herds; others claimed to have no desire to return to what they described as a "life of hardship and want" in the bush.

By the 1970s, immigration to the Loc area from areas outside the valley had significantly waned. The vast majority (80 percent) of people living in Loc in 1988 were born there or in a nearby village. The remainder had immigrated from villages in other regions or from the bush (I did not determine the birthplace of 1 percent of Loc's population). The continual movement that characterized settlement in the earlier decades had largely stabilized, as families became more attached to their neighbors through friendships and marriages, and more attached to specific farms which they cultivated on a rotational basis.

In 1977 the government forcibly relocated the villagers of Cabdow Yusuf, Gora, Loc, and Bunbunle to the site of Loc. At every high flood, the villages of Cabdow Yusuf and Bunbunle would become flooded, and villagers would wait out the flood in Loc or Gora. There was a very high flood in 1977, and the government justified the move on the basis of flooding and because consolidation would facilitate administration. Loc was created as the administrative center for the area, a *beel*. Its jurisdiction covered the village of Maddow across the river,[31] another sedentary agricultural village a few kilometers away, as well as a seasonal Bartire nomad settlement to the west. The nabadoono were replaced by a government-appointed (with village input) village council (which in Loc consisted of the former nabadoono plus a few other men). The six-member village council had the same duties as the former nabadoono, including the authority to grant land to those who requested it and to mediate disputes.

Bunbunle was so far away from the new village site that people began abandoning their farms to the far south, especially in Bancarab. A portion of Bancarab was farmed during the early 1980s by a consortium of farmers who formed a cooperative in accordance with government policy and ideology, but was eventually abandoned (see Chapter 8) and the entire area reverted to bush. Following consolidation, people began claiming and farming land immediately to the south of Loc, greatly expanding Kaxarey and Danballey, which was much closer to their new homes but not as good quality as the land further south. The cultivation pattern in the north was not nearly as altered. Cultivation in Gulmugde and Jeerey expanded, but Erabley and Shanley were abandoned as "lonely places," prone to attacks by wild animals. Several villagers purchased parcels of cleared land in Calibulahaan, marking the first land sales in the northern area.

Taken as an overall picture, the historic pattern of land use within the Loc area shows how well settlers and their children were able to utilize the land base to welcome new settlers while meeting short and long-term needs. As we have seen, villagers consistently cultivated all the dhasheeg areas, keeping the Siimow as a village commons over the last several decades open seasonally and equally to all. Whenever the Siimow was cultivable farmers rushed in to stake out a plot, keeping the village mediators quite busy overseeing boundary disputes. Villagers variably cultivated the doonk and riverbank areas over time. Farmers liked to cultivate farms near each other for companionship and informal labor assistance, and because it reduced the threats from predators (hippos, wild boar, monkeys, as well as the occasional lion) to which isolated farms were more subject. The historical pattern was one where a few farmers would jointly decide to move into an area together to begin clearing individual plots, often followed by other farmers. Eventually some of the farmers would leave their parcels because of weed growth or labor constraints.

Gradually, remaining farmers in that area would also leave their parcels because of the enormous work involved in warding off predators on cultivated parcels surrounded by fallowed parcels or forest. All the land in that area would thus revert to bush, although each farmer would maintain his claim to his particular parcel until he or his heirs decided to return to reclear and cultivate the farm again. This was the pattern in Huriwaa, Shanley, and Erabley, as well as in parts of Gulmugde.

The historical view shows that villagers as a group have been able to make choices—to keep numerous options open—in determining which land to farm over long periods of time. Loc area farmers collectively met the demands brought on by a rising population; the needs of young men to acquire their own land prior to receiving their inheritance; the need to let land rest which had been cultivated continuously for ten years or more in order to combat weed growth; the need for villagers to be able to acquire land close to home as they moved around the area between villages. Abundant land and cooperation between settlers throughout the Loc area ensured agricultural sustainability over the past century.

Community Ties

Following consolidation, Loc became a large village of about five hundred people of different ancestries (Boran, East African, and Somali), different clan affiliations (Ajuraan, Gaaljecel, Laysan, and Bartire), and different personal histories. A breakdown of Loc's population by paternal ancestral ethnicity produced this picture: 27 percent reer Shabeelle, 25 percent Boran, 16 percent descendants of agricultural slaves from the Baay Region (most or all of East African descent), and 9 percent ethnic Somalis who had recently settled from the bush. The remainder consisted of the local sheikh's family from Jilib, who were clearly of Bantu ancestry, but whose family history I did not try to obtain;[32] women who married into the village from the Saakow area upriver; descendants of men who moved into the area two generations ago who were ex-slaves, but no one was sure about exactly where they escaped from, and some who were of unknown heritage (in-marrying women, children of divorced women whose fathers lived elsewhere). A rough approximation of Somali clan affiliation produced this picture: over half the village was Ajuraan, about a fifth was Laysan, and the remainder was equally split between Bartire and Gaaljecel.

The multiplicity of ancestral identities, clan affiliations, personal histories, and occupational histories produced overlapping webs of ties connecting people within the village, the valley, and the region. Differentiation of Loc's population into groups occurred on different bases at different times and in different contexts: under some circumstances villagers regarded themselves as a collectivity, under others they divided up into neighborhood factions, clan factions, ethnic factions, or factions based on other factors such as friendship. Thus while it would be possible, for example, to characterize Loc as an Ajuraan village because of the numerical superiority of villagers claiming Ajuraan clan affiliations (as it was, in fact, characterized by regional officials and pastoralists), such a characterization would not accurately capture the various facets of social identity recognized within Loc.

In the practices of day-to-day life, different aspects of social identity became important in different contexts. The physical organization of the village and the handling of disputes give insights into the significance of Somali clan identities in negotiating social relations within the village. Due to settlement patterns wherein clan membership attracted new settlers, village neighborhoods tended to be organized such that members of one clan lived near each other. This became particularly apparent to me when I spent too much time in one neighborhood or another, to the annoyance of residents of neighborhoods of a different clan affiliation. When we decided to hold the preparations for a feast we were giving the village in the Ajuraan area of the village because there was more open space, a few of the residents of the Laysan area refused to attend, expressing outrage that we had chosen that part of the village over their neighborhood. When conflicts occurred between villagers, each party relied on witnesses for support in stating his case. These witnesses were often of the same clan (usually because they were relatives). In describing to me the settlement history of Loc, some village elders explained that the villages of Gora and Loc did not get along because they were of different Somali clans—thus prompting the move of Loc villagers further south to Loc Yare mentioned above.

If conflicts occurred between members of the same clan, ancestral identities defined potential supporters; such as an Ajuraan of Oromo ancestry versus a reer Shabeelle Ajuraan. This breakdown of support along ethnic lines was often due to the fact that relatives were frequently called as witnesses to support one's case—perhaps evidence of an intangible sense of trust which existed between people of similar background, or perhaps evidence of the strength of family ties. As noted above, marriages were often (but certainly not always) arranged between members of the same clan and same ancestry due to the preference for cousin marriage. Thus we see an ongoing recognition—however muted in daily praxis and sentiment—of ancestral identities by Loc villagers.

While clan and even ethnic distinctions certainly carried an important sense of membership, loyalty, and personal identity, a clear feeling of collectivity—of *village* identity—had also evolved over the more than eighty years of village formation. In talking about the time of consoli-

3. Loc women preparing maize for a village feast. Photo by Jorge Acero.

dation, nearly everyone characterized it as a minor shifting of location rather than a major upheaval because the farmers in all (by that time) four villages regularly visited, helped each other, sometimes intermarried, and frequently lived for a time in each other's villages or even compounds. As one man formerly of Cabdow Yusuf explained, "If a man got married in Bunbunle, people from Cabdow Yusuf would help and participate." Families throughout the Loc area had long worked together in their fields, sharing labor, working in groups to cultivate in turn each group member's farms during weeding or harvesting seasons, forming work groups to help sick or injured neighbors maintain their farms or homes, and lending or borrowing plots of cleared land to friends throughout the four villages. Farmers who cultivated adjoining fields would organize labor rotations to collectively guard groups of farms against predators or would sometimes work together on one farmer's field one day and another farmer's field the next simply for the pleasure of companionship and the chance to chat. Similarly, the owners of a group of neighboring fields would seasonally organize collective work groups to build retaining walls against floods or to dig overflow channels for drainage in their collective field area. Owners of neighboring dhasheeg parcels often helped each other consecutively as the water drained from the farms. Since the opportunity to plant in different areas became available at different times, one farmer could have free time while his neighbor or brother had peak labor needs. Through informal piecemeal assistance, families and friends helped each other meet labor needs.

By the time of my visit, more formal villagewide work associations were also long established components of village life. The *barbaar*, composed of all the unmarried men in the village as well as a number of married men, worked on village construction projects, helped betrothed members build their wedding huts, contributed money for weddings and funerals, and assisted elderly or sick villagers in their fields. The hard work undertaken by the barbaar was matched by their enthusiasm and festive spirit; all barbaar undertakings had great style, marked by dancing, singing, joking, blowing the conch shell and feasting.[33] Men who failed to participate or contribute could be fined. Most village families also relied on the labor-sharing institution of *goob*, found throughout the valley, at least once in the course of a year to pull together large work groups who would donate their labor (which usually included good humor, dancing, singing, and conch-blowing as well) to a farmer for a specific task in exchange for a large meal and a reciprocal donation of labor when another *goob* was called.

In addition to such formal and informal labor-sharing practices, political and domestic matters were considered village matters, rather than simply issues to be addressed within a clan, family, or household. All important village decisions were made collectively by the village council, which drew its members from all ethnic backgrounds and clan affiliations, assisted by any male villagers who cared to participate. Village politics thus drew on the broad Somali pattern of allowing any man to participate in local or clan political deliberations.[34] The council not only handled questions of land distribution, but also mediated all kinds of domestic and civic disputes and figured out how to handle unlawful behavior (for which the village maintained a locked "jail hut" to imprison offenders for a day or two). Villagers had chosen three local men to serve as impartial village judges who could assist the village council in determining fines for wrongful actions. During my stay villagers were fined for offenses like setting an animal trap too close to a walking path (which resulted in a mangled foot on an unsuspecting farmer on his way to weed), for wife-beating, for refusing to participate in a villagewide construction project or to contribute to a village feast, for boundary encroachment into a neighbor's field, and for spreading malicious gossip. The village council frequently mediated domestic disputes, such as a man wishing to divorce his wife because she could not get along with his children from a previous wife, a woman claiming her husband was too stingy, a man angry because the labor of his stepchildren was being claimed by their father, who did not contribute to their support, and a woman angry because her husband was using magic to charm a girl who was engaged to another man. Thus the village as a collectivity mediated the intimate details of villagers' lives *and* livelihoods, overseeing domesticity and morality in addition to distributing land and sharing labor. Love affairs, marriages, divorces, infidelities, and domestic arguments carried equal weight with land distribution as villagewide matters of concern which the village council had not only the right but also the duty to oversee.

As I will discuss in Chapter 6, another important indicator of village cohesion was the fact that villagers paid diya (blood compensation) as a group, no matter which clan with representation in the village was collecting the payment. Furthermore, villagers embarked on a variety of mutually beneficial economic projects together across clan and ethnic lines, such as jointly hiring a truck to carry their sesame production to Jilib for sale.

In addition to political and economic integration, the presence of Sheikh Nasibow's tomb in the center of Loc lent a unifying religious focus to the village. Sheikh Nasibow's son maintained a large compound with a wife and several children in Loc and claimed religious authority over all villagers. Thus he was responsible for overseeing religious rituals, engagements, marriages, divorces, funerals, charges of infidelity, and moral issues. The entire village contributed alms to him, worked to maintain his father's tomb, and honored the anniversary of his father's death by holding an annual festival which drew hundreds of celebrants and dozens of prominent sheikhs to Loc from throughout the valley. Despite the fact that some families (the descendants of the sheikh's early followers in Loc) maintained closer ties with the sheikh's son, the entire village submitted to his authority and viewed him as the religious center of their community.

All of these examples about village cohesion and collective identity should not detract from the fact that Loc, like many small villages throughout the world, was marked as much by division and disunity as by a strong sense of village membership, responsibility, and obligation. Like villagers do the world over, Loc villagers complained that everyone was out for himself, that neighbors didn't trust neighbors; they opened shops in competition with each other, fought with each other, coveted each other's spouses, secretly cleared into each other's fields; they grumbled about the local sheikh's dictatorial ways, about the village headman's incompetence. But my point is that villagers *also* loved each other, trusted each other, and worked together in remarkable and altruistic ways for the benefit of the village as a community. They respected and abided by the decisions of the village council, they took their family problems before the whole village for mediation, they submitted to the authority of the local sheikh, they mourned each other's losses and celebrated each other's happinesses—and they did these things across clan and ethnic lines.

Conclusions

Taken together, Chapters 3 and 4 have introduced several critical dimensions of Jubba valley history which we will continue to revisit, rethink, and refine in later chapters. My brief overview of population changes and movements suggests a dynamic process of cultural production as fugitive and manumitted slaves struggled to create a new world—their world—out of the forests of the Jubba valley. I have described the transformation of the valley landscape—how in-migrating ex-slaves claimed the valley as their place by turning forests into farmlands and villages, by developing sustainable systems of land use and individualized land tenure, and by creating village-based forms of authority, mediation, and negotiation. We have also seen how this transformation of space into place accommodated a multiplicity of social identities, where people could assume or shed clan affiliations, situationally recognize or subordinate personal ethnic ancestries, move between villages, and marry across lines of clan or heritage. Yet we have also seen how this fluidity at the local level came to be increasingly embedded within a process of Somalization which drew valley dwellers into Somali cultural, religious, and social categories. While the Somalization of Gosha villagers did not erase or negate these other aspects of local experience and interaction, it did create new logics, new ideologies, new practices, new ways of being, and, concurrent with the emergence of the idea of a bounded Somali "polity," new forms of authority and community which produced new definitions and categories of identity and structures of domination.

The next section takes us beyond the movements of people in the middle valley and their agricultural practices to look at how settlers and their descendants faced these new categories to imaginatively construct and define their world and their role in Somali society and in the emerging Somali nation-state.

Part III
The Gosha Space in Somali Society

Chapter 5
Hard Hair: Somali Constructions of Gosha Inferiority

From the two previous chapters, we have a sense of how ex-slaves filtered into the Jubba valley, carving out communities, transforming space, forging alliances, and constructing a place of belonging. Through Islam, clan memberships, and trade, ex-slaves were claiming Somali society as their own. Ex-slaves arriving in the middle valley around and after the turn of the century had adopted Somali clan affiliations as an aspect of personal identity, to negotiate social relations, and to build kinship networks. By the 1970s, in addition to considering themselves members of Somali clans and citizens of the Somali nation-state, mid-valley Gosha villagers spoke only Somali dialects, practiced Islam, and shared Somali cultural values. The Somalization of slave descendants bolstered Somalia's image as ethnically, religiously, culturally, and linguistically united. During the 1970s and 1980s, ethnographic descriptions and official Somali rhetoric championed Somalia as democratic, egalitarian, and homogenous.[1] Siyad Barre's nationalist campaign of the late 1970s, which included the outlawing of any reference to ethnic distinctions, patron-client relationships, and all other formal relationships based on social inequality, proclaimed that the master-slave distinction had been successfully transformed by assimilation and the Somali democratic ethos.

Despite these highly touted indications of equality, assimilation, and homogeneity, however, Gosha villagers and other slave descendants continued to hold marked identities which stigmatized them in Somali society. Overt signs of inequality, status distinctions, and social differentiation were readily apparent to any visitor in the 1980s. This chapter addresses these lingering—and powerful—markers of inequality and differentiation by tracing the linkages which have combined to produce the Jubba valley as a place of subjugated "otherness" within the national space.

Over the course of the twentieth century, the convergence of Islamic ideology, colonial policy, and state practice contributed to a construction of racial categories which defined the Jubba valley as a racialized space within Somali society. The status accorded to the inhabitants of that space found symbolic expression in a variety of arenas: regionally through the Somali clan system, locally in Gosha villagers' encounters with Somali pastoralists and state representatives, and nationally in state practice. Tracing the texture of these expressions, this chapter delves into the symbolic significance of slave ancestry in modern Somalia, analyzing the multiple historical factors which contributed to the continuing social and political marginalization of slave descendants.

Hard Hair

The use of the inoffensive term *Gosha* to describe the riverine population provides only an initial hint of a Somali perception of this population as a distinct social group, differentiated on the basis of their environment from the larger—and more "homogenous"—whole. During my stay, other distinguishing and derogatory terms were more widely used by Somalis to label and identify the Jubba valley farmers. Somalis from Mogadishu, upon learning that I was living in the Jubba valley, often offered strong opinions about how different the people in the Gosha were from other Somalis, about their dangerous magical abilities, their questionable Muslim integrity, their distinct physical characteristics, their separate ancestry, their low status occupation of farming. People in Mogadishu told us that we were going to the Jubba valley "to starve" because the poor farmers there had no livestock and barely produced enough to feed themselves. Somali pastoralists moving through the Jubba valley would express astonishment that I could be interested in Gosha villagers. As one man put it: "You should study us [Somali pastoralists]! These Gosha know nothing and they have nothing of value."

In addition to mocking their occupational status and productivity, urban dwellers also warned us about the "licentious" and dangerous dances and rituals performed by valley farmers. Indeed, my field assistant, Cali—who had gained familiarity with and respect for Gosha farmers during his ten years of employment with Swedish health care workers in the middle valley—initially refused to go to local dances, explaining he was uncomfortable with and even a little frightened by the prospect of attending.[2] Valley dances, in which both sexes participated in a highly energetic and skillful series of steps and body movements led by drummers, had a reputation for being un-Islamic, improperly sexual in nature, and insulting to the pious. They were often held in the bush far away from villages in order to avoid attracting attention from disapproving Islamic sheikhs and visiting pastoralists. Gosha dance forms have been the subject of an ongoing campaign of extermination—colonial authorities disdained them as disgusting evidence of the farmers' low level of culture, Islamic sheikhs banned them, and pastoralists condemned them as paganistic.[3]

Beyond denigrating their productive abilities and their piety, urban and pastoralist Somalis sometimes used clearly derogatory terms such as *boon* (person of low status) and *addoon* (slave) to label and identify the Jubba valley descendants of slaves, despite government laws which forbade the use of such signifiers. While *Gosha* was used to specify a particular ecologically delineated territorial space, another term, *jareer*, was more readily invoked to describe the people living within that space. *Jareer*—from *tiin jareer*—literally means "hard hair" and has recently been glossed more broadly as "Bantu" by English-speaking Somalis and non-Somali journalists reporting on the plight of southern Somali farmers during the civil war. Mid-valley villagers themselves, when describing their history and their place in Somali society to me, would say meaningfully, "Our hair is hard." It was clear that having hard hair carried heavy cultural weight, even if outsiders like myself found such hair difficult to distinguish from the hair of other Somalis. Investigating the meaning of this term takes us into the slippery terrain of racial and ethnic constructions within Somali society and its international players. Understanding the kinds of historical factors which have influenced the conceptualization of identity in racialized or ethnicized terms sheds light on what it meant to live as a slave descendant in the middle Jubba River valley in the 1980s.

Theoretically, analyzing the jareer label allows us to probe the territorialization of identity, the racialization of space, and the linked projects of state-building and race-making in producing a space/place/race/identity confluence in the middle Jubba valley. Recent concerns in anthropology with space and identity stem from a frustration with the situational approach to understanding ethnicity,[4] a return of interest in the concept, historicity, and meanings of race,[5] and new attention to the social production of space[6] and the "way spaces and places are made, imagined, contested, and enforced" (Gupta and Ferguson 1992:18). Pursuing the production of racialized space and identity in southern Somalia will allow us to address how the partitioning of space is connected to ethnic inequality,[7] and to see "how global interconnections assert the simultaneous production of difference within a totality" (Watts 1992:123).

Racialized Space

While jareer literally denotes "rough" or "kinky" hair texture, it encompasses a complex of physical features, including bone structure, facial features, and body morphology.[8] For example, the shape of the nose carried special meaning, with broader noses being seen in southern Somalia as significant markers. Somalis said that people in the Gosha had broad, flat noses, and even Gosha villagers directed derogatory teasing at people who had this characteristic. Jareer individuals were said to be bulkier; more specifically, nonjareer Somalis were said to have longer, more slender fingers. The descriptive term used for Somalis in opposition to jareer is *jileec,* which means "soft" (as in "soft-haired), or, more commonly, *bilis* (which is the opposite of *addoon*).

Most significantly, the jareer category is equated with "African"—and thus slave—ancestry, as distinguished from the (mythical) "Arabic" ancestry of Somalis.[9] This emphasis on hair as a representation of difference is emblematic of the global "symbolic potency" of hair type as a potential "symbolic badge of slavery" (Patterson 1982:61). At its most overt level, the jareer distinction marks certain aspects of physical appearance to single out and unite as a group ex-slave descendants.[10] Although Oromo descendants are not individually considered jareer, a separate Gosha Oromo identity has often been overlooked in the colonial and popular conception of the Gosha as a jareer space. Oromo descendants who settled in the Gosha region intermarried with slave descendants categorized as jareer, thus blurring the distinction. The jareer label when generically applied to Gosha residents thus includes Oromo by association.

If this widely used label offers a challenge to prevailing stereotypes of Somali homogeneity, the meanings attached to being jareer clearly undermine academic and popular claims of Somali society as egalitarian and democratic. Analyzing how physical distinctions embodied in the jareer label became correlated with an inferior and stigmatized status is somewhat speculative, but the literature on the ideological construction of slavery and race in Islamic societies and along the pastoralist/agriculturalist Saharan frontier provides some interesting and thought-provoking points of comparison.[11]

Throughout northern Africa, the distinction of slaves being called "black"—regardless of the complexion of their masters—is prevalent.[12] As slaves and populations from which slaves were taken converted to Islam, scholars argue that a transition from equating *slave* with *infidel* to equating *slave* with *black* occurred, with *black* being negatively valued for its association with slavery and its real or purported connection with paganism.[13] As St. Clair Drake has explained, "Prejudice against black people in Arabia and in other parts of the Islamic world had its roots in social relations, not in ideas about 'blackness' as a color that 'carried over' to black people. . . . The allocation of a subordinate role to black people . . . occurred not because they were black, but because they were bought or captured as slaves in East Africa. The most pervasive discriminatory behavior patterns were associated with the institution of slavery" (1990:182).

In a fascinating comparative case, the historian James Webb (1995) describes the construction of racialized identities along the western Sahelian frontier from 1600 to 1850. Regardless of skin color, Webb argues, desert-edge pastoralists along the frontier drew on "older oppositions of Black and White deeply embedded in the Arab conception of world geography" (1995:xvi) to develop regional cultural constructs of "black" and "white" to refer to people south and north of the frontier respectively. In a passage which forces us to consider cultural systems of regional racialization which predate European expansion, Webb argues (1995:xxvi):

> The terms "White" and "Black" are thus deeply inscribed in the history of the sahel of western Africa. These terms have not been borrowed from the cultural constructs of European-American and African-American identities in the Western world, which have been based, in part, upon the cultural perception of skin color. On the contrary, the usage in the Western world of the cultural terms "White" and "Black" to refer, in part, to skin color (pink and brown, respectively) seems to be a distant and refracted borrowing from the Arabo-African past.[14]

Webb's argument for the western Sahel is suggestive of the kinds of Arabic-derived cultural constructs which may have characterized Islamic pastoralist societies across the Sahara into the Horn. The coupling of Islamic definitions of "the African other" as pagan/black slave with such cultural constructs of "white" and "black" along the pastoral/agricultural frontier may have been a potent classification system in premodern Somalia. The use of the term *jareer* to indicate "African" in Somalia may thus be linked to the historical transition in Islamic slaveholding societies from emphasizing paganism to emphasizing racial difference in slaves. When used in modern Somalia, it is a resuscitation of the history of slavery of the referent, clearly rooting him or her in the legacy of subordination and inferior social status.

Comparative studies from coastal East Africa demonstrate the significance of Islamic ideology in defining the moral basis of slave inferiority. Frederick Cooper (1981) argues that Islam was used by East African plantation owners to legitimate a social hierarchy which granted the master the right to dominate the slave. Being a Muslim, the master could conceive of his relationship to his slaves as benevolent (rather than overtly dominant) by seeing as his role the conversion of pagan slaves to Islam. Religion, Cooper says, was thus used to rationalize domination. Ideology, in the form of religious beliefs, was "an active agent, as much a part of domination as whips or social dependence" (1981:278). John Ralph Willis (1985b) and Paul Lovejoy (1983) similarly discuss how the *jihad* (holy war) could also become a raid for slaves, due to the ideology that enslavement, through conversion and eventual manumission, frees a person from the despicable status of unbelief. As Willis says, "parallels between slave and infidel began to fuse in the heat of *jihad*" (1985b:17).

In Somalia, "infidels" were purchased as slaves and remade as "jareer" Muslims.[15] While I cannot claim that Somali slave owners were self-consciously using Islam to justify economic and social power structures, it is clear that Somalis saw the basis of their superiority as religious. Speke recorded in 1855 that Somalis believed the slave trade was their Quranic right,[16] an opinion found repeatedly in colonial documents from the era of abolition.[17] Oral histories indicate that the image of benevolence toward social dependents (slaves) certainly existed, especially among Somalis who captured Oromo for pastoral slavery (often in the context of jihad),[18] and probably among the self-defined "pious" Muslims of Benaadir coastal society.[19] The duty of the master was to convert slaves to Islam. As Cooper (1981:284) says, plantation slavery, and, to an even greater degree I would argue, pastoral slavery, was ideologically constructed as a form of (enforced) dependence (through slavery) and benevolence (through Islam). By converting the slave, the master ensured that the slave internalized the religious basis of his subordinate status; the converted slave could never be "as good" (Cooper 1981:291).

The jareer label, then, while referring to a complex of features believed to physically characterize the Gosha population, had as its greatest significance the cultural values embedded in being jareer. It is a term which refers to history—that of non-Somali pagan slave origins; a history devalued in Somali culture and ideology. The effect in social terms of carrying a jareer identity was a denigrated status within Somali social structure. The people of the Gosha, collectively lumped together as jareer, collectively shared a physicalized lower status identity within Somali society.[20]

Colonial Racial Visions

Colonial intrusion and the imposition of classificatory labels based on imposed Eurocentric racial categories amplified and refined local constructions of identity in southern Somalia. Somalis maneuvered for status within British categories by promoting their self-ascribed Arabic ancestry and emphasizing the Bantu ancestry of the Gosha population.

British colonial administrators, as bureaucratic foot soldiers in the European imperialist project of racializing the world, struggled with the "appropriate" racial categorization of Somalis within the European world view—a difficulty Somalis were quick to apprehend. Archived colonial documents reveal the unwillingness of British administrators to define Somalis as categorically equivalent to other Africans, whom they perceived through a racist lens as distinctly inferior. During the 1920s, for example, Somali leaders and British administrators agitated for a revision of the official colonial racial classification of natives so that Somalis could be categorized as Europeans or Asians rather than "black natives." To this end, the district commissioner for Kismayu District of southern Somalia wrote in 1922 that determining the "racial status" of Somalis was "the most important Somali question of today" and that Somalis should be taken out of jurisdiction of the Native Authority Ordinance and placed under an ordinance of their own.[21] The senior commissioner in Kismayu wrote the same year to the Chief Native Commissioner of British East Africa to emphasize that with Somalis "You are dealing with the most advanced brain on the East Coast" (KNA 1922c). Somalis responded to the British drive for racial categorization by forcefully pleading their case. One letter written (in English) by Somali Darood elders in 1922 to the Chief Native Commissioner says,

> The government officials who have visited our country know we are descendants from Arabia, and this we have already proved and we can prove we assure you we cannot accept to be equalled and compared with those pagan tribes either with our consent or by force even if the government orders this we cannot comply with, but we prefer death than to be treated equally with these tribes for as the government knows well these tribes are inferior to us and according to our religion they were slaves who we used to trade during past years. (KNA 1922a)

The tribes to which the writers refer are all those living in what was then British East Africa which the British colonial authorities included together with Somalis as "Natives" under the authority of the Chief Native Commissioner. In 1924 Somalis rebelled against the Registration Act, believing that the act would cause them to be treated like "Kikuyu" (a generic term sometimes used by Somalis to mean black Africans). Intelligence reports complained that Somalis refused to acquiesce to British desires that Somalis take up farming, saying: "A running story is being spread that if the Somali uses a hoe he immediately becomes a Kikuyu, the result being that agricultural operations have received a very severe setback" (KNA 1924). The connection here between agricultural work, black Africans, and slavery should be obvious.

As these documents attest, questions of race were clearly paramount in the British colonial mentality during the early twentieth century.

Somali leaders sought to ensure that their understandings of hierarchy and difference were translated into official British racial categories. The dialectic of Islamic-inspired Somali perceptions of difference and European notions of race mutually constructed a hierarchy that distinguished and separated people of slave ancestry from other Somalis. A Gosha villager recalled the British affirmation of local racial categories to me in the following terms: "After the British government came in . . . the government differentiated in this way: *reer goleed* [people of the forest] and *reer baydiya* [people of the bush; nomads], or *jareer* and *bilis.*" During another conversation he used different terms: "'This is soft hair [*tiin jileec*]; this is slave [*addoon*]'—during the time of the British they were separated in this way."

These racial distinctions became territorialized in the Jubba valley. While upholding the perception of Somalis as distinct from and superior to the European construct of "black Africans," both British and Italian colonial administrators placed the Jubba valley population in the latter category. Colonial discourse described the Jubba valley as occupied by a distinct group of inferior races,[22] collectively identified as the WaGosha by the British and the WaGoscia by the Italians. Colonial authorities administratively distinguished the Gosha as an inferior social category, delineating a separate Gosha political district called Goshaland, and proposing a "native reserve" for the Gosha. The colonial treatment of the Gosha as a collectivity was historically underscored by the colonial administrations' positioning of Nassib Bundo as a "Gosha chief" in the late nineteenth century (discussed in Chapter 3).

During its early decades, British and Italian racialization of the valley found brutal expression in the Italian forced labor policies of the 1930s. The major thrust of Italian colonial expansion into the area was to develop the valley's agricultural potential for colonial benefit. Concurrent with the historic creation of the Jubba valley as a racialized space for stigmatized ex-slaves, then, was the definition of the valley as an ecologically delineated place for agricultural exploitation. The ex-slaves who settled the valley had built vibrant agricultural communities, even sometimes exporting their surplus production in the Indian Ocean trade.[23] Early British and Italian colonial visitors wrote exuberantly about the stupendous agricultural potential of the Jubba valley—capturing this resource base emerged as a central component in Italy's vision of a great Italian East African empire. Italian colonial administrators viewed the visually identifiable valley ex-slaves and their descendants as the logical and obvious targets for their forced labor campaigns. Somalis, as pastoralists, couldn't be kept on the farm, but Bantu Jubba villagers were "naturally" predisposed to heavy farm labor. According to Menkhaus (1989:238–39), "the division of labor in colonial Somalia of the 1930s was determined along perceived ethnic or racial lines. By the 1930s, the 'Gosha' were collectively designated by the Italian colonial administration to be conscripted plantation laborers." In a passage that neatly describes the Italian colonial use of race to justify forced labor, Menkhaus (1989:246) writes, "Justifications for forced labor leaned more on racially-based explanations of native 'apathy' and 'unreliability,' and a lack of desire to save money. Such cultural deficiencies could only be remedied through the creation of a 'regular, assured, and disciplined native work force.' One article described the 'contract' of colonya as a means of 'overcoming the sort of hesitation and distrust of the black toward all that brings innovation to his primitive agrarian economy.' "[24]

In the late 1980s, elderly Jubba villagers still bitterly remembered how the colonial governments distinguished—using racial terms—Jubba farmers from Somalis in claiming their labor through the Italian kolonya. Recall the speaker quoted in Chapter 4 mimicking the Italians in their insistence that the Gosha were a single Bantu-derived group, officially targeted for forced labor: "I don't accept saying 'I am Mushunguli,' 'I am Bartire,' 'I am Shabeelle,' 'I am Cawlyahan,' 'I am Marexan.' It doesn't exist. You are all lying. You all are Mushunguli Mayasid [Bantu]. You have to participate [in the forced labor system]." Colonial visions of the valley as an ecologically useful racialized place thus played out through forced labor campaigns which enslaved former slaves for colonial agricultural benefit.

Ethnographers imposed the language of "tribe" in their rendition of the construction of Gosha farmers as racially and territorially distinct from other Somalis. The perception of the Gosha as a unified social group within a specific delineated territory dominated the infrequent mention of the Gosha population in the early ethnographic literature. Cerulli, the most prominent Italian ethnographer of Somalia, called the "Wagoscia" a "tribe" formed by ex-slaves (1957:144), as did other Italian ethnographers.[25] Britain's leading Somalist ethnographer, I. M. Lewis, following colonial procedure and perhaps Cerulli, applied the linguistic Bantu "people" category prefix when writing about the "the Wa-Gosha" (1955, 1988). Harold Nelson (1982), drawing on Lewis's and Cerulli's descriptions, generically referred to them as "habash" and "non-Somali." Luling also used the term "Wagosha," while acknowledging that this was "apparently a name given collectively to a number of different groups" (1983:42).

While anthropological awareness of the role of colonial authorities and ethnographers in creating African ethnicities has grown over the past several decades,[26] I am not arguing that British or Italian colonial authorities (or ethnographers) *created* a separate ethnicity for Gosha villagers, but rather that their policies, actions, and descriptions nurtured the perception of "Gosha" and "Somali" as highly distinct and unequal social groups. British colonial preoccupations with racial classification in the Jubba valley prior to 1925, and the Italian colonial use of race to define a legitimate body of agricultural laborers in the valley during the 1930s, contributed to enforcing the separate and unequal status of Gosha villagers during the colonial period.[27] The historical confluence of ex-slave settlement in the Jubba valley, Arabic/Islamic-derived perceptions of physical difference and hierarchy, and colonial race and space classifications produced the Gosha as a racialized space in twentieth-century Somalia. The colonial role in constructing this space in the regional consciousness becomes clearest with the position of Boran slave descendants in the valley. Boran were not considered racially distinct so much as ethnically distinct, and contemporary Boran pastoralists could "pass" unless their Somali neighbors knew their personal ancestry, unlike Bantu descendants, who could never "pass." Colonial policy conflated Boran and Bantu within the Jubba valley to create a racial space for "natives"/jareer/Bantu.[28] The result for the people living in the Gosha was a stigmatized ascribed group identity of inferiority, upheld by definitions of racial difference, applied to people living in a socially conceptualized and ecologically delineated space. As E. Valentine Daniel has written about the "Aryanization" of the Sinhala people of Sri Lanka, "The historicization of a place by its transformation into space is accompanied by the historicization of a people [or of peoples?] through their transformation into a race" (1996:58).

The creation of the Jubba valley as a racialized space was not only affirmed and nurtured during the colonial period, but was also given an incipient class dimension with the Italian claims to Gosha land and Gosha labor for the plantation production of cash crops. This theme of state claims to racialized Gosha bodies and territory proved powerfully enduring and marked the national space occupied by the Gosha place during my stay in the late 1980s. Paralleling what Stacey Leigh Pigg (1992) has described for rural Nepalis, Gosha villagers during the twentieth century have become "incarcerated" (Appadurai 1988) "in a kind of culture-territory. Place and person fuse in the distillation of cultural essence" (Pigg 1992:505).

Structuring Inferiority

The argument of the preceding chapters presents a bit of a quandary for our new understanding of the Gosha as a distinctly "other" space: people living in the upper Gosha considered their Somali clan affiliations central to their personal identities, yet southern Somali history has been a process of distinguishing, racializing, and denigrating Gosha villagers as a distinct and inferior group. How did these differing conceptions of Gosha place emerge in the symbolic and social flow of everyday life? How did Somali ideological conceptions of "inferiority" translate into lived experience? How is subjugation performed, recognized, demonstrated? For answers, we turn to a consideration of the structural organization of Somali society, the nature of Somali-Gosha interaction, and the actions of the state.

Somali Social Categories

The social organization of Somali society accommodated ideological conceptions of "inferiority" through investing clan membership with definitions of lineal purity. Somali clans, while fiercely egalitarian with regard to leadership and political control, contain divisions of unequal status. Bernhard Helander (1986) has called these distinctions of status "nobles" and "commoners." "Nobles" are clan members considered to be lineally pure in that they can claim direct descent from the clan's founding ancestor. The primary division between "nobles" and "commoners" is based on a notion of "lineal purity by which all nobles, regardless of actual clan membership, claim to have a common origin at a mythical level of ancestry" (Helander 1986:99). Several different groups fall under the category of "commoners," including those who are *sheegad* members and those considered "low-caste." Luling (1971) refers to the latter, called *saab*, as occupational castes, as they are known for performing certain tasks, like leatherwork and metalwork. On sight, saab are indistinguishable from "nobles" unless it is known that an individual is of this status. As discussed in Chapter 4, most slave descendants are identifiable as sheegad, due to their physical appearance. Exclusion from "lineal purity" conjoined slave descendants with the other lower status groups in a relation of social inferiority to Somali nobles.

While I. M. Lewis (1955:125) says the distinction between slaves (and presumably ex-slaves) and saab was clear in northern Somalia, in the south these distinctions have been much more blurred, due to a wider variety of "commoner" groups whose relation to each other was quite complex.[29] Furthermore, the villages of autonomous and independent landholding "client-cultivators" in the Shabeelle valley contributed a further dimension. The client relationship binding these villages to specific Somali clans defined them as inferior within Somali society, although less markedly than the occupational castes.

The ex-slave villages established in the Jubba River valley prior to the turn of the century initially resembled the "client-cultivator" villages of the Shabeelle. They were autonomous and independent entities having full control over their resource base. As we have seen, with time new arrivals to the valley began identifying themselves as part of Somali society by using Somali clan affiliation as a mark of social identity. In seeking to include themselves in Somali society through clan membership, Gosha villagers occupied the same general category as low-caste groups, both being defined by lack of lineal purity.

In maneuvering for status, Gosha farmers distinguished themselves (and were distinguished by other Somalis) in several ways from saab groups, however, who were considered ritually impure and thus prohibited marriage or dining partners. While rules of endogamy operated for both Gosha farmers and saab, Somali nobles would eat with Gosha farmers in their homes, yet would not share food with saab individuals. Cerulli (1959) noted that among Majeerteen Somalis, slaves freed through manumission were considered distinct from the low caste of the clan but had some of the same limitations, most notably the limitation on intermarrying with noble Somalis. The willingness of Gosha villagers to describe themselves as jareer may also be seen as an attempt to distinguish themselves from the jileec appearance of the saab groups, ensuring that they were not viewed as ritually inferior.[30] In other words, the basis of their inferiority was that of historical accident (through the misfortune of having been born non-Muslim and captured as slaves), and not destiny, as with the saab.[31]

The ideological basis of Gosha inferiority, which rested on the religious and cultural definition of the status of slave descendants, thus found structural expression in Somali social organization. The distinct physical features of (many) Gosha villagers continued to bear witness to their history of enslavement as non-Muslims. An ideology of racial/religious distinctions subjectively defined ex-slaves and their descendants as a category of people classed as inferior within the kin-based Somali nation. Ideological perceptions of inferiority that legitimated the subordination of slaves in the material context of labor and kinship gave continual meaning and force to the social positioning of their descendants in the Gosha. Notions of lineal purity, blood, and ancestry defined "the bounding of the nation as a collective subject, as a superorganism with a unique biological-cultural essence" (Alonso 1994:384) and excluded slave descendants from blood-based solidarity. Conceptions of race, which crosscut clan, created a distinct and stigmatized identity for jareer Gosha farmers in regional and national society.

Incidents of Indignity and Sites of Subordination

While distinctions of status and purity among Somali pastoralists and Bantu slaves in southern Somalia initially played out in the context of slavery, more recent expressions plumb the deep emotional terrain of human dignity and pride in the absence of physical bondage. The social fact of Somali superiority and Gosha subjugation, structurally captured in the Somali lineage system, is demonstrated over and over again in personalized and localized symbolic assaults that frequently left Gosha villagers raging but unable to vent their rage. The "rituals of subordination" (Scott 1990) so integral to dominance were locally performed in public or semipublic confrontations in the marketplace, the village, or on distant farms; in negotiations over diya payments, over land use, over food; and in countless other trivial but harshly meaningful encounters. Recalling some incidents that I witnessed (or witnessed the aftermath of) provides a sense of the content of these humiliations, revealing the continuing salience of slave ancestry—jareer status—in the 1980s.

Perhaps the most immediately compelling instances were the striking examples of verbal and physical abuse perpetrated by Somalis against Gosha dwellers which occurred regularly during my stay in the Jubba valley.[32] Gosha villagers found verbal indignities, such as the public use of the word *addoon* (slave), painfully humiliating. In one incident, a Loc village youth (one of Sabdow's grandsons) was talking with a Somali girl in the marketplace of the regional town. An older Somali woman (the wife of a government official) interrupted their conversation, loudly (and publicly) remonstrating the girl for talking in public with a "slave." As she was reprimanding the girl ("Can't you find anyone better than this slave to talk with? Why are you wasting time with this type of person?"), she began slapping the youth. He slapped her back and she ran home. The woman's husband contacted the local clan and police authorities, claiming that the youth had beaten his wife and stolen her gold. Although each claimed to be the victim of physical abuse by the other, only the Loc youth was jailed by the police and fined a rather substantial amount, which Loc villagers collectively paid. The woman was not reprimanded or fined for her action.

Loc youths suffered the indignity of arrest on false charges numerous times during my stay—for allegedly stealing from Bu'aale shopkeepers, for not participating in "self-help" projects (which were usually private projects for some government official), and for other petty acts. Although these kinds of charges were eventually dropped, the memories of spending days and nights in jail remained.

Physical abuse also frequently characterized interactions between Gosha villagers and pastoralist Somalis in the area around Loc village. During the long dry season of jilaal (mid-December through mid-March) a string of highly emotional and sometimes violent interactions between pastoralists seeking access to water and graze and farmers seeking to protect their ripening crops from grazing livestock transformed daily life into an ongoing debate about rights, compensation, punishment, and respect. Excessive heat and the high stakes of ensuring crop success and meeting livestock needs contributed to tensions and explosive arguments between pastoralists and farmers, and among farmers themselves, concerning village policy toward pastoralists. While the substance of these conflicts concerned the typical material concerns of pastoralist-farmer conflicts well known to anthropologists, the subtext was one of respect, authority, and pride.

In one telling incident, a Loc boy was working on his father's farm when he noticed some cows entering the field and approaching piles of newly harvested sesame. As he attempted to herd them out of the field by slapping their hindquarters, the nomad youths who were to have been watching the animals for their father attacked and severely beat the Loc boy. The boys were separated by the farmer and the uncle of the nomad boys, but the Loc boy had been beaten quite badly and required several days of medical attention at the regional infirmary. The father of the nomad boys was able, through unofficial gratuities, to keep the case out of the courts, and paid only a small fine to the injured boy's family to cover his medical bills. Despite villagewide public outrage, the victim had little public recourse.

In another example, some pastoralists brought their camels into a village family's compound so the camels could eat the green leaves off the family's large shade tree in the center of the compound. When the woman who resided there attempted to herd the camels out of her home, the pastoralists beat her so badly that she required three weeks of attention in the Bu'aale infirmary. Loc villagers were so outraged and terrified by the prospect of being beaten in their own homes that they referred this incident to the Bu'aale authorities (a rare decision), who sent a policeman to Loc to oversee pastoralist activities in the area. The policeman immediately began arresting Loc youths for petty "crimes" and allowed pastoralists' transgressions to go unchecked.

These two examples represent the most abusive interactions that occurred during that jilaal, although most Loc farmers lost produce to Somali herds over the course of the season.[33] Pastoralists regularly took their animals into Loc farms during the night to eat the ripening crops, but they were rarely caught or forced to pay compensation. Even those pastoralists who maintained "good relations" with Loc villagers would threaten night stealth if their official requests to move their animals through harvested village fields were denied. Loc farmers could only respond to their "damned if you do, damned if you don't" position with exhausting attempts to catch and demand compensation from the pastoralists responsible for grazing animals on unharvested fields. Local elders would mediate in those rare cases where a Loc farmer caught a culprit, but compensation was usually low or nonexistent, and negotiations were couched in the language of brotherhood. The rhetoric of forgiving the pastoralist transgression in the name of maintaining good relations was both commonly utilized in compensation negotiations and widely ridiculed by Gosha farmers in private. One farmer (who had lost a considerable amount of beans to grazing cows) expressed to me his disgust at the negotiations for his compensation, through which he was offered one hundred Somali shillings (about U.S.$1): "Nomads will say 'We're sorry'; 'We are the same people'—they'll just lie, they'll just be nice, to get the farmers to do what they want."

While these altercations might appear to be no more than typical of nomad-sedentary conflict everywhere, the rhetoric of good relations and brotherhood was critical in reminding Gosha villagers of the terms of their membership in Somali society. While Loc village, through the village council, continually acceded to pastoralist requests/demands for access to Loc fields, intervillage relations reached a near breaking point as a result of deep personal anger over pastoralist violations. Beneath the public rhetoric of good relations seethed private rage against village authorities for repeatedly giving in, for allowing pastoralists entry into village fields, for not demanding compensation for livestock grazing on ripening crops, for not standing firmer against pastoralist abuse of villagers' resources. Loc villagers leveled charges of payoffs, weak wills, and lack of leadership against the village council members and especially the village headman, whose attempt to resign his position was rejected by the state government. Yet publicly, in compensation negotiations if an erring pastoralist was apprehended, private rage remained checked and the formal mediation only addressed the material aspects of the dispute: "How much produce was stolen?" "Did the Loc boy injure the cows as he was herding them out of his field?" "Exactly how many beans were eaten by those cows grazing in farmers' fields along the village path?" "How much will medical treatment cost for the woman's injuries?" And so on. The indignity of night stealth, the indifference to farmer subsistence, and the humiliation of physical abuse were never brought into the debate in any overt way. The same Loc farmers who privately railed among themselves against pastoralist abuses publicly adopted the language of kinship and good relations during mediation negotiations. Pastoralist incursions onto Loc farms or violent encounters with Loc farmers were explained in individual terms: a pastoralist who was caught secretly attempting to allow his animals to graze a farmer's crops was excused as being a man who really desired "good relations" with the village; another pastoralist was simply bad-humored and difficult, and thus his physical assault on a Loc farmer was publicly explained as the result of his aggressive personality. The cumulative effect of these incidents of indignity—their collective symbolic statement of subordination—never publicly entered individual compensation negotiations.

Another example of the local gulf between the rhetoric of belonging and the reality of subjugation occurred in the payment of diya. In Somali society if an individual had committed a crime and was ordered to pay diya, his fellow diya-group members were expected to contribute toward the payment of this fine. Thus Gosha villagers, as members of Somali clans, contributed toward the diya payments for crimes committed by Somalis of their clan living elsewhere in the country. When the Somali government planned to execute an urban bureaucrat of the Ajuraan clan who was charged with embezzling state funds, clan leaders negotiated with Barre to repay the amount stolen in exchange for his life. Representatives of the Ajuraan clan from Mogadishu showed up in Loc to inform the villagers of Ajuraan clan membership that they had to pay a certain (rather large) amount as their portion of his fine, which they did. However, I never witnessed—or even heard of—the reverse being true. When Gosha Ajuraan were levied large fines, only Gosha villagers contributed. Ajuraan nonvillagers who were ethnically Somali were not asked to contribute. Certainly, the Gosha villagers' lack of capacity to collectively retaliate gave them little leverage in the regional sphere of diya politics.

The State

These insults, humiliations, and indignities occurred in the face of official rhetoric which denied the existence of status differences. Barre's platform of scientific socialism, introduced in 1970, stressed equality while criminalizing the public or private mention of clan identities. Officially, state rhetoric emphasized "an undifferentiated, nationalistic Somali identity, in which traditional divisions were totally annulled" (I. M. Lewis 1988:210). While explicitly rejecting kinship (expressed through the clan system) as the basis for Somali unity, however, Barre's irredentist campaigns implicitly continued to draw on descent and blood as the basis of their legitimacy. The kinship basis of state-claimed space was made clear in Somalia's paramount symbol of state sovereignty and national unity: its flag. The flag's five-pointed "Somali Star" (I. M. Lewis 1994:173 n. 17) represented the hoped-for unification of Somalis divided during the colonial era into the five colonial territories of Kenya, Italian Somalia, British Somaliland, the Ogaadeen, and French Djibouti. While using descent in order to define the limits of irredentism, the state used the language of homogeneity to force Gosha villagers into "bleeding for the nation" (Williams 1989:436) by involuntarily entering military service. During the late 1970s and early 1980s, the military regularly kidnapped Gosha villagers into the military, where they were sent to serve far from home on the Ethiopian front and against rebel clans in the north.[34] Gosha villagers made ideal soldiers because they were visually identifiable as comrades by other government soldiers and because they were more easily caught if they tried to escape into the northern countryside where they were clearly out of place. State rhetoric and practice gave a cruel reality to Brackette Williams's observation that "All bloods are not equal, but the precepts of nationalist ideologies demand that all subordinate groups bleed equally for the nation" (1989:436).

State efforts to claim national homogeneity, combined with state irredentist practices defined by descent, contributed to the marked differentiation of jareer in the nationalist milieu. Legislating homogeneity —*requiring* it—served to heighten the local and national awareness of the difference between lineally pure Somalis and lineally foreign jareer. Rhetorically homogenizing the nation while targeting visually distinct bodies to serve as soldiers in nationalist campaigns provided a state sanction of Gosha subordination in the official realm. As Ana María Alonso observes, national self-identity is affirmed through such a "construction of internal Others, whose markedness assures the existence of a national identity that . . . is successfully inscribed as the norm" (1994:390). Gerald Sider captures the coexistence of official Somali nationalist rhetoric and differentiating state military practice in his observation that "state power must not only destroy but also generate cultural differentiation—and do so . . . in the center of its grasp. . . . The historic career of ethnic peoples can thus best be understood in the context of forces that both give a people birth and simultaneously seek to take their lives" (1987:3); quite literally, in the Somali case.

Thus global racial categories elaborated during the colonial period reinforced preexisting local ethnic constructions, ensuring a national hierarchization of ethnicities and their accompanying privileges, statuses, rights, and meanings within the political community condensed into being by postcolonial state power.[35] In other words, the hierarchizing project of state-building reinscribed local identities of *jareer* and *bilis* on the national level, supported by the affirming symbolism inherent in global hierarchies of racial difference extended through the technologies of colonial categorization.[36] The Somali nation-state defined itself as a polity of "citizens," but *state* proclamations of homogenization produced heterogeneity, as the people of the Gosha became a racialized ethnic group viewed as outsiders to the *nation* of blood-based descent.[37] The Gosha itself, as the physical location of these outsiders, became an ecologically delineated racialized space of otherness.

Conclusion

The Jubba valley of the late 1980s, on the eve of a brutal civil war, had been spatialized as a place of racialized otherness for 150 years. Beginning with the entry of fugitive slaves in the 1840s, the racializing of the valley was officially delineated by the colonial authorities until the 1940s, highlighted by ethnographers until the 1980s, and taken advantage of by the Somali government throughout the 1980s. Despite the inclusive rhetoric of segmentary lineages and clan, and the homogenizing rhetoric of the Barre state, the Jubba valley remained a place of subjugated "others" within the Somali kinship network and the Somali nation-state. Rather than breaking down the barriers to unity, Barre's ban on the linguistic recognition of status or kinship served to make the jareer status officially and publicly unacknowledgeable and undiscussable. Gosha villagers were denied any political voice as minorities and indeed lacked any political representation.

By denying the existence of race, ethnicity, and status distinctions, the Somali state denied Gosha farmers' experiences of humiliation and separation as a legitimate or even existent aspect of nation and state in Somalia. Wanting to participate as clan members in the web of Somali kinship rights, obligations, and identities, and wanting to be viewed as citizens of the Somali nation-state, Gosha farmers struggled for dignity in a system that denigrated them and for equality in a state that disproportionately claimed their male bodies for nationalist campaigns. Such symbolic assaults on the dignity and humanity of Gosha peoples represented a form of violence that foreshadowed later assaults on their bodies in the midst of civil war.

The ambiguous position occupied by Gosha farmers in Somali society is reflected in thousands of sites of domination around the world. In reflecting on European domination over Native Americans, Sider writes:

> The peculiar intimacy between dominators and dominated—from above, an intimacy that comes packaged with brutality and contempt; from below, an intimacy riven with ambiguity—seems particularly important to the historically unfolding process of domination and resistance, though perhaps more directly important to understanding resistance (and also nonresistance). It is in trying to unravel the interwoven paradoxes and ambiguities of this intimacy that we can most clearly see what seems to be the fundamental *cultural* contradiction of the process of domination . . . : between domination as a form of incorporation, of bonding together, and simultaneously domination as a form of creating distance, difference, and otherness. (1987:11)

We have seen how this condition came to characterize the postcolonial Somali state, as Gosha people were absorbed as citizens while being particularized as sanguinially distinct. The sanctification of the Somali state as based in the blood of nationhood (manifest in the flag, the Ogaadeen campaigns, Barre's harangues about Somali unification) positioned jareer Gosha people as the internal other: racially, occupationally, and historically distinct citizens of the state who were nevertheless called upon to fight for the blood of the nation. In the next chapter, we examine Gosha peoples' struggles with their contradictory position: as belonging and being different; as a created "other" incorporated within a single system of social and cultural domination.

Chapter 6
Between Domination and Collusion: The Ambiguity of Gosha Life

Over the past hundred and fifty years, through enslavement, escape, conversion, and manumission, through colonial categories of racial definition, through ethnographic labeling, and through the state's encompassing technologies of power, Gosha villagers have become Somali and non-Somali at the same time, incorporated into the Somali nation-state while being created as distinct others. The dimensions of being incorporated while denigrated, and of being created while dominated, resulted in profound ambiguities for Gosha villagers in the 1980s. Gosha farmers accepted the Somali social order—clan and kinship—as legitimate and sought a place within it, yet this order defined them as inferior. Their rejection of the denigrating ideology interwoven within the hegemonic kinship-based social structure produced a tension for Gosha villagers, forcing them to mediate between the poles of inclusion and exclusion, of belonging and subjugation. The preceding chapter described instances of abuse and humiliation experienced by Gosha farmers, who frequently accepted low compensation, allowed abuse to go unpunished, or framed such instances in personalized rather than systemic terms. Such passive responses did not indicate a tacit acceptance—a "false consciousness"—of their position or a lack of awareness of their subjugation.

The burgeoning literature on resistance strategies of dominated peoples has clearly demonstrated, time and again, the myriad and complex styles of resistance to a variety of dominating forces, discourses, and mechanisms of power. Bedouin women express otherwise unacknowledgeable sentiments in private moments of poetic exchange while publicly upholding dominant values of strength and honor, rural Malaysian women seeking modernity through factory work which disciplines and subjugates them experience spells of spirit possession while on the job, Malaysian peasants maintain a "hidden transcript" of resentment toward the wealthy while outwardly remaining deferent and obedient; such well-known studies are all examples of resistance by people who appear to be putting up with—indeed, *upholding*—the system that subjugates them.[1] The power of these studies is in demonstrating the complex struggles of dominated groups seeking dignity within the confines of their social circumstances. Far from overturning the social order, these groups and others like them throughout time and space are rather working within their societies—using the language of popular values, using acceptable cultural practices—to win acknowledgment of their humanity and their agency. They use the tools available to them—official rhetoric, hegemonic forms of social organization (gender, family, kinship, class), popular symbols, as well as private discourses of gossip and fantasy—to claim social membership and to assert better terms of belonging. Such subjugated groups inhabit the enormous gray area between domination and collusion, a confused space of imagined alternatives, public acquiescence, and private rage.

Although the space between domination and collusion is awkward and uncertain, Gosha farmers, too, were struggling, fighting, in subtle and sometimes overt ways for their pride, dignity, and humanity. Subjugated peoples everywhere find ways to privately rage within this awkward space; this chapter looks behind Scott's (1990) "public transcript" to get a sense of what was happening within Gosha villages as Gosha farmers privately—and sometimes not so privately—wrestled with the tensions of domination and collusion.

Fighting Back

Throughout my first eight months in Loc, I felt that I was perpetually witnessing abuse without retribution as Gosha farmers appeared to react regularly with passivity—until one remarkable day in January during the jilaal season. That afternoon we were returning to Loc by car from another village where we had spent the day recording oral histories. Loc was in an uproar. Women and girls were dashing about the village, crying and agitated. The men around were outfitting themselves with spears, bows and arrows, knives, and machetes and running off into the bush. The daughter of one of our friends was running after her brother calling for him to stay in the village, saying, "Let the old man [their father] go and die, but don't you go as well—what if you both die? You have to leave us one!" He ignored her and followed his father into the bush. The village head, a quiet and peaceful man, was at his home although his son had left, and he and his family explained to us what was happening. Two Loc youths had been out in the bush, miles away from the village, collecting a root used to make baskets that villagers sold to itinerant traders. The boys became separated in their work, and one boy heard some nomads approach his companion, who was hidden from him by the bush. He thought he heard the nomads attacking his friend, stealing his watch and beating him severely, as the friend screamed out the names of his father and the prophet. Rather than come to the aid of his friend and risk being murdered, and thinking he was being pursued, he ran the long distance back to Loc, arriving exhausted and hysterical and saying that his friend had been attacked by nomads and was probably dead. The villagers immediately reacted. Almost every fit man and youth in the village took up his weaponry and headed off on foot for the spot described by the boy. We had arrived just as the last men were leaving.

The remainder of the afternoon and evening was spent tensely, with women nervously talking about what could be happening, how they were sure their men were being massacred, as nomads are often armed with guns. The wife of the village head paced for hours around the compound, angrily lamenting, "What if they're Marehan or Cawlyahan? They have guns! What is this *reer goleed* thinking about bows and arrows? They'll be useless against their guns!" We were also very upset, feeling helpless. The men gradually began returning at about eight in the evening. The hysterical boy's story had resulted from his avid imagination. When the nomad youths approached the other boy he had become a bit nervous and had called out to his friend. The boy had heard him calling and immediately took off running, thinking he was being attacked. The boy left behind, however, was neither robbed nor attacked—the nomads just wanted to know the time. The men, who had run many miles, were quite angry at the boy who had reacted so extremely, saying they would never believe him or come to his aid again.

What turned out, fortunately, to be a non-event had provoked a remarkable reaction. In direct contradiction to their routine public passivity in the face of injustice, on this day the village men reacted quickly and violently to the alleged attack on one of their sons. They had no intention of letting such an attack go unrequited, and seemed to be quite willing to put their lives on the line to this end. This event occurred just after the attack on the Loc boy in his field and after several other incidents involving damage to farmers' fields by pastoralists' livestock. Loc villagers were fed up and spurred into action with the news of the most heinous attack yet.

I was startled by the vehemence of the village's collective response, especially after witnessing the countless minor humiliations Gosha villagers lived with, and seemingly ignored, every day. Realizing that their violent response had not appeared out of nowhere but rather had to have been born out of some ideological community of resistance, I began to listen more closely and watch more carefully. It gradually dawned on me that the numerous trivial humiliations experienced by Loc villagers rarely passed ignored or unremarked. I realized that resistance took form in poetry, fantasy, and magic, in the historical imagination, and through asserting alternative facets of social identities. At the same time, however, these subtle dimensions of resistance contained contradictions and ambiguities, reflecting the complex location of Gosha farmers as citizens and foreigners, Somalis and non-Somalis, clan members and jareer. In what follows, I explore some of these ambiguous dimensions of resistance to denigration and racial/ethnic homogenization in order to probe Gosha peoples' viewpoints of their position within the Somali nation-state.

Fantasy Retaliation

A world of poetry and fantasy stories existed in Gosha folklore, in which Gosha villagers outwitted Somali nomads for love, for money, for dignity. These artistic forms of resistance tended to be subtle and private, retold in intimate moments around a compound campfire in the evenings or woven into poems recited occasionally by local poets for family and friends. Particularly prominent among these stories were themes dealing with the historic ability of Gosha villagers to control crocodiles and send them to do their bidding, usually to redress grievances. Stories about Gosha men longing for, but being repudiated by, Somali girls often contained an element of revenge; the Gosha man would send a crocodile to kill the girl who had rebuffed him, and sometimes her family as well, or to forcibly bring her to him. One man described to me such a scenario:

> Now, you want a girl, a *bilis* girl. When she is in the Gosha [selling milk] you tell her, "I want to marry you." [She responds] "You slave! How can you marry me! You can't have me!" When she brought milk two or three times to this village you fell in love with her, and then you tell her, "I want to marry you. Leave the hardship life of the bush. Here there is good bathing, there is soap." Then she responds, "You slave! How can you marry me?" and then you go and ask her parents. They refuse you. They say "Kirrrrrrr! [which one would say to a donkey to mean "Go!"]. You and me, we are not the same people." That's the time that you send the crocodile. And then the crocodile will grab her and bring her to you.[2]

Although Gosha villagers claimed that such magical knowledge of crocodiles had been lost—that no one alive knew how to control crocodiles—these mythical stories of magical power played upon Somali fears about the magical abilities of Gosha villagers. Throughout southern Somalia, Gosha farmers were known for their magical abilities: their knowledge of the special properties of roots and plants, of incantations, and of crocodiles.[3] When I first arrived in Somalia, people in Mogadishu told me many stories about Gosha magic; I had great difficulty hiring an

4. Young nomad women selling milk in the village. Photo by Jorge Acero.

assistant from Mogadishu who was willing to work with me in the Jubba valley for this reason. When I hired Cali, who had been living in the middle valley for ten years, local sorcerers offered to make him magical amulets to protect him during his stay in Loc village—although whether their intent was to protect him or to remind him of their powers should he step out of line remained unclear. Colonial documents reported in detail on Gosha knowledge of crocodile magic, such as this entry in the Gobweyn Record Book cited in Menkhaus (1989:144): "It is a fact that many WaGosha own crocodiles and that each individual knows its master and answers to its call." Despite the fact that the practice of magic was illegal and punishable by imprisonment (or death) under Barre, Somali fears of Gosha magic continued to be quite strong. It was not, of course, accidental that Gosha villagers chose to emphasize magical knowledge in their fantasy stories, which were well-known outside the valley.

While using stories of their magical prowess to intimidate Somalis from outside the valley, however, Gosha villagers also were very much concerned with magic that villagers might perpetrate against each other. The most serious conflict within the village during my year-long stay was a case in which a Loc man of notorious magical abilities attempted to kill a Loc married woman who had spurned his amorous advances. As the woman lay unconscious following his magical attack, village authorities forced him to reverse his spell, and then, after two days of serious deliberation, decided to involve district authorities. The district authorities referred the case to the district court. An attempted murder through magic was horrifying to villagers, who felt this man had to be removed from their village, despite his wide kinship network within the village.[4] It was, of course, equally terrifying to pastoralist nonvillagers who heard about the case (through the remarkably effective "bush telephone"), confirming their stereotypes of Gosha villagers as a bunch of evil sorcerers.

Regional fears of Gosha magic were affirmed through widespread knowledge of less scandalous cases than this one as well. During our stay, a man living in Loc believed he and his family were plagued by illnesses caused by local sorcerers, manifest in headaches, skin lesions, stomach pains, or persistent vomiting. This man was originally from the regional capital, but had made use of his connections to bureaucrats to make legal claims on parcels of land owned by other villagers in Loc under customary law. Although his stories of the magical retaliations he suffered for stealing land from villagers did not seem to be stemming the tide of land grabbers, such stories bolstered fears of Gosha sorcery. Loc villagers delighted in attributing this man's illnesses to magical punishments for his transgressions.

Gosha villagers thus viewed magic as both a defense and a source of pride; all villagers knew of the historic ability of Gosha men to control crocodiles, spoke of magic as a useful and effective—although very dangerous—form of retaliation, and related with verve and pleasure the glorious tales of Nassib Bundo's use of magic to thwart Somali nomads in the turn-of-the-century Somali-Gosha wars. This pride in a powerful heritage of magic was mediated by their own personal everyday fears of magic, however, making Gosha magic from a villager's standpoint look more like a weapon held by a knowledgeable few rather than a widespread tool of resistance available to all. In other words, villagers' stories of the *historic* uses of magic to seek dignity and redress grievances celebrated a powerful Gosha *heritage* rather than an effective community tool for contemporary villagers, who feared the potential of being harmed by fellow villagers as much as they reveled in the stories of the historic triumphs of Gosha sorcery against outsiders. The use of magic was thus an ambiguous kind of resistance—a power held by some but dangerous to all; a power which seemed to have a positive community heritage but a more uncertain contemporary role. The memory of magic as a successful form of resistance for early villagers in the Gosha paralleled the narratives of Nassib Bundo's fame. Every man and woman in the Gosha had heard the magnificent story of how Nassib Bundo conquered and massacred the Somalis who had been troubling nascent lower Gosha settlements after the turn of the century. This story had become oral tradition and was the only traditional narrative that pitted Gosha against Somali, celebrating Gosha dominance. The widespread knowledge of this story is indicative of a certain pride villagers throughout the Gosha held of their past resistance to Somali domination. But this narrative occupied an ambivalent place in the historical consciousness of upper Gosha villagers, who frequently accompanied the story of Nassib Bundo with an explanation that since Nassib did not rule the upper Gosha, upper Gosha villagers had nothing to do with this warfare against Somalis. The ambiguity remains: memories of collective resistance—through magic and under Nassib Bundo's leadership—were retold with pleasure but then quickly discounted as holding any contemporary significance for people in the upper Gosha as a community. Rather, magic becomes an individual power to be used against outsiders *and* villagers, and Nassib Bundo's exploits become a legacy of a only few villages in the lower Gosha.

Furthermore, in my search for Gosha responses to subjugation, the poetic recollections of a past in which Gosha villagers triumphed through magic over nomad adversaries directly contradicted everything else I was hearing about the history of Gosha farmer–Somali nomad relations in the valley. Indeed, sorting out the history of this relationship proved to be a journey into the complexities of historical consciousness, popular memory, and the uses of the past.[5]

Historical Consciousness

A question which interested me greatly during my stay in Somalia was the nature of local pastoralist-farmer relations in the middle valley following abolition. In discussing this time period during my village interviews about local history, village elders recounted their past autonomy from and equality with surrounding Somali nomads in terms which flew in the face of the daily injustices they lived with in the present. Time and again in their stories to me, Gosha elders portrayed earlier decades of life in the middle Jubba valley as marked by independence, freedom of choice, and relative autonomy from surrounding Somali pastoralists.[6] They argued that their ancestors not only chose to affiliate with Somali clans of their own free will after reaching the valley, but that their ancestors were free to choose with which clan to affiliate. If Gosha villagers as a group had identified themselves as part of a Somali clan prominent in the Baay Region, for example, local elders claimed they had the absolute freedom to do so. Conversely, some villagers had chosen to affiliate with Somali clans powerful in the Jubba valley. Again, such decisions were described by my elderly Gosha interlocutors as having been a matter of choice, not a result of coercion or force by powerful Somali clans. The Gosha villagers' version of their history was a history of life relatively unaffected by the actions of Somali pastoralists, where Gosha farmers had full and complete control over their territory, their farms, their production, and their persons.

Although I repeatedly heard this version of history in numerous middle valley villages, I grew increasingly skeptical about the likelihood of such historical autonomy, free choice, and equality given the persistence of subjugation and domination I continually witnessed in the present. Knowing that Gosha villagers were frequently treated with contempt, that Somali pastoralists allowed their livestock to graze villagers' ripening crops without permission, and that despite their claims to clan membership upper Gosha villagers usually paid diya compensation as a village rather than as clan members, I wondered about the extent of such practices in the past. My initial foray into the British colonial archives in Kenya during my fieldwork turned up numerous reports of Somali raids on Gosha villages, abductions, and massacres.[7] Curious about the historical vision of this time period held by local pastoralists, I began interviewing local pastoralist elders from three different clans whom I had come to know in order to get their version. Their version dramatically contradicted the villagers' version, painting a picture of pastoralist control and oppression. In one remarkable conversation with the regional head of the pastoralist Cawlyahan clan (who were historically notorious as aggressors and warriors), he denied any Gosha historical agency:

> After the Elyan wars,[8] Cawlyahan occupied from Baardheere to Mareerey [encompassing the entire mid-valley area]. Everyone living there came under Cawlyahan. We took Gosha for whatever we wanted—to work our fields . . . when we were moving with the cattle we picked young people to help with the moving. We would take young people and they would live with us, as our slaves. In the hot season we came close to the river, into the Gosha. The Gosha worked their fields and Cawlyahan's fields. Families had links to particular families, so when your family heard you are near, they came running with baskets of corn and food to help you and serve you. At that time they were all *sheegad* to Cawlyahan. . . . Everyone was Cawlyahan, came under Cawlyahan, had to work for Cawlyahan, and pay tithes to Cawlyahan.

While this image of Cawlyahan preeminence undoubtedly reflects the clan membership of the speaker, elders from other pastoralist clans agreed that pastoralists oppressed Gosha people in earlier decades. A Bartire herdsman explained, for example: "Gosha were just poor people and Cawlyahan used to swallow people. . . . They used to rob the Gosha. They were hard to them. . . . People in the Gosha used to be oppressed." This image of early upper Gosha villages being subject to forced affiliation, oppression, and raiding by dominant Somali clans was hotly contested by Gosha villagers themselves. The consistent vision of their history presented publicly by groups of Gosha elders and in village council meetings was that of independent Gosha villages rarely, if ever, affected by surrounding Somali pastoralists. Whereas pastoralist elders stressed their former ability to dominate Gosha villages at will, to make demands, and even to control Gosha labor, Gosha elders claimed there had been virtually no contact between farmers and pastoralists during the earlier decades of upper Gosha settlement.

Pursuing these conflicting versions of history with various groups of elders in the upper Gosha consistently turned up the same story. In public discussions of valley history, village spokesmen downplayed Somali pastoralist involvement in the affairs of Gosha villages. In my struggle to make sense of what I was hearing, to sort out "what really happened," what was self-interest, and what was good-natured fabrication, I grew increasingly uncertain about the project of doing meaningful historical anthropology that relied almost completely on oral histories collected from an ex-slave population with a denigrated history. I had begun to feel that what I believed was probably true—a localized history of subjugation—was so effectively denied by contemporary Gosha villagers that maybe they had erased their past—what I thought of as their subaltern history—in the face of official state rhetoric and hegemony. But I was also uncomfortable imagining that I had a clearer sense of their history than they did, having witnessed such claims to "objective authority" suffer a recent death in anthropology.

Then one day in a private conversation, a Gosha elder and widely respected local historian with whom I had an ongoing working relationship offered an alternative view of local farmer-nomad historical relations. I arrived in his village for our scheduled discussion to find him enraged because in the previous days pastoralists had come into his fields and grazed their animals on his crops, finishing them off, while he was away visiting another village. In anger he, who had been quite adamant that Gosha farmers had had a great deal of autonomy and independence, discussed the history of injustices committed against Gosha farmers by surrounding pastoralists:

> *Reer goleed* [people who live in the Gosha as farmers] farmed farms and land. The pastoralists just used to come down for water to the river, especially in the hot season, but they didn't farm here. It was *reer goleed* who started to farm the land, and *reer baydiya* [people of the bush, pastoralists] only came to take it when the crop was ready. Like now, when they don't have enough and the government is not close by, then they take the crop by force. . . . When the crop is mature or when it's on the stalk, even until they were burying it [in underground storage pits] *reer baydiya* used to take it by force. On the other hand, they would even come into the storage pits and take a portion. . . . If you imagine the way of thinking of *reer baydiya*, in just the two days I have been in [another village], my field which you see here in which I had grass bushes, beans, potatoes, squash . . . just like the way they used to force the people before, they let the cows go in and finish the stalks and everything! I just came from planting in the *dhasheeg*, I just washed my feet now, so these two days we had these problems. Even now they are a bit afraid of the soldiers and the government or they would have robbed everything like before.

Even his description that day of the nature of the *ku tirsan* (leaning on) relationship was a radical departure from his previous characterizations of it as complementary, supportive, and protective. In this discussion, he framed the relationship as one of exploitation, abuse, and extraction: "Everyone [in the Gosha villages] was robbed by the person he was leaning on. A person who leaned on one clan could not be robbed by another clan, because the latter would be afraid of the clan you are leaning on. A Cawlyahan can't rob a Bartire. He would be afraid of Bartire. They only robbed their own."

Listening to him that day, it seemed as though the public mask had slipped (to borrow from Scott [1990]); that the immediate experience of material loss (of crops to the stealthy livestock and their owner) and

5. A pastoralist family migrating in the hinterland of Loc. Photo by Jorge Acero.

humiliating injustice (he was a village headman and a local celebrity of sorts) had become irreconcilable in that moment with a history of equality, autonomy, and peaceful coexistence. The events of the preceding days reverberated back through history, reconfiguring its representation in the present. As the days of jilaal wore on, and pastoralists allowed more frequent incursions into village fields, villagers began to occasionally share similar sentiments and reminiscences in private conversations or metaphorically in poems and proverbs, but never in "formal" public discussions of history. Individuals would make passing remarks about historic pastoralist dominance or injustices or would privately relay stories about such matters, but these were never reflected in public discussions of history.

The contradictory versions of history went even further. Another point of contention in the histories told by pastoralist and Gosha elders was that of the choices available for clan affiliation and the changes brought about by independence and the revolution. After Somalia received independence in 1960, clientship and institutionalized forms of authority were officially banned. After the 1969 revolution, Siyad Barre introduced what we might call the "laws of nationhood." One man echoed the sentiments of many Gosha villagers when he proclaimed to me that with these laws "our being foreigners ended. . . . We all became one. All before that we were foreigners. Now there is no distinction between *reer baydiya* and *reer goleed.* Somali is one. This is soft hair [*tiin jileec,* "lineally pure" Somali], this is slave [*addoon*] ended."

Local pastoralists suggested a much narrower conception of the change in status that the Gosha villagers received with these laws. Pastoralist elders argued that the laws gave Gosha farmers the freedom to choose with whom they wanted to affiliate, a decision which had been forced upon them prior to the revolution. The Cawlyahan elder quoted above emphasized the restriction on their ability to dominate Gosha villagers as a result of the laws: "At that time [before the 1969 revolution] the Gosha were all *sheegad* to Cawlyahan. After the revolution, they all affiliated with their original [Somali] clans like Ajuraan. If they had said they were another tribe before the revolution, they would have been punished [by Cawlyahan]. The Gosha were not free until the revolution, because then the government said everyone is Somali, no more slaves."

Several pastoralist elders emphasized the official protection from overt forms of dominance the laws granted Gosha villagers, but without noting that any greater degree of acceptance of Gosha people by Somali society occurred with the laws. In a particularly striking way, one pastoralist elder extended the image of the *ku tirsan* relationship to say that Gosha people are now "leaning on" the Somali government.[9] His implication, of course, is that Gosha people had "affiliated" with the Somali state, which now protected their interests against pastoralist claims.

The conceptions of local history emerging through these interviews were thus quite different. For the settlement period of the upper Gosha (the teens through the early 1950s), Gosha farmers told a story of autonomy and independence whereas Somali pastoralists remembered subjugation and oppression. For the period following independence and the revolution, when the laws of nationhood were introduced, Gosha claimed these laws effectively confirmed their equal status, whereas Somali pastoralists saw only how the laws undermined their own local authority.

What are we to make of such different versions of history? Are we hearing resistance or observing hegemony? Are Gosha villagers denying their own past in conformity with the official present or are they using the official present to reclaim a history of dignity rather than humiliation? And where do we (and do we even have to) locate truth?

In the postabolition context of what was happening in the valley after the turn of the century, perhaps these apparently contradictory versions all captured an aspect of historical reality. These different portrayals of the history of relations between Gosha farmers and local Somali pastoralists were not necessarily mutually exclusive, although the interpretations of different events were contested. There was agreement, or at least acknowledgment, that Somalis did raid Gosha villages, although all agreed that the Gosha farmers were in full control of the land they farmed, being in no way tenants or squatters on land owned by pastoralists. The Gosha version, which was not part of publicly acknowledged history, but which occasionally emerged in informal ways, painted a picture of Somalis opportunistically taking advantage of Gosha villages as easily targeted settled communities. Conversely, Somali elders portrayed their domination and raiding of Gosha villages as having been their right and having been much more extreme than Gosha farmers generally claimed. These different portrayals may be a factor of the different significance "raiding" held for farmers and pastoralists. For Somali pastoralists, who argued that Gosha farmers were required to give allegiance to particular dominant local pastoralist clans, such raids might have been considered a forceful way to exact owed tribute. For Gosha farmers, such raids may have been seen as only occasional events during a time characterized largely by peace. While frequency of raiding may be inaccurately represented in everyone's accounts, colonial documentation and Gosha farmers' private acknowledgments of pastoralist raiding suggest that local Somali pastoralist groups were able to exert domination, however infrequently, over Gosha villagers.

Furthermore, there was agreement that independence and the revolution brought changes to the Somali herder–Gosha farmer relationship, but the form these changes took was contested. Gosha farmers claimed the laws of nationhood gave them a sense of belonging in Somali society, reinforcing their desired status as equal Somalis. Local Somali pastoralist elders ignored any change in status these laws were to have brought Gosha people, emphasizing instead that the laws lessened the ability of the pastoralists to overtly dominate Gosha villages.

The pastoralist version of the historical relationship thus emphasized a patron/client aspect, where Gosha farmers were subjects or pawns with no choice in the construction of their social identity. Conversely, Gosha farmers emphasized their historical autonomy from surrounding groups of pastoralists in their forging of a social identity within Somali society. Particularly important to the Gosha villagers was their formal legal recognition as equal members of Somali society, which they translated as true membership status in Somali clans.

Viewing both conceptions of history as legitimate—as having historical truth—means focusing on the question of how people were sifting through their history to make choices about what to emphasize and what to ignore. Most significant are the different meanings contained in contemporary interpretations of past relations given by Gosha farmers and local Somali pastoralists, as each group attempted to mold its vision of history to serve modern ends. Gosha villagers, in their struggle for an accepted, equal Somali identity, minimized past conflicts based on inequality and emphasized legal recognition of their equal status. Anger and resentment about raids, which clearly did happen, emerged in private conversation, but public history did not include a recognition of postabolition subjugation. Pastoral Somalis had nothing to gain by recognizing or accepting a change in status of Gosha peoples. They refused to acknowledge a rise in status—or were unable at that time to step out of their ideological conceptions of people in the Gosha as ex-slaves.

This story of collective memory and historical interpretation is interesting because it underscores the refusal of Gosha villagers to construct themselves as a subjugated group. The desire by Gosha elders to deemphasize a history of oppression is particularly intriguing as it runs counter to the tendency of denigrated groups to rally around a history of oppression. Subjugated groups around the world use their history as a source of cohesion, of group identity, and of solidarity. In contrast, Gosha people used their history to reclaim agency—their rightful membership standing in clans of their choosing, their freedom from subjugation within those clans, their economic independence as farmers and producers, their standing as free and equal citizens. Contradicting the unofficial but predominant history of Gosha subjugation held by local Somali nomadic clan members, the Gosha elders' construction of a "subaltern" history relied on the themes of equality, dignity, self-reliance, and pride which were so integral to Siyad Barre's rhetoric of scientific socialism. Although Gosha villagers viewed most aspects of state intervention in local life negatively, in this one area they co-opted official rhetoric for their own purposes—extending Barre's official proclamations about the future to reconfigure their past. Popular memory thus became a source of pride and dignity rather than a remembered series of humiliating events. That such events occurred was acknowledged in private reminiscences which continued to be evoked in times of anger and tension as alternate knowledges. But such knowledges remained private and privately expressed. A history of subjugation was not something Gosha farmers celebrated, but rather was something denied, rejected as not meaningful, kept hidden. In their desire to be Somali citizens, Gosha people sought meaning in remembering a history of dignity and autonomy, not one of humiliation.[10]

As I sat listening to these conflicting and competing versions of local history, I thought back to the words of another researcher, Virginia Luling, who had worked two decades earlier with jareer people along the Shabeelle valley. While calling for more research to be done on these peoples in Somalia by arguing that, as with any group, they have a history worthy of being told, she nevertheless wondered about the effect of such research: "Would it only serve to stir up the embers of old prejudices, and confirm the low status they are striving to throw off? Or might it, by asserting that they have a past of their own worthy of attention, help them to claim a place of respect in a changing Somali society?" (1983:52–53).

The implications of this question, of course, speak to the project of historical anthropology in general: the right to publish, claim authorship, freeze time, establish "truth," define "meaning," as Richard Price (1983) has so eloquently discussed.[11] I suspect that the Gosha elders who so carefully explained to me their history a decade ago have now refashioned that history following the years of brutal warfare which tore apart their communities and took the lives of their neighbors. While I do not know the contemporary form of Gosha "mythicohistories" (Malkki 1995), the militant voices of those few jareer who have left the Horn and of other subjugated groups in Somali refugee camps in Kenya suggest that a radical reconstruction of local, regional, and national Somali histories is underway.[12] I will return to this point in the Epilogue.

Alternative Identities

Another aspect of ambiguity and resistance (and ambiguity in resistance) in local life was the nature of local identities. Colonial discourse, ethnographic descriptions, and the Somali popular imagination treated Gosha inhabitants as a "tribe," an undifferentiated population defined as a group on the basis of a shared heritage of slavery. State kidnapping practices that targeted Gosha bodies for military service supported the popular conception of Gosha inhabitants as a separate and homogenous "group." Gosha villagers met the homogenizing gaze of colonial authorities, the modern Somali state, and Somalist ethnographers with a variety of locally meaningful identities which contradicted their representation as "the WaGosha." The gulf between a "tribal" representation and Gosha villagers' conceptions of local identities reveals the divergence of structure and practice, certainty and ambiguity.

Far from imagining themselves as some kind of a "tribe," the people who lived in the Gosha recognized differences and similarities among themselves according to a variety of criteria, which included clan affiliation, residence, affection, and ancestry. Gosha villagers were not interested in recognizing ethnic boundaries of the sort identified by Frederik Barth (1969), but rather strove to challenge the legitimacy of boundaries based on constructions of race, which they perceived as discriminatory rather than desirable. In other words, while recognizing their "racial" distinctiveness within regional and national life, Gosha inhabitants looked to other facets of identity as more meaningful markers for social interaction in local, regional, and national arenas, using most of these markers to undermine notions of "race" or "ethnicity."

As discussed in previous chapters, within and between Gosha villages a vitally important aspect of identity was Somali clan affiliation. Clan membership provided an important basis (in theory) for residential patterns, for diya payment, for marriage transactions, and for personal identity. By their second year, toddlers were already being drilled in patrilineal "family history," learning to recite their clan lines back to the founding Somali ancestor of their (adopted) clan-family. In my strolls through the village fields, I occasionally heard children, who were often charged with guarding their families' farms against birds, pass the time by reciting their patrilineal clan names. One day a little girl, no more than four or five years old, ran crying through my compound to find her father because her father's friends were teasing her by saying she wasn't a Bartire but rather an Ajuraan (which was her mother's clan affiliation). Her father assured her that she was Bartire, and that his friends were just jesting with her in good fun.

By asserting their membership in Somali clans rather than their unity as a racially identifiable group, Gosha villagers resisted racial stereotyping and its accompanying ideological denigration. By claiming membership rights in Somali clans, Gosha people challenged the validity of race as the master symbol of group identity, demonstrating instead their right to transcend boundaries of race through their clan memberships.

At the same time, however, other aspects of identity muted or superseded the importance of clan affiliations (as well as a racialized identity) in villagers' minds. In the practice of everyday living, clan affiliations shrank in importance, and other aspects of identity became much more significant. As we have seen, membership in a village community offered a critical set of political, economic, and affective ties. Jubba villagers emphasized territorial ties as a basis of communal solidarity and identity, regardless of the distinct clan affiliations claimed by village members. Villages, rather than lineages or clans, held and allocated land, and the village often functioned as a single entity in the payment of diya. Because of its heterogeneity, Loc provides a good example of how village unity transcended clan divisions even within the practice of clan-based mediation. With outsiders, the village stood as a single unit. If a villager was involved in a dispute with an outsider, the village as a group stood as his support and contributed to pay his fine. In the case of the young man who had struck the prominent woman from Bu'aale who had called him a slave in the marketplace, the entire village, regardless of clan affiliation, contributed toward the payment of his fine. When an Ajuraan leader came to Loc to inform Ajuraan villagers of their share of the fine levied by Barre against the Ajuraan civil servant for embezzlement, all villagers, Ajuraan or not, contributed toward the payment. Villagers regularly contributed toward a diya payment owed by a clan represented in their village other than their own. Villagers explained to me that clan memberships did not make a difference when fines were levied by clan authorities; if a member of the village *community* was fined, the *community* paid.

Increasingly, village compositions cut across ethnic and clan lines. The government policy outlawing territorial control by clans effectively supported the practice that anyone could live and get land anywhere, regardless of clan affiliation. In southern Somalia, high mobility and the importance of village integrity functioned to reduce the essence of clan as the single most important aspect of identity. Throughout southern Somalia, in fact, mobility and acquisition of land encouraged flexibility in clan membership. Helander (1996) describes the myriad ways in which interriverine agropastoral Somalis shifted kinship affiliations on the basis of territorial interest. In a telling example, Helander was several months into his research before he discovered that the village in which he lived, called the "Capital of Hubeer" (a Rahanweyn clan) actually counted only four men of Hubeer ancestry among its inhabitants; the rest were Hubeer by affiliation (for purposes of acquiring property rights), not birth. Even some of the newest arrivals to Loc in the 1980s had taken on new clan memberships in order to maximize their (new) kinship networks within the village.

Furthermore, other kinds of ties frequently superseded clan affiliations in daily life. Friendships, love affairs, and, increasingly, marriages cut across clan lines to unite people on the basis of sentiment and affection rather than patrilineality. While neighborhoods in Loc did reflect clan divisions, some of the closest friendships in the village were between people of different neighborhoods and different clan affiliations, as were some of the most enduring marriages. As just one example, Sheikh Cabdi Nur's family—who will be discussed again in Chapter 8—encompasses many cross-clan and cross-ethnic ancestry marriages. Almost thirty years ago Sheikh Cabdi Nur, a prominent local healer of Ajuraan reer Shabeelle ancestry, married Xalima, a Laysan woman whose father was one of the earliest immigrants to Loc from the Baay Region. Their eldest daughter, Robiye, married one of the Boran-descended Ajuraan reer Sabdow immigrants, Xeffow. Following the preference for cousin marriage, Xalima arranged for her youngest daughter to marry the son of her Laysan brother, which in this case produced another generation of cross-clan marriage. Sheikh Cabdi Nur and Xalima had arranged for their son to marry the daughter of another local reer Shabeelle family, but before the marriage took place the son eloped with a girl unknown to the family from Baardheere. Thus within this one family marriages occurred across at least two clan affiliations and three ethnic backgrounds. Furthermore, an example of the help Robiye received when she had difficulty conceiving demonstrates the nature of the collective village support system. After Robiye and Xeffow had been married several years without children, the three oldest women in the village—including Khadija, the daughter of Loc's founder, Isaaq (of Laysan/Tolomoge clan affiliation); the daughter-in-law, Xalima, of Bunbunle's earliest settler, Sabdow (of Boran ancestry and Ajuraan clan affiliation); and one of the original immigrants to Cabdow Yusuf (of reer Shabeelle descent and Ajuraan clan affiliation)—held a special ceremony to pray together for Robiye to conceive.

In addition to ties of clan, ties of locality, and ties of affection, other markers distinguished people within the Gosha from each other as well, serving to undermine a sense of Gosha-wide solidarity or ethnic homogeneity. Linguistic divisions separated people in Loc (as well as elsewhere within the valley). Some villagers spoke Maay-maay, the dialect of the Baay Region, while others spoke Maxad-tiray, or "standard" Somali. While dialect differences did not impede village dialogue, I became aware of the connection between dialect and identity whenever I addressed a Maxad-tiray speaker in the Maay-maay dialect, or vice versa. The first time this happened, I used a standard Maay-maay greeting to say hello to a woman I did not know well, who responded that I had addressed her using the language of "*those* people who live on *that* side of the village." The differences in dialect reflected the different histories of villagers: people of Boran heritage tended to speak "standard" Somali, while people whose ancestors had lived as agropastoralists and slaves in the Baay Region spoke Maay-maay. I have already mentioned the secret language shared by a few men of reer Shabeelle origin (including Sheikh Cabdi Nur), who used this language as a mark of their friendship and in remembrance of their boyhood days.

Finally, ancestral, preslavery heritages continued to play a small part in village interaction. While these histories of ancestry were not celebrated, they were acknowledged and recognized as private knowledges. People knew whose ancestors were Boran or reer Shabeelle or from elsewhere in East Africa, and they recognized that this knowledge had once been important—that it had played a role in structuring residential and marriage patterns until recently. While not uniformly celebrated as a central component of personal identity, the fact of diverse ancestral non-Somali heritages belied the idea of a "WaGosha tribe" in the eyes of Gosha villagers.

In fact, whereas Gosha villagers would refer to themselves as jareer ("we here in the Gosha are jareer"), I never heard villagers refer to themselves as "Gosha." People in the Gosha would say, "We here in the Gosha believe . . ." not "We Gosha believe . . ." Their acknowledgment of racial difference did not extend to a self-perception of ethnic coherence. Gosha people, while recognizing their racial distinctiveness, did not view themselves as a tribe, a clan, or even a valleywide "community." Rather, Gosha villagers resisted colonial, ethnographic, and popular attempts at ethnogenesis, choosing instead to privilege other aspects of identity adopted from outside the valley, such as clan affiliation and dialect, and developed in microlevel interactions within the valley, such as village ties, friendships, and ancestral heritages.

In contrast to the geographic term *Gosha* (or "WaGosha") as an ethnic label commonly used by ethnographers, colonialists, and Somalis from outside the valley, when referring to Gosha inhabitants in the collective the people living in the Gosha typically used *reer goleed* or "people of the forest." In their minds, *reer goleed* contrasted more sharply with *reer baydiya* (people of the bush; pastoralists) in emphasizing what villagers saw as a highly significant distinction between occupations (people who farm versus people who have livestock). Whereas *Gosha* tied people to a specific historically constituted and symbolically laden space, *reer goleed* was a more general, and thus a more ambiguous and flexible, signifier.

The State

The role of the state in local life may have encompassed the most extreme experience of ambivalence for Gosha villagers.[13] The state stood as both protector and predator; navigating between the poles was a constant aspect of daily living. In their interactions with the government, many Gosha villagers shared the very pragmatic Somali view that one never knows where help may come from, yet anyone could be your enemy as well. Throughout their dealings with state officials, Gosha villagers maintained a healthy skepticism marked by occasional opportunism. While the experiences of state kidnapping, extortion, police bias, and unfair laws were very much a part of Gosha villagers' conceptualization of the state, they also knew that they could sometimes receive state distributions of food during floods or droughts, that they could sometimes use government agricultural machinery (which government publicity claimed was for local villagers but which usually was commandeered by state officials), and that they could utilize the state rhetoric of equality as a matter of personal pride and community defense.

For the most part, Gosha villagers avoided interaction with the state, viewing most state intervention in their daily lives as detrimental. Villagers paid their land taxes, occasionally received some state food assistance following floods or droughts, and always listened politely when a state representative showed up in their village, but they had very little faith that state institutions regularly could—or would—assist them. Although Siyad Barre's state laws were designed to introduce state control over matters typically handled by village councils, elders, and families, matters such as land distribution, dispute mediation, inheritance practices, marriages, divorces, and female infibulation, villagers avoided complying with these laws whenever possible. Only after extended deliberation would the village council decide to refer an internal matter to state officials for resolution. Their reluctance to involve the state was born not only out of insularity, suspicion, and a sense of village responsibility for villagers' affairs; more importantly, it resulted from the knowledge that the state officials who mediated disputes often kept compensation payments for themselves rather than awarding them to the victim. Yet at the same time the state was useful as a mediator when villagers did not want to take responsibility for making a difficult decision. When Sheikh Cabdulle tried to murder the woman who did not reciprocate his love through magic, villagers were frightened to speak out against him because, as was the custom, as an elder he attended all the village deliberations. Furthermore, the defendant was a close relative of the mayor of Bu'aale (both were Ajuraan reer Shabeelle), a locally powerful state representative who very much wanted a resolution in favor of Sheikh Cabdulle. Caught between wanting to banish the man yet fearing magical repercussions *and* government repercussions (from the mayor), the village council agreed to fine the perpetrator if the mayor would quietly arrange a permanent change of locale for the man. The mayor's superior, the district commissioner (who had been notified of the case by the village council!), refused to accept this compromise and insisted that Sheikh Cabdulle be imprisoned pending a state trial—a decision that came as a great relief to many villagers. They had been able to demonstrate leniency toward the offender, please the powerful mayor, *and* get what they wanted in the end (although in the short term only, because Sheikh Cabdulle did eventually return to the community).

Loc villagers found themselves dancing carefully around the mayor of the regional capital on several occasions. They could not alienate him because they never knew when his kinship, clan, or political links might be useful, yet they could not always bow to his sometimes tyrannical demands. On one occasion, he threatened to block the use of state machinery in Loc if villagers did not provide him with a jerry can filled with honey. Loc farmers were desperate—they needed the state Caterpillar to come build a retaining wall against the rising river which was threatening to flood into their fields of maturing crops, but honey season had not yet come to Loc and no one had access to honey for the mayor. So villagers tried secretly to go around the mayor. They heard the Caterpillar working in the next village south (which had been able to provide the mayor with honey), so they sent a delegation to negotiate with the driver. He asked for money, diesel, and motor oil (the latter two obtained from me) in exchange for doing the work. Unfortunately, the villagers lost their gamble because the driver decided the water was too high to accomplish the work and went back to Bu'aale keeping the payment, diesel, and oil.

One final story helps capture the delicate balance Loc villagers maintained between submitting to government demands and trying to protect themselves and their interests. One night, two pastoralist brothers drowned in the center of Loc. They had come into the central grassy area of Loc to water their cattle, but one cow had become stuck in the muddy river bottom. Three of the four brothers watching the cattle waded into the river to free the cow, but only one emerged. The frantic cries of the two surviving brothers brought villagers out of their beds at about three in the morning to see what was going on and eventually to help. Two villagers used the village canoe to save the cow and to search for the bodies of the two drowned brothers, while several villagers went to inform the Bu'aale authorities. Other villagers tied up the two surviving brothers, who were slashing their bodies with their daggers in grief, and put them in the jail hut for their safety.

The Bu'aale authorities told the Loc delegation that the village was responsible for taking care of the situation, for finding the bodies and arranging the funeral, preparing the feast, and hosting and caring for the grieving relatives. While the nomads were not known to the villagers—they had no relatives in common but had just come into the village to access the river—the villagers were obligated to spend the next several days working on the funeral and attending to the bereaved families. Loc women dropped their own domestic tasks and labored for hours preparing the funeral feast, while the pastoralist men ordered them around, hollered insults at them for their slowness, and demanded drinks and snacks. As hosts, the Loc villagers did not share in the feast, but served the many pastoralist guests arriving for the funeral, prepared the bodies, and dug the graves. While complying with the government edict that they put themselves at the service of the nomads (and certainly feeling compassion for the family's tragic loss), the Loc villagers managed to hold their own in the face of uniformly rude treatment. In one scene that unfolded in the village head's compound, the Loc women were resting in the shade enjoying a cup of tea after working their second eight-hour day of feast preparation in the jilaal heat. Some pastoralist male guests came into the compound and began screaming at them to put down their tea and get back to work, demanding to know how they could dare to drink tea when instead they should be offering it to the pastoralist men, insisting that they hand over their cups to the men immediately, and berating the Loc women in vehement terms for being slow and lazy. I tensed as I waited for the women's reaction: they uniformly burst into gales of laughter and sat sipping their tea while blatantly ignoring the men. The angrier the men got, the harder the women laughed. They did eventually hand over their cups and serve tea, but in their own time. Furthermore, the village headman managed to claim for himself the sack of sugar provided for the feast by the government, which he later sold at a nice profit.

These short vignettes demonstrate the sorts of binds Gosha villagers frequently experienced as they tried to comply with government requirements while continuing to do things their own way, as they worked to stay in the good graces of government officials without sacrificing their principles or livelihoods, and as they tried to avoid penalties while extracting benefits whenever possible. They viewed the government presence in their lives much as many villagers in Loc undoubtedly viewed me: as an uninvited, undesired, and unavoidable intrusion which nevertheless brought some potentially positive benefits—an official mediator for a difficult village argument, the occasional ability to use government-owned equipment, the possibility of food aid, an unexpected sack of sugar (or, in my case, the occasional ride, medicine, contribution to a family ritual, support in a land dispute with an outsider, or source of entertainment). While government intervention in village affairs was generally negative (characterized by land stealing, kidnapping, extortion, and the like), Gosha villagers recognized that *sometimes* state and local agendas converged, and that maintaining ties with local state representatives and nominally following government laws—which was in any case unavoidable—might, now and again, bring unexpected rewards. Maintaining ambivalence toward the government was a form of keeping one's options open: today the mayor may be demanding the impossible as your superior, but tomorrow he may save your life as your clansman.

The relationship between Gosha farmers and the state was also made ambivalent by the popular Somali perception of Gosha people's dependence on the government. Excluded from blood-based membership in the Somali nation, the status of Gosha farmers as citizens of the Somali state depended on state recognition of this status and thus Gosha farmers were often seen as allied to the state (rather than to some component of the Somali nation). Southern pastoralists complained about "state protection" of Gosha villagers (recall how one local pastoralist characterized the *ku tirsan* relationship between Gosha farmers and the government); northerners associated jareer with the state because the only jareer in northern Somalia were government soldiers, seen as representing the interests of the state against the northern population. In the Jubba valley regional sphere of social interaction, pastoralists highlighted this ambiguous position in their situational approach to Gosha farmers. Pastoralists sometimes familiarly positioned Gosha farmers as "fellow clan members" (such as during compensation negotiations for pastoralist violations, when seeking permission to graze their livestock on farmers' fields, or when trying to access government food relief distributed to Gosha villages), and sometimes bitterly positioned Gosha farmers as "*ku tirsan* to the state" (such as when they were unable to exact desired goods or services from Gosha farmers). In other words, *everyone* struggled with, opportunistically used, and tried to manipulate the ambiguous location of Gosha farmers relative to the state.

Ambivalent Locations and Ambiguous Resistance

We have seen how ethnographic discourse, historically contingent understandings of race, and state technologies of power over bodies and categories of identity combined to create the Gosha as a racialized space inhabited by a distinct population. This chapter argued that the "distinct population"—the "WaGosha"—was struggling to define a very different conception of their identity and their place in the national milieu. People who lived in the Gosha resisted the derogatory and distinguishing labels foisted upon them by emphasizing clan membership over racial identity, by recognizing their diversity rather than an encompassing "Gosha" homogeneity, by viewing their history in the valley as one of rugged independence, autonomy, and equality rather than one of subjugation, and by drawing on sources of "secret" power to effect or imagine revenge. At the same time, however, we have seen how people in the Gosha maintained a public face of accommodation to the society and state which denigrated them—by submitting to pastoralist demands and not requiring adequate compensation for crops lost to livestock or for physical or verbal abuse, by using the official rhetoric of the state which inhumanely claimed their bodies for warfare, by claiming a history of freedom rather than confronting historical oppression. We have seen the ambivalences contained within Gosha people's resistances of magic as available to few but frightening to all; of history claimed as a source of public pride but also containing privately remembered humiliating events; of the ambiguity of identity as a blending of race, ancestry, clan, village, and citizen; of wanting little to do with the state—the Loc headman even rejected the possibility of a state school in the village—yet aggressively utilizing state rhetoric of equality in envisioning local history.

The practice of resistances thus was not uniform or communal, but was rather personal, ambivalent, and ambiguous. In other words, while people in the Gosha resisted racially based and historically defined subjugation, they did so individually by denying any essentialized group identity on the basis of race, history, or oppression. Memories of historical abuse remained private recollections unacknowledged in public forums, personal choices of clan affiliations took preeminence over forging a homogenized "racial" unity, and magical prowess existed as an individual art used for personal vengeance.

Given their rejection of a group history of ethnogenesis forged out of oppression, what exactly were Gosha villagers resisting in their versions of history, in their magic and fantasy, in their recognition of multiple facets of identity while adhering to the Somali clan system? What do these individualized responses to subjugation mean? Examining these examples of resistance provides more than a satisfaction at hearing the muted speak up—what Lila Abu-Lughod calls the romanticization of resistance; it also serves as a "diagnostic of power" (1990:42). Abu-Lughod suggests that forms of resistance can "tell us more about forms of power and how people are caught up in them" (1990:42). Let us pursue this idea.

In recounting their history, Gosha elders' reminiscences mirrored their contemporary responses to pastoralist invasions when describing pastoralist exploits as opportunistic and personalized. Gosha elders did not publicly construct pastoralist behavior—historically or in the present—as symptomatic of *group* subjugation, confirming their refusal to essentialize themselves as a subjugated group who were collectively dominated. Their historical narratives emphasized dignity and equality, just as their contemporary mediations with pastoralists were framed in the equalizing language of brotherhood and good relations. Similarly, Gosha people overcame humiliation in their poetics and fantasies of retaliation. In these tales, they were not imagining a revolution or a magical role reversal; rather, they were fantasizing about having the magical ability to *demand* equality and status.

In their identity politics, while individually resisting their denigrated status within Somali society, Gosha people were also resisting being excluded into a "community" of homogenized—albeit Somalized—foreigners. They sought to claim their rights to equal status as individuals, not as a "minority group," and viewed abuses as individualized assaults on personal dignity. Their dynamic recognition of multiple facets of identity—their view of themselves as a group of people of diverse origins and experiences who happened to live together as farmers in the river valley—undermined their representation as a "tribe" or an "ethnic group." They saw themselves as split by differences—of heritage, of clan affiliation, of village residence, of affection—which minimized their self-perceptions of group unity. They refused to find unity through celebrating, through publicly remembering, a communal history of slavery. Rather, they buried their history, ignored it (indeed rewrote it?) in order to claim status as equal Somali citizens. Rather than holding a "class-action suit" mentality, Gosha farmers negotiated retribution for abuses on an individual basis, explained exploitation in personal terms (the woman in the marketplace had a bad temper; the nomad who beat up the Loc woman had a violent personality), and fought for dignity in the immediate context of face-to-face interaction. The ethnicized hierarchy which took form in the context of state-making had created the Gosha as a racialized ethnic "internal other"—but this other refused to assume an "ethnic group" self-consciousness.

Such forms of resistance indicate that Gosha people were struggling against categorical definitions which excluded them collectively into a category of denigrated "other" on the basis of race, history, and occupation (as easily exploitable farmers). They were rejecting denigration, but they were also rejecting the tyranny of categorization—the constituting of "the Gosha" as a collectivity that first took place in the political economy of the colonial period, informed by the dominant ideologies of race, and that later developed as an unacknowledged offshoot of Barre's nationalist programs which highlighted difference while claiming national homogeneity. The projects of colonial domination and post-colonial nation-building depended on race-making in order to claim bodies for state use and to define the essence of the nation. These projects categorized "the Gosha" into existence as a subjugated racialized ethnic group within the Somali nationalist milieu. Dreaming of membership in the Somali nation, Gosha people were thus fighting against the categorizing power inherent in state-making and nation-building processes.

In struggling against their distinct categorization, Gosha people were not necessarily striving for "belonging" in a patriotic or even nationalistic sense, however: they wanted clan affiliations, but they wanted other options too; they wanted state rhetoric but did not want a local state presence or to bleed in state-waged irredentist wars. And rather than striving for full assimilation, which was an ambivalent goal, they wanted acceptance on their own terms—humane terms of dignity, equality, and mutual respect. Their struggles against their position within nation and state, against the power of categories, against the ideology of denigration, and against the contemporary role their history defined for them in hegemonic cultural-religious discourse took place in the highly localized arena of face-to-face interaction.

Indeed, such positioning is perhaps the most immediately effective and most possible form of resistance. Just as the state arrives at the local level in the embodied form of bureaucrats and state agents, so subjugation is symbolically experienced in the form of innumerable tiny acts of denigration and humiliation. These personalized instances become the most pressing sites of resistance, the public forums in which struggles for dignity and pride are waged. Chipping away at minor injustices, appealing on a personal level to a looting pastoralist or a power-hungry local policeman, retaliating against a small indignity with a slap, a poem, or a story—these are the locally meaningful encounters within which Gosha people measured their standing, evaluated their status, and pressed their case for equality. People in the Gosha used state rhetoric—a national tool—to resist the denigrating symbolism manifest in local experience. They had a lot at stake in this discursive war, namely their ability to claim agency over and ownership of their identities and bodies. As Sider says, "One of the most remarkable facts about domination is that it is never simply political and economic, but always entails attempts to humiliate the dominated" (1987:21). Gosha people's resistance strategies suggest that, in their eyes, a good way to fight domination was to deny the experience of humiliation. Perhaps rare instances of explosive rage—such as running en masse into the bush to find the pastoralists believed to have attacked a local boy—resulted in part from the knowledge of impotence in the face of larger and less tangible abuses. Disproportionate targeting by the military, unequal participation in the diya system of compensation, loss of land to government bureaucrats through deception and subterfuge (to be discussed in Chapter 8), and a generalized atmosphere of racial inequality were much more difficult injustices to confront. People respond to what they can, and in ways available to them; to take on the military, the state, or regional clan elders would have been suicidal. In a highly militarized world where most pastoralists were equipped with AK-47s and where the government had control over huge stocks of weaponry, the Gosha people held no illusions about their ability to match fire with fire. They understood their categorization at the national level and their inability to effectively challenge a nationalism built partly on racial and hierarchical exclusion.

And yet throughout these daily face-to-face battles—these ongoing skirmishes over symbolic domination that pit rhetoric against experience in defining reality—we can imagine other historical trajectories. Gosha people obviously recognized the vast discrepancy between official rhetoric and local experience; they individually recognized that the rhetoric of belonging and equality opposed the local knowledges they each carried and that the official rhetoric they drew on came from a state which oppressed them in every other way. Such discrepancies certainly produced a tension, similar to what Antonio Gramsci (1971) called an "unease." People in the upper Gosha only had to look a few miles south to find an alternative response to their position. The Mushunguli of the lower Jubba never adopted Somali clan identities, never became Islamicized, and managed to maintain their ancestral language and customs to claim an "ethnic group" status. Why didn't this model permeate throughout Jubba valley society, as ex-slaves filtered in to build new communities? Why didn't ex-slaves throughout the valley reject Somali society as a source of identity, of meaning, and of legitimacy, refusing to accept or to nurture Somalized identities? Why didn't all ex-slaves in the valley look to their past as a source of strength, drawing on this past to develop a recognized political "minority" voice? In the next chapter, we will pause to reimagine history, to briefly ponder the historical circumstances that contributed to shaping the actual outcome rather than another, imaginable one.

Chapter 7
Negotiating Hegemony and Producing Culture

A decade ago the social historian Hermann Rebel chastised anthropologists and historians alike for celebrating the resistances of those we study while overlooking the often brutal facts of their daily lives: "One of the strongest tendencies in recent work by both anthropologists and historians has been to downplay the degradation and terror experienced by victims of exploitation and persecution. The new tone is one that stresses such extant aspects as the discovery and wielding of power even from weakness, the development of 'cultures' of resistance, the achievement of some sense of social identity and belonging as a benefit derived from participating in even the most debased circumstances, and so on" (1989:117). Anthropological acknowledgment of the experience of terror, violence, and brutality has certainly grown since Rebel wrote these words, and many who continue to focus on historical consciousness, resistance, or agency of subjugated people(s) explicitly recognize the realities of historical or contemporary violence within which resistances take shape.[1] It is impossible to understand agency or experience in the absence of knowing something about historical circumstances. In other words, understanding the very real conditions contributing to violence is essential to our ability to grasp the choices and to honor the experiences of those suffering through violent times and conditions. Historical circumstances shape quiescence as surely as they produce rebellion.[2]

The previous chapter described some of the ways in which the farmers of the Gosha symbolically coped with the denigrating and humiliating experiences of their daily lives. I argued that Gosha people resisted degradation in part by emphasizing in the regional arena their Somali clan memberships rather than a unifying racial categorization and by using Barre's socialist rhetoric of national unity to claim equal status as citizens of the Somali nation-state. Their resistance to racialized homogenization and degradation—their claim to membership in the Somali nation-state—however, occurred in the face of persistent injustices, humiliations, and racial categorizations which seemed to be losing none of their force or dominating power, a fact viciously demonstrated in the murderous campaigns against Gosha villagers during the early 1990s. Our postgenocide vantage point impels us to ponder not the effects but the premises of these practices of resistance pursued by Gosha villagers in the 1980s. In this chapter, I revisit some of the historical conditions that propelled ex-slaves settling into the middle Jubba valley over the past one hundred years to continue to seek a place within a society and nation-state that oppressed them.

As we have seen, most former slaves and their descendants sought independence from enslavement and from their former masters while simultaneously seeking to locate themselves *within* the hegemonic kinship system of Somali society. The historical record suggests ex-slaves throughout Somalia generated few alternatives to the clan model. With the exception of the earliest maroon settlements in the lower Gosha, all communities formed by ex-slaves utilized Somali clan structure as their basis for social organization. Yet we have also seen how this choice directly contributed to their ongoing denigration as commoners in a world of nobles, as foreigners in a world of lineal purity, and as contributors but not receivers of clan-mediated diya payments. Considering the onerous ideological baggage of race and status attached to *jareer sheegad* clan members, it is interesting to ask why the ex-slaves of the middle Jubba valley and their descendants did not reject Somali social constructions as imposed, alien, or undesirable, in favor of creating new forms of non-Somali identity. What are we to make of the continuing desire (as of the late 1980s) of most ex-slaves to claim membership in Somali society through a clan system that denigrated them and through adopting the equalizing rhetoric of a state that was built on stratification? Why didn't a self-styled Gosha elite emerge to challenge Somali hegemony and mobilize local people as a collectivity in the national arena? Can we simply claim that their continuing use of clan is an indication of the power of Somali hegemony, in the negative sense (Gosha villagers experiencing false consciousness, unaware of the drawbacks of the system to them)? Or is there more to their participation, their legitimation of clanship as part of their identity?

While I have already suggested in Chapter 4 some of the historical conditions which perhaps made it expedient for ex-slaves arriving in the Jubba valley to adopt Somali clan affiliations, I would like to pause again to consider the questions raised above a bit further, as they strike at the heart of ongoing anthropological debates about false consciousness, domination, collusion, and resistance. Although much about middle valley history remains unknowable, I will attempt to recapture some of the historical contingencies and conditions which may have shaped the identity politics of ex-slaves and their descendants in the middle Jubba valley in the twentieth century. While this endeavor may be more speculative than concrete, sometimes imagination better captures lived experience than a silent historical record.

Slaves as People Without History (or Culture)

One easy response to the question of why ex-slaves took on clan memberships is to think of the new slaves arriving in the valley as cultureless as well as kinless, who "naturally" adopted the hegemonic clan-based social blueprint of the dominant society. Indeed, ex-slaves in many parts of the world have been characterized as cultureless, desperately attempting to acculturate or assimilate themselves to the dominant society. In his book on black consciousness in the United States, Lawrence Levine reviews the abundant scholarly literature on African-Americans, which he criticizes for its assumption that African slaves in the New World "emerged from bondage in an almost culture-less state" (1977:442). For all its insights, Orlando Patterson's (1982) description of slaves as "socially dead" unintentionally reinforces such a vision. The Africanist literature on slavery which emphasizes belonging as the antithesis of slavery contains numerous examples of ex-slaves seeking to "pass" or quietly assimilate into their host societies, choosing to deny their pasts, their ancestral identities, and their slavery experiences in favor of embracing completely new ethnic or national identities.[3] Similarly, as Liisa Malkki (1995) has noted, refugees (among whom we can count fleeing ex-slaves) are often imagined as examples of bare humanity, stripped of all cultural traits; empty vessels in need of new content.

Such assimilationist views (which are supported by popular conceptions of involuntarily transported peoples)[4] would allow us to envision cultureless ex-slaves arriving in the Jubba valley—itself an empty slate, an ecologically bounded space (something akin to the misused biological concept of "niche")—faced with the process of reculturing themselves. This scenario could nicely explain the tendency of ex-slaves to adopt Somali clan affiliations.

Against this image, Malkki's (1995) wonderful and painful analysis of refugee Hutu identities demonstrates the ways in which refugees *deepen*, embellish, and persistently grapple with cultural identities, experience, and constructions of history. Her point is relevant for slaves too, in reminding us that slaves are not people stripped of culture. Throughout the processes of enslavement, slavery, and escape or manumission, they remain, of course, fully cultural beings, struggling with similar issues of cultural identity, experience, and constructions of history, and retaining cultural practices and knowledges such as dance, art, song, and medicine. We can adopt the Comaroffs' (1992:27) view of culture as "the semantic space, the field of signs and practices, in which human beings construct and represent themselves and others, and hence their societies and histories," and draw on Michel Foucault's (1980) understanding of the productivity of power to see how the status of slavery is culturally productive (albeit within constraints defined by unequal arenas of power), not culturally repressed to the point of cultural absence. Although all would agree that slavery is a highly repressive system of power, Foucault argues that

> the notion of repression is quite inadequate for capturing what is precisely the productive aspect of power. In defining the effects of power as repression, one adopts a purely juridical conception of such power, one identifies power with a law which says no, power is taken above all as carrying the force of a prohibition. . . . What makes power hold good, what makes it accepted, is simply the fact that it . . . traverses and produces things, it induces pleasure, forms knowledge, produces discourse. *It needs to be considered as a productive network which runs through the whole social body, much more than as a negative instance whose function is repression.* (1980:119; emphasis added)

In short, while slaves and their descendants lived under conditions defined by others (recall Marx's famous words [(1852) 1973:146]), they still managed to actively and continually forge new communities, identities, historical understandings, and cultural practices within the spaces available to them.

What many slaves—especially child slaves—lost was not "culture" (however defined), but rather, unlike the camp refugees in Malkki's (1995) account, a meaningful sense of ancestry, of heritage, tied to a specific location and a specific group of people who inhabit that location. Envisioning culture as something akin to ancestry—or replacing the notion of culture with the notion of heritage tied to place—thus becomes tricky, for it suggests that people who have lost their emotional attachments to a particular place, like many slaves, are somehow unmoored, free-floating, lacking notions and sentiments of community. To the contrary, although slaves may have lost an intimate connection to their ancestry, cultural productivity—which may or may not draw on notions of ancestry or heritage—becomes their survival strategy.[5]

A lack of historical ancestral knowledge is a feature of slave descendants throughout the world. Nowhere has slavery been considered an admirable or desirable condition. People of servile origins have often sought to deny, hide, or even reject this fact of their ancestry. As Klein (1989:212) says, "Slaves are essentially people without history," or, to be precise, people who cannot or will not reveal much about their history.

The condition of slavery hindered the retention of personal genealogies, and free descendants of slaves usually know only the barest facts of their enslaved ancestors' experiences. Patterson's characterization of the slave as a genealogical isolate is moving and apt description. The slave has a past, he writes, "but a past is not a heritage. . . . Slaves differed from other human beings in that they were not allowed to freely integrate the experience of their ancestors into their lives, to inform their understanding of social reality with the intuited meanings of their natural forebears, or to anchor the living present in any conscious community of memory" (1982:5).

The acceptance of Somali clan affiliations by Jubba valley ex-slaves suggests that Somali society provided a fully hegemonic model of kinship and social organization which genealogically severed ex-slaves had no choice but to adopt. The condition of slavery in general would seem to support this scenario. There is no more bald example of subordination—both ideologically and in the division of labor—than slavery, one of the most extreme forms of domination. Enslavement often originates in a violent act of warfare and/or kidnapping, where an individual is ripped out of his or her homeland, stripped of kin, personal autonomy, and a localized history shared with a group, and injected into a foreign society as a social dependent.[6] This status as a person divorced from a collective ancestral history is passed on to those born into slavery.

The context of slavery thus appears to present a perfect scenario for the imposition of new cultural and social patterns and ideologies on those enslaved. It is hard to imagine a clearer case of hegemonic dominance, in both the ideological and physical arenas, and the adoption of Somali clan affiliations seems to provide an indication of successful hegemony. Yet I have argued that slaves should not be viewed as cultureless—as empty vessels—but rather as people who produce all kinds of cultural forms while enslaved and following slavery which are not just assimilationist, but are creative and new and meaningful for them. I am also arguing that slaves do this in the absence, usually, of personal, preslavery genealogies. We cannot conflate a lack of personal ancestral history or community heritage with a condition of social or cultural vacuity.

Furthermore, anthropology's fascination with resistance has demonstrated that people everywhere, in the grips of many genres of hegemonic dominance, resist in myriad ways—privately, silently, ideologically, ritually, morally. As we saw in the previous chapter, ex-slaves and their descendants resisted much in Somali society, even while they persisted in the collective use of Somali clan identifications. To simply argue that the condition of slavery facilitated a hegemonic acceptance of Somali identities and social mores is not explanation enough. We must query the notion of hegemony and what it means to say that Somalia's social structure was hegemonic. Rather than agreeing with the assimilationists and the refugee specialists critiqued by Malkki that it is "natural" for people "without history" (slaves, refugees) to remake themselves in the image of their new home, we must query history, to whatever extent possible, asking why certain outcomes emerged and why certain choices were made. We cannot imagine that the historical trajectory of identity and hegemony in the middle Jubba was inevitable or predetermined, or that clan memberships carried the same meaning for jareer slave descendants in the Jubba valley that they did for other Somalis.

Envisioning ex-slaves and their descendants as active agents in controlling their destinies allows us to see them as people who create physical and social spaces for themselves—within historically shifting larger structures—in ways which are meaningful to them, if perhaps initially invisible to others. We have only to look at the rich ethnographies of such spaces in the Caribbean for examples of the intensely productive cultural creativity of New World ex-slaves.[7]

In what follows, I attempt to capture some of the ways historical processes shaped the choices made by ex-slaves as they forged local and personal identities. I explore some aspects of master-slave paternalism, Islamic inclusiveness, the sentiment and emotion of kinship, and historical pragmatics in order to offer my thoughts about why ex-slaves accepted the Somali genealogical model as legitimate and sought to participate in it. This discussion is undoubtedly incomplete and tentative, and I introduce it as a way to provoke further discussion and more historical research on the politics of identity beyond clan in twentieth-century Somalia.

Paternalism, Childhood Slavery, and Islamic Conversion

In one of our private conversations, Jimcale, the pastoralist-turned-farmer who was released from slavery/clientship as an adult shortly before settling in Loc, poignantly explained to me the impact of childhood enslavement on his (pastoralist slave) father: "[The master says about the slave-child], 'This is my child,' and then when you grow up you will be told your history [by your master/father] and then you will understand that you don't belong to them. But you were brought up by them and are affiliated. You won't talk about your former tribe because you grew up with this tribe. Children only know who they're brought up by."

His explanation that "Children only know who they're brought up by" brought home to me the extraordinary significance of being enslaved as a small child after being kidnapped from one's parents. Because many of the slaves acquired by Somalis were children during the time of their enslavement, they grew up speaking only Somali and practicing Islam, often as part of Somali households. Slaves were identified as part of a particular clan by virtue of association with their masters, whom they usually called father. Enslaved female children were not only culturally indoctrinated into Somali families and clans, but were physically remade as Somalis as well. Jimcale recalled how captured Boran girls underwent the Somali practice of female circumcision and infibulation, emerging from the operation as newly embodied Somali women. Bodily inscription accompanied cultural indoctrination.

The kinds of paternalistic dynamics suggested in Jimcale's recollections of his father's enslavement have received broad scholarly recognition. Hegel's master-slave dialectic—in which master and slave are seen as psychologically and emotionally codependent—received new life in Eugene Genovese's (1974) pathbreaking analysis of the forms of paternalism which he saw as inherent in southern American master-slave relations. The paternalistic relationship that bound slave to master and defined the master's role as both legitimate and humane, Genovese argued, ensured that slaves identified with the dominant society. Paternalism "undermines solidarity among the oppressed by linking them as individuals to their oppressors. . . . Paternalism created a tendency for the slaves to identify with a particular community through identification with its master; it reduced the possibilities for their identification with each other as a class" (1974:5–6). Genovese describes the American slave-owning master as a patriarch in control of a large household of black and white dependents who were all subject to his paternalistic authority. In this way, slaves were categorized with other subjugated household members as part of a family, not a class.

Cooper (1977) similarly argued that the paternalism of master-slave relations in precolonial coastal East Africa undermined potential class awareness on the part of subjugated slaves. While slaves shared cultural practices, such as dance forms and a sense of common origin, their closest bonds were with their masters. The patriarchal nature of coastal society, reinforced by Islamic ideology and law, ensured that ties of dependence and paternalism were pervasive in master-slave relations. "Only through the master did slaves share in the political strength and social ties of communal groups" (1977:214), defined by Cooper as closely knit kin-based groups that shared a sense of common origin, identity, and relations with "outsiders" (Cooper 1977:5). The language of kinship (such as the father-son terminology used between male master and male slave) rationalized master-slave relations "in terms of the patriarchal structure of the family" (Cooper 1977:226).

Such visions of the force of patriarchy and paternalism in binding slaves ideologically to their masters offer insights into the Somali situation as well. In the Somali context, the newly imported slave was thrust into a new society with a strong grid of social organization that defined the social identity of his or her owner. This identity, in altered form, was extended to the slave as the personal property of the Somali owner. Cooper's observation that slaves accessed "communal groups" only through their masters in Islamic precolonial coastal society has implications for how slaves could participate in the "political strength and social ties" of clan groupings in Somalia. While the dispersed nature of pastoralist life clearly militated against the formation of a class consciousness among pastoral slaves, even plantation slavery provided effective barriers, due to the prevalence of children slaves and the sanctioning ideology of Islam.

Through their direct or indirect incorporation into the Somali clan structure through their owners and their conversion to Islam, slaves began to see themselves (and this is particularly true for the children of slaves) as participants in Somali clans. Especially in contrast to people enslaved as adults who bore children only after obtaining their freedom, slaves brought to Somalia as children or born in Somalia were understandably more inclined toward an involvement in the Somali clan structure. Childhood enslavement was perhaps the single most important factor distinguishing the ancestral slavery experiences of the middle Jubba communities established on the basis of Somali clan affiliations from the lower Jubba fugitive slave communities established on the basis of African—especially Mushunguli—ethnicity. Middle Jubba villagers retained so little knowledge of personal preslavery ancestries most likely because the vast majority of their ancestors were enslaved as children, either on plantations or in pastoralist households. The continuing cultural and linguistic distinctiveness of the Mushunguli of the lower Jubba is due largely to the fact that their ancestors arrived together in Somalia as adults, escaped together to form maroon communities, and remained intact as a group. Their *collective* historical experience stands as a continuing reminder of the significance of childhood enslavement on personal identity for most other slave descendants in the valley. The ancestors of most slave descendants in the middle Jubba had experienced childhoods of slavery within paternalistic households whose social position was defined by clan status, a status which extended to all household members whether free, enslaved, or born free to an enslaved mother.

Religious conversion rooted slaves more firmly in Somali conceptions of the social order. Comparative studies show that slaves' acceptance of dominant social patterns in Muslim areas, while never complete, occurred to greater degrees than in areas where there existed non-Muslim groups which ex-slaves could join.[8] Few non-Muslim communities existed in Somalia during the latter half of the nineteenth century. In the lower Jubba, the earliest fugitive slave arrivals in the mid-nineteenth century did not join the non-Muslim Boni hunter-gatherer groups, but rather fought against them for control of the area, eventually pushing most Boni away from the river. Islamic sheikhs were successfully spreading Islam throughout Gosha villages by the late nineteenth century, and by the turn of the century most arriving ex-slaves were already converted. Many middle Jubba valley ancestors had attained their freedom through manumission, an Islamic act that served to bind Somali master and converted slave.[9] Jimcale described to me the paternalism inherent in the act of manumission:

> The child you yourself took, you will make him a slave. If he is obedient to you, you will set him free [when he's old enough]. You will give him livestock. You will give him a wife. If it was a woman, you will give her a man. You will set her free. The small child who was stolen [enslaved through warfare or kidnapping], if he reaches the age of [late teens] and is mature, you set him free. If he was obedient, accepted his service, wherever you sent him, he fulfilled it: you set him free. You give him one animal. You call people, you call him himself: "Cali [a man's name], come." "This morning this man's head is free." Or you will say, if I was your slave, "The man called Jimcale, he was obedient to me. This morning I want to set him free, to give him an animal." Other people are called. They will be witnesses. You can't set a slave free on your own. After that the man who used to be owned, tomorrow in the morning he can go where he wants.

The paternalistic practice, however often it actually occurred, of a master providing his slave with a spouse and an "inheritance" of livestock established a bond that ideologically connected the new free generation—produced by the ex-slave with a wife acquired through fictive kin ties and supported by the livestock inherited from the former master/father—with the former slave owner. In a symbolic sense, the master paid the bridewealth for his "son."

Another middle valley elder who was locally revered as a knowledgeable Islamic teacher and village leader described his enslaved father's experience in a way that captures some of the sense of mutual personal obligation felt by master-fathers and slave-sons:

> My father was stolen from Mombasa when he was fifteen years old by a friend of his father's. The man's name was Macallin Iidore, and he brought my father to Somalia by tricking him, telling him, "You will earn a lot of money if you come with me," and my father believed him. Macallin Iidore brought my father by ship, and after my father arrived in Somalia he understood that he was deceived. Macallin Iidore sold my father to another Bartire [a Somali clan] man living in eastern Somalia. My father's Swahili name was Ulilya, but the Somali man who bought him named him Nassib, which means "I got him by luck." The man liked my father because of his obedience. The Somali people used to kill those who were infidels and uncircumcised, but my father was brought up among Arabs (on the Swahili coast) and he was circumcised.[10] When the man saw this he kept him as his own son. My father served for this man as his own son for some time.

> My father adopted Bartire because the man who owned him was Bartire. . . . During that time there was a war between different tribes, like Bartire, Galadle, and Eelay, and they used to steal camels from each other. The worst war was between Eelay and Galadle. So many people were killed on both sides. That was the time when my father got his freedom. He was set free because he took a good role during the war with Eelay, fighting for his tribe Bartire. Many other slaves were released by Bartire after the war [in recognition of their service].[11]

Following his release from slavery, the speaker's father migrated to the Jubba valley with his "cousins," where he met and married the speaker's mother, settled down, and began farming. All of his descendants have continued to claim affiliation with the Bartire clan.

The role of Islam in legitimizing and naturalizing the genealogical structures of Somali society for converted ex-slaves and their descendants was probably enormous. My informants in the middle Jubba often spoke of the role of Islamic holy men around the turn of the century in mediating peace among ex-slave communities and between them and surrounding Somali pastoralists in the lower valley, in supporting the actions of clan leaders in warfare and decision-making throughout the valley (such as Nassib Bundo and the Ajuraan leaders of the middle Jubba, Sheikh Cabdow Kheyr and Sooyan), and in introducing "the way of life in the Gosha as we now know it," in the words of one man.

Islamic leaders, in their capacity as mediators, legal experts, and moral guides, invested heavily in Somali genealogies for their unifying and legitimizing power. In discussing the role of Islamic leaders in nurturing a vision of Somali nationalism prior to 1900, Cassanelli suggests that Muslim sheikhs used genealogy to closely bind religious and personal identities in Somalia. His words are worth quoting at length, because his argument captures the role of Islam in permeating Gosha villages with a religious sensibility that tied adherents to a genealogically united Somali heritage:

> One can reasonably argue that it was the Muslim sheikhs, both Arab and Somali, who first planted the notion of a wider Somali identity. They propagated stories of Arab ancestry and facilitated the construction of genealogies that linked the ancestors of the various clans they served to the Qurayshitic lineage of the Prophet or to some prestigious immigrant from Arabia. Only the sheikhs maintained written Arabic manuscripts that recorded the genealogical connections, at the highest levels, among various clan founders. The practical effects of such links were, of course, limited since there existed in Somalia no large-scale political organization to give substance to the concept of a total Somali genealogy; yet the ideological basis for the recognition of a larger Somali community was there.
>
> We might speculate that through their activities of political mediation, social consolidation, and religious propagation, the saints helped both to forge and to reinforce the notion of a shared religious heritage among the Somalis. They provided to the various groups on the ground a sense of common history; and they

encapsulated that history in the genealogies which every Somali maintained to define his place in the social system. To this extent, then, the work of the saints contributed to the fusion of Islamic and Somali identities. *If today one can almost automatically say that to be a Somali is to be a Muslim, historically it can be said that to accept Islam was to accept membership in a larger Somali nation.* (1982:128–29; emphasis added)

For slaves in Somalia, converting to Islam meant accepting, or at least acknowledging, the sanctification of Somali genealogies by Muslim sheikhs and the importance of finding a place within these genealogies. Somali Islam affirmed the religious significance of Somali genealogies, and offered a combination of religious adherence and Somali identity to slave converts.

In passages such as those above, the testimonies of slave descendants who had some knowledge of their parents' or grandparents' slavery experiences reveals the paternalistic force of the slavery experience in Somalia. Undoubtedly, many enslaved children brought up in Somali families and cut off from contact with and knowledge about birth parents and natal communities—whether Boran pastoralist children or east African children laborers—accepted and became attached to Somali social categories as an essential part of remaining social beings. These attachments remained important after manumission, in part because of their significance to Somali Islam, and became part of an inherited body of knowledge passed down through the generations.

Affective Ties

The loss of a powerful sense of personal non-Somali African heritage must have been acute for enslaved children and those born into slavery in both pastoralist and plantation settings. In the middle Jubba, people whose ancestors were believed to have been plantation slaves had retained the least amount of preslavery ancestral family knowledge, or were the least inclined to share such knowledge publicly or privately with me. These men and women, most likely through lack of knowledge rather than recalcitrance, were unable to relate more than the barest details of where their parents (or grandparents) had come from or what their lives had been like. The elderly Bartire man quoted above recalled that his mother's mother had huge holes in her earlobes. Since he had heard as an adult that women "from the West" (Kenya, Tanzania, or Malawi) wore earplugs, he assumed his maternal grandmother had been enslaved from this part of Africa. He had no recollection that her natal birthplace or early life experiences were ever mentioned during his childhood. While his father had recounted his childhood experiences to him, his mother had never told him anything about her past.

Although Loc villagers tended to know many intimate details of each other's lives and histories, even those most knowledgeable and willing to describe details about villagers' slave ancestries were unable to relate information about plantation slavery except to point out those villagers believed to be descended from plantation slaves. Mid-valley villagers of Boran descent retained a greater sense of ancestral identity and a few could recite some Boran words, but most found this association devoid of great meaning. Although the most elderly living Boran descendants willingly acknowledged their ancestral ethnicity, their children, grandchildren, and great-grandchildren found this ancestry increasingly insignificant to their daily lives, and spoke much more readily about how their ancestors simply had been pastoralists who had lost all their livestock, rather than acknowledging their enslavement or clientship, or mentioning their ancestral ethnic origins.

Aside from the Mushunguli of the lower Jubba, an enduring reconstitution or renaissance of original ethnicity along East African tribal lines never occurred among slave descendants in Somalia. Although recognition of ancestral backgrounds continued to some extent, these preslavery identities lacked the force of sentiment and affection and were rapidly disappearing. A lack of continuous social interaction within those structures and communities had gradually weakened them as potential aspects of unification or common identity. While some cultural practices such as dance forms and medicinal knowledge were retained, the cultural significance of preslavery *identities* did not survive the experience of slavery with enough force to symbolically bind together ex-slaves, most of whom no longer spoke their ancestral languages or practiced the ancestral religions. Generating a common sense of identity based on preslavery identities was also difficult due to the sheer diversity of these identities. Thus, although alternative discourses of heritage in the most general sense were still available, they were devoid of meaning. The alternatives did not provide an effective basis for collective action, consensus, or communal identities. Ancestral ethnic commonalities were increasingly de-emphasized in favor of stressing Somali clan affiliation—which for most individuals had been their lifelong orientation—and Gosha village bonds, which provided a far more important basis of social interaction.

The influence of reer Shabeelle, who began arriving in the 1920s, further nurtured Gosha individuals' choices to seek and/or maintain Somali clan affiliations. Reer Shabeelle provided a model of a group which saw itself as both distinct (on the basis of race) and thoroughly part (on the basis of culture, language, religion) of Somali society—a model that was adopted throughout the upper Gosha. Furthermore, and importantly, reer Shabeelle people held a strong sense of pride in their local political power, their historical resistance to colonial authority, their Ajuraan heritage, and their social membership within Somali society. Their long-standing participation in a Somali clan of "near legendary" (Cassanelli 1982:84) fame which claimed pockets of membership throughout southern Somalia including pastoralist, agropastoralist, and agricultural groups, gave them a strong sense of belonging in the Somali nation. Despite their jareer appearance, no locally established oral traditions clearly linked them with an enslaved or non-Muslim past, thus providing them with a sense of having a fully Somalized heritage. Their pride in their identity—as racially distinct Somali clan members with a rich individual *and* clan history—demonstrated a way to reconcile foreignness and belonging.

In constructing social identities, individuals living in the upper Gosha thus drew from a variety of sources, including a superficial knowledge of a personal ancestral past, a recognition of an ascribed racial identity, affiliation to a Somali clan, and village membership. Different backgrounds were recognized in general (Oromo, East African Bantu, reer Shabeelle), and had some importance in shaping personal identity. These ancestral backgrounds provided a link to the past, however tenuous and muted its recognition. Although this knowledge was widely shared among the Gosha, it was not necessarily culturally transmitted across generations as part of a body of information to be proud of, because of the association with slavery (although this was less true for reer Shabeelle). As Jimcale explained to me about his father: "He didn't say, 'Where is my father from? Which tribe was he?' He didn't ask for that. He was told after some time where his father came from, but he himself didn't ask about his father. 'Father where are you from?' he didn't say. But we, when we were mature enough, our father said to us, 'I am Yabadalay. I am Ajuraan. I am Waaqle. I am Wale Mage' [all Somali clan and lineage names]. He just told us those."

Non-Somali ancestral backgrounds structured interaction only to a very limited extent. With an increasing incidence of intermarriage, the basis for a recognition of differing ancestries was rapidly losing its significance. Young men and women tended to be uninformed about their grandparents' histories, and, more importantly, they were not interested in the details. By the 1980s, people lived, married, and argued primarily along Somali clan lines with only the occasional superficial acknowledgment of their different ancestries (such as when I came around asking questions about such things).

For many ex-slaves and their descendants, then, Somali clan memberships offered a more immediately compelling social identity than the much hazier memories of a pre-Somali heritage. While middle valley villagers did not seek to deny their non-Somali ancestry—a fact they were reminded of every day—they also did not publicly seek to incorporate this ancestry into their daily life in personally meaningful ways. Their preslavery heritages, however recalled, remained for most little more than a historical fact, not a sentimental source of personal knowledge.

At the same time, however, the connection to ancestral heritages varied among middle valley farmers in important ways. The reer Shabeelle pride in their distinct identity (as "reer Shabeelle") *and* Somali clan affiliations (as Ajuraan) grew out of an attachment to a geographic place of origin, a memory of great heroes and deeds, a sense of common history and experience, and ongoing interaction within a regional Ajuraan network. Oromo descendants recognized their ancestry and could identify the Oromo geographical domain, which was locatable if not personally meaningful. Their heritage as pastoralists, whether free or enslaved, remained their most significant common marker. In contrast, east African slave descendants held the least connection to a remembered geographical area of origin or sense of common historical experience.

The personal and sentimental significance of Somali clan affiliations were also variable, however, and hard to gauge. This is an important point. A lack of ancestral connection for slave descendants did not translate into complete devotion to a Somali clan. Somali clan memberships did not just fill an identity vacuum, but rather were integrated into personal identity as one aspect of social life. While all slave descendants in the middle Jubba claimed clan membership, we have seen how other kinds of social relationships, such as friendships and village ties, often eclipsed these memberships in day-to-day life, rendering them of secondary or even marginal importance. In fact, it could be argued that the pragmatics, rather than sentiment, of claiming a clan identity provided the overwhelming logic of clan affiliations for most ex-slaves and their descendants.

Pragmatics

The pragmatic reasons for claiming Somali clan affiliations are perhaps more straightforward than the messier reasons of sentiment and affect. In addition to the benefits secured by affiliating with locally powerful Somali clans, over the course of the past century Gosha villagers utilized their clan affiliations to justify their independent rights to land, labor, and freedom. As discussed in Chapter 4, Somali clan affiliations were used to avoid re-enslavement and, more unsuccessfully, to avoid forced conscription as laborers on Italian-owned farms during the colonial period. Following the example of the client-cultivator non-Somali communities along the Shabeelle, Gosha villagers used clan affiliations as networks for trade and loans. Claiming a clan membership status allowed slave descendants in the Gosha to negotiate in the economic arena using the discourse of kinship. While this discourse was often used to their disadvantage by pastoralists and urban bureaucrats, mid-valley villagers recognized the (at least rhetorical) importance of appropriating the language of clan to negotiate loans or facilitate financial transactions with Bu'aale shopkeepers. In other words, while the tangible financial benefits may have been slight, having access to the rhetoric of brotherhood provided villagers with a widely accepted basis for interactions with Bu'aale moneylenders, government representatives, and the world outside the valley.

As we have seen, Gosha villagers used their status as clan members in their discursive struggle for social status within wider Somali society. At various points during their history, Gosha people individually and collectively used their clan memberships in strategic and pragmatic ways to claim social rights, to bolster economic opportunities, to develop support networks, and to justify their rights as members of Somali society. Such a strategy made eminent good sense in a state dominated by patronage politics. Locating themselves within the grammar of patronage politics through identifying with Somali clans offered Gosha villagers the possibility of appealing to state-backed local clan mediators (whose title had been changed from *clan* mediator to *state* mediator after the revolution) for protection from state repression or representation in regional disputes. In the terrifying years of the 1980s when state repression reached a peak, local and regional clan networks offered the best mediation outside state channels and the best way to negotiate within the state justice system. As we have seen, Gosha villagers did not often benefit materially from their participation in clan-mediated negotiations, but the important point is that clans offered the framework for conducting negotiations. Even when a Gosha villager brought close friends or kin of a different clan to serve as his witnesses or mediators, negotiations with outsiders took place within the rubric of clan mediation. In other words, claiming membership in Somali clans at least gave Gosha villagers a place at the bargaining table, a way to access clan-mediated negotiations, even if the basis of their involvement in their eyes was as villagers, farmers, or relatives, rather than as clan members. In the two cases I described where pastoralists physically assaulted Loc villagers during the 1987–88 jilaal, the Loc village council first mediated directly with the pastoralists to assess the fines for medical expenses, but then referred both cases to regional clan authorities for further mediation. The clan authorities mediated (the Loc farmers were represented by the regional Ajuraan leader),[12] but the Loc village council members—regardless of their personal clan affiliations—served as witnesses for the injured Loc farmers.

Hegemony and Identity

In his critique of the way the term *hegemony* is used to explain why dominated classes don't revolt, Scott argued that it amounts to an explanation "of the institutional basis of false consciousness" (1985:315). As such, Scott claimed it overlooks the "hidden transcript" of resistance and the revolutionary potential of silenced ideological resistance. But I think he overstates the point; rather, hegemony can be used simply to refer to the accepted state of affairs—the uncontested common ground which exists at particular historical moments in every society. In a defense of the concept's utility, the Comaroffs argued that, if used carefully, hegemony offers "a cogent way of speaking about the force of meaning and the meaning of force—the inseparability, that is, of power and culture" (1992:28). As an analytical tool, it links the ways in which power and culture are mutually constituted in networks, institutions, discourses, and so on, to influence people's lives in ways unthinkable or unquestioned, "suggesting a more fluid vision of the way power interacts with culture [than a] simplistic model in which economic elites plot to control their world" (Nordstrom and Martin 1992:6).

Indeed, its usefulness as an analytic tool is evidenced by its wide deployment—it has been extended by anthropologists to describe relations such as those based on gender, age, religion, or ethnicity, in addition to class. Yet to say that a system, an ideology, or a discourse is hegemonic is not to explain it, and it is this effort to understand which must be foremost. Explaining hegemony requires a genealogy of the particular historical factors which have rendered normal an acceptance of the hegemonic order; it demands processual, not structural thinking. It also requires a rejection of the reductionist view that "hegemony equals false consciousness" in favor of continually remembering that the concept refers to a historically situated (and shifting!) state of affairs that is more or less unquestioningly accepted by most members of society (including both beneficiaries and the subaltern) during a particular time period.

William Roseberry (1989) emphasizes the mutual constitution of power and culture when noting that it is not only dominant groups that produce culture (to which subordinate groups must adhere), but rather that dominant and subordinate groups participate *together* in the process of cultural production. This process, however, takes place in a context of inequality, of "unequal fields of power" (Roseberry and O'Brien 1991:9), which results in different experiences for the dominant group and the "ordinary" or subordinate group. In his words, understanding the role of "hegemony" in culture and experience

> requires, first, the recognition of differential experience: the differential experience of persons . . . ; of particular generations in particular times and places—and the understanding of that differential experience in terms of individual life courses but also in terms of structures of inequality and domination. Yet it also requires a recognition that across this differential experience, and to a certain extent across time, some common understandings emerge, along with common forms of language and modes of interaction, common sensibilities of self and place and history. (Roseberry 1989:48)

Using the term *hegemony*, then, to refer to the force of the Somali clan system in Gosha community formation can be useful to the extent that we allow room for the shifting nature of social relationships and forces over time within an overall continuity. The argument of the previous chapter used local tensions, ambiguities, and resistances as diagnostics of what Gosha people accepted and what they rejected, of which hegemonies were naturalized and which contested. We have seen how Gosha people accepted a clan basis of social interaction (the overall continuity) but rejected the accompanying denigrating ideology (produced through the shifting nature of social relationships and forces over time). At the same time, however, I also argued that the clan basis of social interaction, while naturalized and legitimized throughout the middle Jubba, did not dominate or control social life to the exclusion of other aspects of identity and experience. Gosha villagers were painfully aware of the negative implications for them of the Somali clan system, with its inherent hierarchies, statuses, and points of exclusion. Yet they also chose to utilize the benefits of participating in Somali society through accepting its genealogical basis, as manifest in their Islamic faith, their adherence to clan as an important aspect of personal identity, and their ability to interact with people from outside the valley under the auspices of kinship. (During the 1980s, middle Jubba villagers increasingly recognized that the latter "benefit" had more often become detrimental, as we shall see in the next chapter.) The psychological and emotional effects of childhood enslavement and conversion to Islam combined with the pragmatic use of clan in the political and economic arenas to make Somali clan affiliations compelling, meaningful, and desirable for upper Gosha ex-slaves and their descendants.

In characterizing Somali kinship as a "common ground" of continuity, however, we must also remember that this common ground is itself never fixed absolutely; that is, the overall structure of continuity is itself constantly being reproduced. This important point reminds us that while the system of clan and genealogy may have served as a hegemonic "common understanding" which ex-slaves adopted, utilized, and legitimized, the meaning and use of clan and kinship has always been, and will undoubtedly continue to be, the *contested* backdrop of Somali society. Ex-slaves and their descendants saw clan affiliations as important, necessary, and personally meaningful, but they made choices about those affiliations and those meanings which should not be reduced to an image of socially dead, culturally vacant ex-slaves naturally adopting an unchanging culture produced for them by dominant society.

Rather, in the face of the imaginable alternative of rejecting Somali society and its encompassing kinship networks—of generating a self-conscious collective identification as an "ethnic group" or several "ethnic groups"—settlers to the middle valley chose another course. I have attempted to provide a sense of why this was the case through revisiting some of the historical circumstances surrounding these choices. The slavery experiences captured in Gosha villagers' memories of their parents' stories (and their silences), the ideologies inherent to Islamic conversion, and the pragmatism of clan affiliation in the twentieth century shaped mid-valley settlers' choices in critical ways.[13] The settlers in the mid-valley used their experiences and knowledges in ways that allowed them to articulate with and exist within the hegemonic social structure. Here is where we glimpse the productivity of power (the power of enslavement, the hegemony of kinship): in the cultural practices and emerging social identities of middle valley villagers as they resisted denigration while seeking national belonging, as they adopted clan affiliations while employing anticlan state rhetoric and superseding clan ties with other aspects of social identity in practice, and as they remembered their ancestral identities while adhering to Somali Islam and its exclusively inclusive genealogical vision.

Ex-slaves and their descendants have thus been waging ideological battles within the confines of what was possible in order to define the terms of their existence by borrowing and adopting state rhetoric *and* the discourse of kinship to forge their identities. It is in this sense that Somali genealogical hegemony can be seen as productive, not repressive, for ex-slaves and their descendants. They have not been forging a uniform "Gosha culture" or "Gosha history," but rather have been working collectively, in groups, *and* idiosyncratically to creatively shape a place in contemporary Somali society. While accepting the imperative of genealogical inclusion as legitimate, they have at the same time been pursuing a subtle transformative agenda—namely, to be included on their terms, with dignity, equality, and honor, to reshape the significance of clan in the living of daily life, to use clan as only one out of many aspects of identity. That they have so far been largely unsuccessful in their appeal for dignity and equality in no way indicates passivity or an encompassing false consciousness of their position, but rather stands as symptomatic of their struggles.

Part IV
Violence and the State

Chapter 8
The Political Economy of Subordination

The hegemony of clan and its accompanying genealogical exclusivity, the ideology of superiority, and the weight of history—these are some of the themes I have called upon in the preceding chapters to describe the status of Gosha villagers in the Somali nation-state of the 1980s. In the regional sphere of social relations and power dynamics, Gosha villagers were striving to assert membership in Somali society, to demonstrate personal dignity in the face of symbolic subordination, to build village-based coalitions as a critical source of mutual support, and to maintain some degree of economic and political autonomy from the state. Their success lay in their ability to exact compensation for wrongs committed against them (sometimes), in their ability to transcend race, history, and denigration in forging alliances based on mutual respect with local pastoralists or to extract benefits from the state (occasionally), and in their ability to protect their livelihood. It is to this last point, which was increasingly tenuous in the 1980s and destroyed in the 1990s, that we now turn.

If symbolic acts of subordination such as those described in Chapter 5 are enraging and humiliating, the material implications of domination may be the most directly life-threatening. Several scholars have noted that material domination often accompanies symbolic humiliation and that hegemony always facilitates appropriation. As Scott claims: "The bond between domination and appropriation means that it is impossible to separate the ideas and symbolism of subordination from a process of material exploitation" (1990:188; see also Sider 1986:127–28). Whereas Part III described the texture of and struggles against symbolic subordination in Gosha village and regional life, this chapter examines the other side of the equation—the material side—to see how symbolic subordination underwrote material appropriation in Somalia's Jubba valley. In particular, this chapter explains how the racialized space of denigrated "others" became reenvisioned as a national space of potential wealth claimed by the state.

Nineteenth-century slaves arrived in Somalia as appropriated beings, as people whose bodies were claimed for material production and exploitation. For many, their struggle to reclaim their bodies—to reclaim their right to their own labor and production—took the various forms of physical flight to the Jubba valley, armed resistance, agricultural innovation as smallholder farmers, and ambivalent and carefully mediated acquiescence as Muslims and Somali citizens. With the exception of several bleak years under Italian colonization, during much of the twentieth century their descendants have been fairly successful at maintaining autonomy, avoiding state and/or elite appropriation, and controlling their land, bodies, and production.

In the regional society which emerged from the dynamic ferment of the late nineteenth and early twentieth centuries, Gosha farmers had successfully carved out a new space over which they maintained authority and control. By defeating the hunter-gatherer Boni and pushing the pastoralist Ogaadeen Somalis away from their settlements, the earliest maroon settlers staked their claim to economic independence and uncontested control of farmland in the Jubba valley. Fugitive ex-slaves created a new place in the regional topography: a frontier space of smallholder agriculture, of magic, of danger, of otherness. While pastoralists occasionally attempted to enter this space to claim Gosha bodies or Gosha produce, they certainly never attempted to claim riverine Gosha *land*, which held no intrinsic value in the pastoralist system of production. Pastoralist appropriation took the form, as I described in Chapters 5 and 6, of occasional opportunistic appropriation, but was not a fact of daily life or a persistent threat to subsistence. The arrival of Italian colonialists to the lower valley brought the first sustained threat by the state to Gosha farmers' hegemony over agricultural land. The transformative agenda of Italian colonists in their bid for a lucrative settler colony redefined the Jubba valley as a place of great agricultural potential and Italian domination. Between 1935 and 1940, Italian expropriation and kolonya policies turned thriving and productive agricultural communities in the lower Jubba into impoverished and malnourished villages living on the edge of starvation alongside large, state-supported export-oriented Italian plantations.[1] The Italian colonial government expropriated fourteen thousand hectares of prime agricultural land along the river south of Jilib for Italian-owned banana plantations, relocated several Gosha villages onto plantations as permanent labor, and pursued a policy of producing export crops in place of subsistence crops—policies that cumulatively resulted in local food shortages and a devastating famine by 1938 that only ended with Italy's loss of Somalia in 1942 to

Britain.[2] As we have seen, Italian policy and discourse had redefined the valley as an agriculturally promising space inhabited by racialized laborers. At the conclusion of Italy's colonial era, lower valley villagers reclaimed their transformed landscape of uprooted villages and banana plantations, having gained a new awareness of the potential for outside interest in valley *land* as well as local bodies. Villagers in the middle valley emerged from this abysmal chapter of colonial history relatively unscathed, but with village populations enhanced by the arrival of fleeing farmers from the lower valley.

During the decades of the 1940s, 1950s, and 1960s, Gosha villages all along the Jubba reinvigorated their smallholder agriculture, experimenting with cotton as well as different manual irrigation techniques. These decades were marked by a virtual absence of state or elite interest in the Jubba valley or its agricultural potential,[3] allowing lower Jubba villages to recover to some extent from colonial land and labor expropriation policies, and allowing middle Jubba villages to establish a highly flexible and adaptive system of customary land use practices as immigration waned and their settlements stabilized.

The 1970s and 1980s brought radical changes in the political economy of the Jubba valley as the valley was once again redefined, but this time by the postcolonial Somali state, as a state resource to be developed with international donor funds and projects. This transformative shift in state policy toward the Jubba valley was accompanied by changes in the national socioeconomic structure which together altered the nature of social relations, power dynamics, and production practices in the Jubba valley. State claims to the valley resulted in the large-scale appropriation of valley farmland by national elites from outside the valley. Staggeringly costly state farms, internationally funded multimillion dollar development projects, and new government policy toward land tenure in an era of economic collapse and intense militarization of the state brought elites into the valley to claim dominance on the basis of their access to wealth, state power, and weaponry. The land rush of the 1970s and 1980s dispossessed local farmers of their land and production, irrevocably altered regional power dynamics, and precipitated a period of unprecedented violence. In the process, valley farmers lost control of their livelihoods, many lost control of their persons as they became landless laborers for wealthier landholders, and most lost their hope of a brighter future for their children. These two decades transformed the valley from a place of productive smallholder agriculture to a place of falling productivity and environmental destruction; from a place of freedom and autonomy to a place of immiseration, landlessness, and terror; from a racialized space for incorporated "foreigners" to a state-claimed space appropriated by national—and postnational—elites.

This chapter chronicles these devastating past two decades on local life, livelihood, and environment in the Jubba valley, revealing some very unflattering general truths about the effects of development wisdom, foreign aid, and donor-supported state-building processes on minority groups in African states. We will see how the geographic and ecological space of the middle Jubba valley, once a remote backwater peripheral to the postcolonial state, became in the 1980s a national target of elite appropriation. Tracing this transformation addresses the broader issue of class formation in Somalia—who were the land-grabbing national elite, why did they want land in the valley, and how did they go about claiming it?—and the intertwined nature of class formation and state-building. In order to address these questions, I will move back and forth from the local scene to the national arena, charting the dialectics of class formation, racialized ethnicity, state formation, and donor funding. We begin at the local level with a detailed discussion of the political economy of production in Loc on the eve of its destruction. This portrait of Loc provides a baseline by which we can measure the changes in productive relations brought by state policy, donor funds, and national/regional power hierarchies. Our story of land use, land tenure, and village production in the middle valley picks up where we left off in Chapter 4, in the early 1970s, just prior to the transformative events of the late 1970s and 1980s.

Middle Valley Customary Tenure

As described in Chapter 4, by the early 1970s middle valley villages each controlled a clearly demarcated area of farmland overseen (after 1977) by their respective village councils. Loc's land tenure practices (which were representative of other middle valley villages) provide a picture of how one Gosha village managed its land base (of about 751 hectares), minimized risk, strived for sustainability, managed the thorny dilemmas of stratification in a small community, and handled gender divisions.[4]

In Loc customary practice, only men acquired or inherited land, with which they were expected to support their families. Thus a man would typically obtain his first parcel of land in anticipation of his marriage, later acquiring more parcels as his family expanded through children and additional marriages. In theory, women could not independently hold land (although a few did in 1988); rather, women were to labor on their father's land until marriage, their husband's land after marriage, their brother's land after divorce, and their son's land in widowhood. While women were not typically granted independent rights to land, a husband was obligated to provide enough land for his wives to feed themselves and their children. A failure to meet this obligation was grounds for divorce. A man and his wife usually worked the land together, but in polygynous households the husband assigned to each wife a plot on which she grew maize for household consumption. Men either gave their divorced sisters separate plots, or, more usually, provided them with small rations in return for their labor.

To ensure that each household had a sufficient land base to minimize risk, the village customary tenure system, as it evolved through the emergence of *nabodoono* and the appointment of village councils, provided a number of ways for men to acquire land: through inheritance, by request through the village council, through purchase, or as a short-term, long-term, or permanent gift. Farmers regularly lent and borrowed land to meet seasonal needs as well. A brief description of each means of obtaining land clarifies its significance within the overall land tenure system.

Inheritance

In 1987 and 1988, most village households had inherited a significant portion of their land, reflecting the fact that Loc population growth had been largely the result of births rather than immigration since the 1970s. Under customary tenure land generally passed from a father to his sons, even though Islamic law and Somali state law (Law No. 23, Article 155) stipulated that daughters must inherit land as well (another indication of Loc villagers resisting government intervention in their lives). Sometimes sons chose to divide each individual parcel, especially on dhasheeg land, but more often sons divided up the parcels intact among themselves, weighing the factors of location, size, and soil type. Resident sons could claim the land of nonresident sons only until the latter returned to the village. If a man died leaving only young sons, a grown daughter or the widow could manage the farms until the sons came of age, but the man's brother or older sons by another wife could also reclaim the land until the young sons grew up. The two widows in Loc living under these conditions were nearly destitute, dependent on handouts from their former brothers-in-law and their brothers.

Villagers reported that inheritance disputes have been rare in Loc. In fact, one of the most bitterly remembered inheritance disputes recounted to me involved a daughter who tried to inherit a parcel of land following her father's death. As the widowed mother recounted the story, of her three sons and one daughter, one permanently ill son wanted only one small farm and a second son left the village to take up pastoralism, claiming none of his father's land. The third son was to inherit the rest. He left some of the parcels fallow, as the total was far more than he needed or was able to farm. The daughter's husband divorced her, leaving her without any independent means of support. Backed by her mother, she pleaded with her brother to be given a parcel of land from which to support herself and her children. The brother refused, and the mother went so far as to take the matter before the village council. She described to me how she "screamed and screamed, but they wouldn't listen." In 1988, the daughter was working for the brother on his inherited land in return for the food he provided. Loc men and the vast majority of women were adamant that women were not supposed to inherit land but instead should labor on male-held land.

Village Council Allocation

The second most common way in which Loc households had acquired their land by 1987–88 was through the village council. Either a man could find a piece of bushland himself and then obtain clearance to farm it from the village council, or he could ask the village council to find him a free area of land. The council's responsibilities were to ascertain the boundaries of each new farm and to make sure that newly claimed farms had no previous claimants. The presence of the council ensured a community oversight of village lands, but the council had no authority to reclaim or redistribute land, to monitor sales, or to block outsiders from acquiring land. If a villager had a very large parcel of land of which he farmed only a portion, the council could legitimately ask him if he might be willing to give up a portion for someone else, but it had no way to enforce such a request. Conversely, if a farmer had more land than he needed and no one to whom to give, lend, or sell the excess, he could tell the village council to reallocate it to someone else. Sheikh Cabdulle, who tried to use sorcery to murder the woman who did not return his love, provides an example of the minimal degree of control maintained by the village over villagers' individual farms. Following Sheikh Cabdulle's forced departure from the village, his kin (he had no immediate family) harvested the maize on his farm and sold the production to pay the fine owed the victim. During the next season, a relative used the field for his own crop. When Sheikh Cabdulle quietly returned six months later, he began planting his field again. The village council had never discussed what was to be done with his land after his departure or his right to it once he returned, since this was considered a matter for Sheikh Cabdulle and his extended family.

Although the village council held authority over mediating disputes, in no way did villagers view the council as the owner or authority over what individual men/households/families did with their farms. In this sense land tenure in Loc represents a variation on the common African model of individual/household usufruct rights to community land. Loc villagers placed much more emphasis on individual rights to land than on community controls over land use, did not view rights over land as symbolically vested in the council or the headman, and did not practice any collective form of organized periodic redistribution.[5]

Land Sales

In addition to acquiring land through inheritance and with the approval of the village council, villagers also were regularly buying and selling land to each other and to immigrants by the 1970s. Although population pressure is commonly considered the prime impetus for land sales within African customary tenure systems, land sales in land-abundant Loc resulted from a number of other factors as well. Until the mid-1980s, villagers primarily sold land to newcomers—people who went on to acquire land through the village council within a few years. One of the last reer Sabdow arrivals provides an example of this process. Weheliye settled in Bunbunle with his siblings as an adolescent in 1974. After arriving in Bunbunle, he and his older brother bought their first farm, a cleared doonk parcel in Iskorex of less than half a hectare. Four years later, the village council approved Weheliye's request for nine-tenths of a hectare of riverbank land in Danballey in anticipation of his marriage.[6] With the imminent birth of his third child in 1986 the village council approved his request to clear a third farm of three-fifths of a hectare on the northern side of Dhasheeg Loc. His elderly ailing mother, Xalima, moved into his compound that year as well, as did Weheliye's wife's sister from Baardheere to help with childcare and farm work. Weheliye's trajectory as a farmer over the fifteen-year period (1973–1988) shows the common progression from newcomer to villager and from young bachelor to husband and father of a growing household. As Weheliye's history shows, sales allowed more recent newcomers (post-1970) a way to demonstrate their desire to become villagers and to more rapidly move into farming than if they had to clear a new farm. Sales also provided people moving away from Loc with an opportunity to earn a few shillings for cleared land, and villagers saw the purchase of cleared doonk land as an opportunity to avoid the enormous labor inputs required to clear a parcel of virgin forest. Furthermore, buying a parcel of cleared land granted far more tenure security than borrowing it.

As is typical throughout much of Africa, fruit trees could also be sold separately from the land they grew on, and a few Loc villagers sold a tree or two in the past. I found no indication in oral histories that land or tree sales had ever been controlled by the *nabadoono* or the village council, and by the 1980s farmers permanently leaving the area always sold their land or trees to whomever they wanted, even to nonvillagers. While the sale of land has never been prohibited, the practice and prices have always been low. By the late 1980s, land sales to outsiders were increasing and were of a very different nature, as we shall see.

Gifts

While not as common as inheritance, individual claim through the village council, or purchase, sometimes a person received a gift of land from a friend or neighbor. About a quarter of Loc's households in 1988 had received a parcel of land as a gift from friends with more land than they needed. While such transactions were not marked in any formal or public way, Loc villagers recognized gifts of land as a legitimate transferral of tenure rights.

Loans

Loc households depended on meeting their changing seasonal needs through the widespread practice of borrowing farmland. Lenders never required a payment; rather the lending of land was an integral, reciprocal, and mutually advantageous aspect of local tenure. The reciprocal obligations involved in lending and borrowing were to avoid starvation, not to amass wealth. Thus no farmer would refuse a request to borrow, as to do so might very well jeopardize the subsistence of the would-be borrower's family. Most households borrowed land in most seasons, and reported doing so for as long as they could remember. The motives varied: after a flood people would borrow high land; during a drought or jilaal, dhasheeg land was in high demand; a young newly engaged girl might borrow a small plot to earn some income for household items prior to her wedding. Women benefited from the ability to borrow land independently of their husbands. Although the amounts women borrowed typically measured just a few square paces which yielded only a few baskets of corn or sesame, women could plant what they wanted and use the production for petty cash, for a daughter's wedding gifts, or for household food needs beyond what was allocated by the husband.

The Overall Picture

The piecemeal fashion of acquiring land, combined with the desire to spread landholdings over the three different land types of dhasheeg, riverbank, and doonk, produced a risk-minimizing pattern of fragmented landholdings. In 1987–88, Loc households held an average of 3.8 parcels of land each, cultivating in that year an average of 3.4 hectares of land per household scattered throughout the village land base.

Most Loc households also had land in bush which had not been cultivated in years, but over which they still maintained full and recognized rights. Most (about two-thirds) of Loc households did, in fact, have parcels of land spread over the three land types. The few families in 1988 without dhasheeg land held extensive farms in productive doonk areas, but were able to borrow parcels of dhasheeg whenever they desired.

Loc families rotated their use of their fragmented parcels depending on the season, the climate, their access to labor, whether adjoining farms were being cultivated, or whether they needed maize for food or sesame for cash. The fluctuating nature of household composition—due to deaths, divorces, marriages, births, fostering, illnesses, and so on—meant that families had to balance the possibilities for cultivation resulting from the climate each season with their available labor pool. The extent of household indebtedness also affected the family's choice of what to plant where in any season. A family with food needs and higher than normal needs for cash to pay back loans would probably have to work harder (farm more land) than it would under less financially strained conditions.

An example of the choices for cultivation made during 1987–88 by the relatively successful household led by Sheikh Cabdi Nur demonstrates this family's strategy over the course of a year. Sheikh Cabdi Nur was a man in his late fifties in 1988. His first wife, Xalima, was also in her fifties, and they had three children living at home with them: a son, Keerow, twenty years old; another son, Axmed, sixteen years old; and a daughter, Xabiba, fifteen years old. Their twelve-year-old grandson by a daughter who lived in Bu'aale also lived with them. Cabdi's second wife Caddey was twenty-six years old and had a one-year-old baby daughter. Cabdi had three farms: a doonk/dhasheeg farm of 2.1 hectares (Farm 1), a doonk farm of 1.7 hectares (Farm 2), and a 2.8-hectare doonk/dhasheeg farm (Farm 3).

The devastating 1987 flood wiped out all of the growing crops on Cabdi's Farms 1 and 3. Some corn was left standing on Farm 2. The water receded from Farm 2 first, and Cabdi and Xalima replanted all at once with sesame in early June, as they needed to repay debts to a Bu'aale businessman incurred for purchasing food during the peak of the flood. As water receded from Farm 1, Cabdi lent three plots to relatives whose land was still under water. He assigned Xalima a large plot on which to grow maize, which she and her children planted bit by bit beginning in early June as the water receded. Cabdi planted the rest of Farm 1 (the dhasheeg portion) in sesame, beginning in early June, planting bit by bit as the water receded. By the time he had finished planting his sesame in late July, it was time to weed the sesame on Farm 2 and the maize on Farm 1. Harvesting of the sesame on Farm 2 was accomplished in late

August, after which the gradual harvesting of maize on Farm 1 began, continuing into September. In early September harvesting of sesame on Farm 1 began, which continued for several weeks as it matured.

By late September Cabdi's Farms 1 and 2 were completely harvested, and water had finally begun to recede on Farm 3. Cabdi had acquired this farm in 1970 after the birth of his first son, but he had left it idle since 1977. In 1986 Cabdi and Keerow recleared it in order to grow crops for Keerow's marriage. Beginning in late September 1987, Keerow planted some maize, but primarily sesame to be sold to finance his wedding. Since both Keerow and his younger sister Xabiba were marrying that January (1988), neither Farm 1 nor Farm 2 were planted that dayr (1987), as there was much work to be done at home in preparation for the weddings and not much rain. After Keerow's crop was harvested, Cabdi and Xalima borrowed a portion of dhasheeg from friends in the next village to the north of Loc on which to plant sesame to cover their remaining wedding expenses and to get them through until the spring crops were ready.

This description shows how Cabdi was able to allocate labor over the course of the year to different farms and different crops in order to meet the household demands for food, cash, and the differing abilities of individual household members (a young wife unable to work much, an older wife with several unmarried children to help her, an older unmarried son and daughter whose labor he still controlled). The next year undoubtedly brought changes in his strategy of land use and allocation of labor, with the loss of control over the labor of his son and daughter, the increased working ability of his young wife (providing there was not a new child) and grandson, and a different set of priorities for food versus cash crops.

Thus households made choices about how they would use their land in response to the highly variable conditions of life (and health), climate, and microecologies. Having access to enough land to cover their bases and having the option of abandoning land for periods of time without losing claim to it were critical to the success of local farmers in maintaining themselves year after year. Customary tenure as it evolved over eight decades in Loc offered local farmers flexibility, adaptability, and tenure security—three critical components of household sustainability in the middle Jubba.

Local Stratification

While offering tenure security and sustainability, customary practice and regional infrastructure inhibited the growth of stratification within mid-valley communities. There is no evidence to suggest, for example, that Loc's customary tenure practices benefited some but excluded others, or that certain categories of people (identified on the basis of clan, ethnic ancestry, age, and so on) had better access to land or opportunities for wealth than others. This is an important point, for several scholars have written about the ability of local elites in African communities to amass resources (through land concentration) to the detriment of their neighbors.[7]

With little opportunity for any mid-valley villager to hold livestock or to obtain off-farm—especially government—employment, the agricultural sector offered one of the only avenues toward wealth accumulation and thus stratification. Up through the time of my visit, Loc villagers found themselves collectively denied access to possibilities for wealth accumulation within agriculture as well, although not for lack of effort. For example, during my stay a group of Loc villagers tried to form an irrigation association by digging channels to connect their farms and pooling their money to buy one of the diesel-powered water pumps brought to the middle valley by a visiting civil servant/businessman. Despite their hard work and optimism, they were unsuccessful; the pumps were unofficially reserved only for civil servants. Bank loans in general were completely unavailable to villagers, although local businessmen or government officials offered private loans at usurious rates which villagers struggled to pay back. Just prior to my arrival in Loc, for example, everyone in the village except six or seven people borrowed money from a Bu'aale businessman after the late gu flood destroyed their crops. He required repayment in sesame from the dayr harvest at a rate of 2,200 Somali shillings per *kintal*,[8] when the going rate in Mogadishu and Jilib for sesame had reached 7,000 to 9,000 Somali shillings per *kintal*. With no other options, the villagers had been forced to accept these terms.

Road conditions equally handicapped everyone's attempt at marketing surplus or cash crops in towns outside the middle valley, a situation that encouraged farmers collectively to hire trucks or contract with itinerant traders from Mogadishu to buy their surplus. Some farmers did occasionally receive periodic windfalls—from a bumper sesame crop or a honey collecting excursion—which they unilaterally reinvested in small stores that opened and closed rapidly along Loc's central walkway. The stores stocked tiny amounts of household basics, such as sugar, tea, matches, powdered soap packets, and oil (which people bought by the tablespoon), serving as household pantries for the proprietor as much as places of business for the community.[9] Many Loc farmers had experimented over the years with different cash crops, such as watermelons, tobacco, and cotton, but found seeds difficult to obtain and marketing unpredictable. Many farmers' attempts to plant fruit trees (mango, papaya, banana) on their riverbank land were consistently thwarted by floods or wild animals, although several kept trying.

Given the limited opportunities available in the middle valley for acquiring wealth through off-farm employment, commercial ventures, or through improving agricultural productivity or marketing cash crops, wealth in land and labor served as two of the only markers of intravillage stratification. These two factors were strongly correlated—larger households farmed more land than smaller households and the larger landowning households supported more people than smaller landholding households—suggesting that differentiation in land and labor was based on factors relating to the household life cycle. To get a sense of the degree to which households with different amounts of land and labor also had different amounts of cash available, I collected annual budgets from several households of varying sizes and landholdings. Their similar lifestyles, diets, and material goods hinted at what turned out to be their similar incomes and expenditures per capita. In fact, one of the only indications of inequality I uncovered in Loc was a slight differentiation among households in the quality and quantity of their dhasheeg holdings. Although the practice of partible inheritance and the rapid acquisition of dhasheeg land over the past five decades was evening out the amount of dhasheeg land held per household, descendants of Loc's first settlers (especially Isaaq's son) continued to hold more and better quality dhasheeg land per household than others.

Several aspects of village land use besides partible inheritance mitigated this stratification in dhasheeg holdings, however. The widespread practice of lending and borrowing land between households ensured that families with limited dhasheeg holdings would be able to borrow more for free if needed. The existence of the dhasheeglike commons, the Siimow, helped equalize access to dhasheeg land. Finally, when dhasheegs were full of water, individual tenure rights ceased and anyone could harvest lily tubers, fish, and utilize the water of the dhasheegs.

While inequities in dhasheeg holdings represented one form of (rather limited) stratification, gender stratification was another inequity that was not easily mediated within the village. Rights to land guaranteed to women through both the shariʿa and state law were locally ignored, and the vast majority of women never received rights to land independently of men. While a few women had been able to inherit land, particularly where there were no male heirs, a number of Loc women complained to me that their system—which made women dependent on men for accessing land—was inequitable. In order to get around customary constraints on women's independent access to land, many women in polygynous households with grown sons avoided their husbands' control by forming farming partnerships with their sons, who as men could acquire land, but over whom they retained parental authority.[10] While these partnerships afforded women some independent income and production, the women still operated within the male-dominated system of tenure.

A final aspect of intravillage stratification was perhaps the most ominous and indicative of future trends. During my stay, there were two local men who had formed state political connections outside the village which they used for personal gain at the expense of their neighbors. Both were born in the regional capital and had lived most of their lives in town, but had family connections in Loc. Both inherited land in Loc and eventually came to live in Loc as adults in order to farm their land. One was the local party representative, appointed by the government. Through his connections in Bu'aale, he was able to register his farm, but in the process also registered as his own a neighboring farm then in bush (for a combined registered area of six hectares recorded in the registry). The owners of the neighboring farm learned of their loss when the party representative brought in a bulldozer to clear the parcel they had left fallow. Many villagers treated him with polite and civil dislike, and he continually suffered from lesions, boils, and painful skin ulcers which he blamed on sorcery perpetrated by the family whose farm he surreptitiously registered.

The other man was once the official marketing representative for the village (farmers were required to sell all their production to the national marketing board until 1984), but was charged with embezzling from village accounts and served time in prison. After his release, he was able to return to Loc, where his parents, siblings, wife, and children still lived, and resume his farming activities. While serving as the marketing representative he had registered an area of land which included his farm and a large portion of the Siimow, over which he had not yet attempted to exercise his legal rights in 1988 (for a total of nine hectares recorded in the registry). He had also registered another nine-and-one-half-hectare farm in the name of his son, who worked as a driver for the Ministry of Livestock in Bu'aale. While he was much more a part of village life than the local party representative and participated in village affairs as an elder, villagers considered him untrustworthy, and they humorously and not so humorously joked about his tendency to steal other men's belongings, including their wives. He was not an ambitious farmer, and being unclear about the boundaries of his registered area he was not in a position to physically dispossess his neighbors of their land.

Despite their somewhat ambiguous position as part villager and part outsider, both of these men lived in the village and could participate in village affairs. Aside from gossip and sorcery, villagers had little ability to limit their actions outside of the village. While these men were perhaps marginally better off than other villagers (as a result of their political connections and their land titles), the disparity was not reflected in a higher standard of living, greater local influence (if anything they had less influence over village affairs than other men), more material goods, better diet, or better health. More important was the fact that they were able to gain registered rights to their neighbors' land for their personal benefit while continuing to live as villagers. They represented the first local expression that things were changing in the middle Jubba in ways over which villagers had little control.

In sum, stratification within Loc was neither obvious nor important in structuring social or economic life. There was no local ruling village elite, no class or group that was economically better off, and no group that was politically better connected than other villagers. While there were at least two individuals who were able to establish political connections with regional or national level figures or agencies, their influence was extremely limited, although their behavior was indicative of the tenure changes beginning in the middle valley. The major threat to the economy and subsistence of Loc and other middle valley villages was located to a far greater extent outside of these villages, in the form of regional "big-men" (Goheen 1988) from Bu'aale and national elites.

But who were these regional big men and national elites? The next section initially takes us outside of the valley and back in time to assess in summary fashion the wider context of regional and national political economy in the twentieth century that produced regional big men and national elites. Events outside the valley—new forms of wealth accumulation, the increasing political marginalization of agricultural southerners, growing state and international interest in agriculture, the influx of foreign aid funds—contributed to a dynamic situation of class formation, regional stratification, and state efforts to assume control of productive activities and resources. These trends culminated in land grabbing, ecological destruction, and agricultural decline in the Jubba valley by the 1980s when these elites began arriving to claim rights over valley land.

Regional Stratification in the Pre-Barre Years

Up until the 1980s the prevailing academic understanding of Somalia as a "pastoral democracy" (I. M. Lewis 1961) grounded in an egalitarian ethos overlooked any hint of significant class stratification. Viewing Somalia as an egalitarian nation of pastoral nomads masks the kinds of inequalities, class differences, and economic pressures that contributed to the speculative and violent rush for agricultural land in a previously marginalized corner of Somalia. Over the past decade, several scholars have developed alternative views of Somali society which trace the regional stratifications and class divisions that emerged during the colonial period and expanded after independence. These studies argue that during the twentieth century new occupational opportunities, new export markets, and Somalia's increasing involvement in the world economy differentiated and stratified the Somali population, transforming Somalia into a class-based society.[11] These national and regional transformations reverberated throughout all areas of Somali society, finding particular expression over the last two decades in the political economy of land tenure in the Jubba valley.

The North

The colonial period nurtured some forms of stratification and introduced others in different regions of Somalia. Several scholars writing about northern Somalia have argued that class-based cleavages arose in the north through the British-directed commercialization of the livestock sector and the creation of a class of traders, through colonial and postcolonial state expansion and the emergence of a class of state employees, and through the influx of remittances from Somalis working in the Arabic peninsula.[12]

Britain's establishment of a garrison at Aden in 1839, which served as a station for ships sailing between India and Europe, introduced the first significant demand for Somali livestock abroad. Aden's need for meat precipitated British interest in the Somali coast as a supplier of livestock and livestock products.[13] By 1886, a very few British authorities settled on the northern coast to ensure an uninterrupted flow of livestock to Aden. By the turn of the century, "livestock had unquestionably become the most important commodity in the Somali trade with the outside world" (Abdi Samatar 1989:32). Over the next five decades, the steady demand for livestock and British colonial interest in the trade resulted in a reorganization of internal Somali production practices and trade arrangements to ensure a continual supply of livestock to the northern ports. British-supported Somali traders and urban merchants gradually replaced the traditional clan-mediated caravan system of trade in the Somali interior, resulting in the emergence of a state-backed "merchant class." Abdi Samatar (1989) describes how pastoralists throughout the north were drawn into the sphere of merchant capitalism, to the benefit of the colonial government and the new Somali mercantile class. "Born in the pastoral nomadic sector (for the most part), but with subsequent commercial, urban, and overseas experiences, the Somali petit-bourgeoisie was an amalgam of truck owners, traders, clerks, teachers, drivers, and livestock brokers . . . [but] was not a dominant class whose members owned and controlled the means of economic production" (Geshekter 1985:32). Rather, scholars claim that this loose group constituted a clearly differentiated mercantile-state class which exploited the pastoralist class through merchant capitalism.[14] Lidwien Kapteijns (1991:9) argues that after World War II, the "commercial capitalist way of life" of the Somali middle class which invested capital in the import-export trade gained hegemony through the support of the colonial state, and became wealthy and powerful "at the expense of an increasingly intensely exploited pastoral sector." Together, Kapteijns (1991) and Samatar (1989, 1992) argue that the commercial capitalism fostered by urban merchants backed by the colonial state transformed and destroyed (traditional) Somali society by nurturing consumerism, by introducing unfair terms of trade which favored the merchant and state class to the detriment of the pastoralist class, by discouraging the reinvestment of resources into the pastoralist sector, and by introducing a new basis for political power in class rather than traditional corporate kin groupings.

Several scholars contest this argument. Their studies suggest that despite wealth differentiation, wealth from trading did trickle throughout the producing population, that strong personal ties linked pastoralist producers and traders, and that some pastoralist producers were wealthy enough to extend financial support to less secure traders.[15] Although the extent of class differentiation may be unclear, the twentieth century clearly witnessed the growth of a commercially oriented livestock export economy in northern Somalia, supported by the colonial government, which introduced a new form of differentiation in the region. Licensed livestock exporters could also take advantage of the *franco valuta* system by investing their hard currency profits—derived from the difference between the official rate and the higher price actually paid by the buyer—in imported consumer goods for resale.[16] Furthermore, the departure of hundreds of thousands of mostly northern Somalis to the Arabian peninsula during the 1960s and 1970s brought a flow of remittances to family members at home. Many of these laborers abroad also participated in the *franco valuta* system through which they invested their foreign currency earnings in consumer goods, later sold for a profit in Somalia.

The South

In the south, class differentiation proceeded at a slower, if steady, pace. The end of slavery meant waning fortunes for Shabeelle slaveholding clans as the avenue toward wealth accumulation through exporting cash crops closed. Livestock marketing increased following abolition, although Peter Little (1996) argues that a class of large export-oriented livestock traders did not emerge until after the 1960s. Incipient stratification of the southern livestock sector had begun after the turn of the century with the large-scale immigration of Herti pastoralists and traders, who competed for local ascendancy with the Maxamed Subeer pastoralists and traders.[17] In the agricultural sphere, Italian policies to develop an export-oriented plantation sector funneled profits into Italian, not Somali, hands. Rather than producing a class of Somali/Gosha market traders and commercial businessmen, agricultural commodities produced by forced labor were sold by Italian middlemen. The cumulative effect of these policies in southern Somalia was, as we have seen, the creation of stratified racialized groups. The Italian colonial period also produced a class of Somali civil servants dependent on state employment for their livelihood. By the 1950s, the economic and political dominance of Italian plantation owners together with Somali civil servants constituted what Menkhaus (1989:312) called "a collaborative Italian-Somali elite [which] governed affairs."

The Postcolonial State in 1960

Following independence and unification in 1960, two significant and linked economic changes further contributed to the creation of national elites and to regional stratification within the unified postcolonial nation: the tremendous influx of international aid and the huge growth in public employment. Somalia received more foreign aid per capita in the 1960s than any other African country, creating what David Laitin called "the first generation of millionaires" (1976:452). "This [aid] helped to pay for increasing numbers of bureaucrats and parliamentarians, who lived ostentatious and opulent lives in Modagishu, and for a five-fold increase in the size of the Somali army" (Laitin and Samatar 1984:62). David Laitin and Said Samatar (1984:62) estimated that by the mid-1970s about 40 percent of the paid work force in Somalia drew government salaries. With this trend, Somalia's postcolonial state resembled other independent African states in its "rapid crystallization of a state bourgeoisie, which took form around the political and bureaucratic apparatus of the public sector" (Young 1982:81).

The expanded opportunities for amassing wealth through government employment and overseas employment during the 1960s and 1970s were not evenly distributed throughout the population, however. Somalis in the south, including riverine farmers, found themselves increasingly removed from national politics, from access to international aid, and from domestic and foreign commercial opportunities. Wage labor opportunities abroad were overwhelmingly available only to northerners. The success of the Somali Youth League (SYL) party, which drew its support from the central and northern regions, in dominating the national government after independence meant the increasing exclusion of southern members of the Xisbia party. As a result, southerners not only lacked a strong representation in the postcolonial government, but they also lacked opportunities for obtaining government jobs, for claiming control over or rights to foreign aid, and for commandeering government resources.[18] As Cassanelli explains, "Apart from their underrepresentation in the national assemblies and legislatures of the 1960s and 1970s, people from the Jubba valley and Baay regions were virtually absent from ministerial positions, diplomatic posts, and national educational and cultural institutions throughout the post-independence years" (1996:17). Furthermore, Barre's choice of Maxad-tiray in 1972 as Somalia's official language linguistically as well as politically marginalized southern Maay-maay speakers.[19] By the mid-1970s, riverine and interriverine southern farmers and agropastoralists formed a self-sustaining, subsistence-oriented, politically marginalized, lower-status occupational class within the context of the Somali nation-state.

The Jubba Valley

In addition to the emerging forms of regional stratification described above, Menkhaus (1989) notes that two new forms of stratification developed within lower Gosha communities during the decades of the 1950s and 1960s. First, a small number of Somalis, with some Arabs and even a few Gosha villagers (Menkhaus names four) managed to develop small export-oriented plantations along the lower river. This is remarkable not because of the numbers involved, which were few (totaling forty in 1960), and not because of their impact, which was slight as many never developed or quickly failed entirely, but rather because their presence signaled the initial interest of regional and urban-based elites in Jubba valley land. Most of the Somali landlords were deputies in Parliament or held other high administrative posts who were looking for investment opportunities and the prestige of owning a banana plantation.[20] The limited export market for Somali bananas stifled the investment value of Jubba valley land, however, especially since other, more profitable investments were available, such as in livestock marketing or urban real estate.[21]

Second, these decades witnessed the increasing commercialization of lower Gosha villages "in sale of land, labor, grain, and cash crops" (Menkhaus 1989:337). Growing commercialization resulted in emerging forms of stratification within lower Gosha communities, as wealthier villagers earned money from selling cotton or grain, with which they bought riverbank land, hired wage laborers, or invested in small local shops. Local class distinctions became evident in the changing base of support for the southern-based Xisbia political party, as a few wealthier Gosha farmers deserted Xisbia for the nationally dominant SYL, which offered the possibility of patronage politics.[22] This shift in political alliance by wealthier Gosha farmers echoed the political opportunism demonstrated by the opposition after the SYL victory in the 1969 elections: the entire parliamentary opposition except the former premier abandoned their parties to join the SYL.[23]

During these decades, the middle Jubba remained almost completely outside of national politics, cut off from export markets because the lower Jubba "banana belt" of export-oriented production did not extend upriver, and largely outside of domestic commercial market opportunities. Middle valley farmers grew some cotton and sold some grain, but marketing opportunities remained limited due to poor or impassable roads.

Several trends which proved to have significant implications for the political economy of the Jubba River valley had thus emerged by the early 1970s. First, new forms of wealth accumulation had begun to differentiate classes at the national level. The marginalization of southern farmers from national politics, in language, and from participation in the global economy had become an enduring aspect of national political and economic life, which reflected their social standing within the Somali "nation" as well. The one southern export, bananas, fell from 50 percent of national export earnings at independence to just over 10 percent of export earnings in the late 1970s.[24] Furthermore, export earnings from bananas remained in the hands of the tiny class of mercantile-state elite in the south and were not by any means distributed throughout the southern agricultural population. Second, the development of this mercantile-state elite class marked the first glimmers of national elite interest in Jubba valley land, which remained slight during the 1960s, but which forecast a devastating future. Third, the huge influxes of foreign aid under the control of a growing class of civil servants typified the boom years of the 1960s. While Western aid to Somalia virtually ceased during the 1970s when Somalia was under Soviet patronage, the 1960s anticipated the effects of the return of Western development funds and "wisdom" a decade later.

Accelerated Stratification: The Barre Years

The 1970s marked a transition in Somalia's economy, when Barre, under the banner of "scientific socialism," attempted state-directed economic development through extending state control over many areas of the economy and production. His new policies nationalized financial institutions and the few industries operating in Somalia, established state marketing boards for construction materials and agricultural produce, developed state farms, and enacted new laws to bring control over lucrative sources of capital under the state. Two significant events helped to derail his hopes for economic growth and national integration. The great drought of 1974–75 interrupted a state-supported national literacy program, when hundreds of thousands of drought-stricken nomads were resettled into relief centers, state farms, or state fishing cooperatives at tremendous government, and eventually donor, expense. Three years later, following the enormous expenditure of state funds during the unsuccessful Ogaadeen war and faced with rising foreign debt, Somalia once again received a huge influx of more than a million war refugees who flooded into government relief centers throughout the country.[25]

When the Soviets abandoned Somalia for Ethiopia in 1977, the Somali economy was on the point of collapse due to the combined effects of war, drought, and Barre's unsuccessful economic policies. Livestock exports, still handled by private traders rather than the state, had become almost the sole source of export earnings by the late 1970s.[26] Into this context of massive population dislocations and economic deterioration, foreign donors began pouring billions of dollars in international assistance. While the initial assistance was primarily for drought relief, the influx of donor funds quickly took on a political patina during the next decade. The reasons for high donor—especially American—interest in Somalia in the late 1970s and early 1980s have been discussed at length by policy analysts, who argue that Cold War geopolitics, American fears of Middle East oil embargoes, and a perceived need for military bases in the Horn resulted in a flood of politically motivated foreign aid.[27] David Rawson calculates that foreign donors spent over $2.5 billion—an absolutely staggering amount—between 1980 and 1989 in Somalia on development projects, economic programs, and military technology (1994:171). Tapping into development funds became the biggest national industry.

In the face of a rapidly deteriorating domestic economy with few opportunities for wealth accumulation, accessing state resources became the primary avenue for personal enrichment as well as family subsistence for Somalia's wealthier urban classes. Numerous observers of Somalia's political economy during the late 1970s and 1980s describe the frenzied atmosphere of private profiteering from government resources which characterized the boom years of development aid. While these observers have written from different theoretical viewpoints about Somalia and have presented differing analyses of Somalia's collapse, their descriptions of the postcolonial private accumulation of Somalia's public resources are depressingly similar. A few quotations from various sources illustrate this point. Abdi Samatar and A. I. Samatar explained how

> the absence of a dynamic and expanding productive base made access to state resources, and their distribution, the central objects of competition and envy. . . . The entire country has suffered severe setbacks caused by economic inertia, intense inflationary pressures induced by the [Ogaadeen] war, and the cost of a large and unproductive bureaucracy. The disorder engendered by this process has led to the misappropriation of the nation's wealth by officials in ways that were previously unimaginable. It is usually in the upper echelons of the public service that the bulk of the sacking of the commons takes place, while most bureaucrats, whose salaries have been virtually swallowed by inflation, garner whatever they can by exploiting their offices. (1987:681,684)

Martin Doornbis and John Markakis described how "the new social strata that emerged [during the postcolonial period]—merchants, petty bourgeoisie, intelligentsia—found their material and social welfare depended very much upon the state. For the latter two groups, the state became their sole employer and patron. With the influx of foreign aid—Somalia was especially favored . . . the state emerged as a relatively abundant source of resources and, inevitably, it became the bone of contention" (1994:86). Analyzing the impact of foreign aid, Rawson wrote about some of the effects of private appropriation of development funds: "Development programs became channels for winning that struggle [between elites] for power and perquisites, rather than investments in Somalia's welfare and economic future. . . . From the Central Bank, the Commercial Bank, and the Ministry of Finance, counterpart currencies flowed into private hands, fostering demand for imported goods, creating an acute trade imbalance, and generating inflationary pressure within the economy. . . . Both parliamentary and military governments tended toward arbitrary rule and control of economic resources for the benefit of the ruling elite" (1994:158,171). Laitin and Samatar (1987:95) estimated that government officials embezzled 40 percent of each development contract; Rawson writes of "an 83 percent rate of implementation slippage" (1994:180) in Somalia's twelve largest development projects while claiming greater slippage existed in smaller projects. Writing about the final months before collapse, Simons described how economic uncertainty and unpredictability encouraged urban civil servants to take what they could as quickly as possible:

> [F]oreign aid projects . . . were all temporary. Likewise, who remained in charge of them was continually shifted by those in control of the government who, themselves, were often demoted or replaced. Therefore, for many people it only made sense to get all they could while they could, whether through means others

would label corruption, graft, or nepotism. As a result, with money and other opportunities having been siphoned off by the men at the top, resources would often dry up for those below, as well as for those the project, agency, or ministry was intended to assist. Thus, one lesson learned by government employees attempting to work their way up the snakes-and-ladders board was to seize opportunity, and money, whenever possible. (1995:126)

Cassanelli described how "those who got rich quick by milking the cows of international refugee relief, foreign development aid, and military assistance," together with livestock traders, overseas workers, and import-export merchants, "managed to educate their children overseas, build lavish villas for themselves or for rental to foreign expatriates, and purchase fleets of cars with hard currency that was supposedly scarce in the country" during the time period when Somalia was officially one of the world's ten poorest countries (1996:20). Daniel Compagnon minces no words in his description of the effects of private appropriation of national funds:

Embezzlement of public funds, corruption of ministers and civil servants in connection with public markets and development projects, baksheeshes at all levels of the bureaucracy, illegal trafficking by relatives or friends of the president—all these were tightly linked to a direct access to state power. . . . [I]nvestment capital was predominantly oriented towards speculative trading activities and all kinds of illegal trafficking detrimental to the productive side of the economy. A stratum of wealthy and corrupt businessmen (many of whom were penniless in the early 1970s) arose from all the clans. (1992:8,9)

Crawford Young (1982:81) notes a similar process of bureaucratic class practice linked to parallel market development throughout Africa.

Together, these writers (and many others) describe the national economy of the late 1970s and 1980s as one of increasing uncertainty, inflation, and competition among urban elites for private claim to state resources. The result was not a solidified class of entrepreneurs, civil servants, and politicians engaged in a mutually supportive effort at class domination and accumulation. Rather, private appropriation of state resources was an atomistic, inchoate, and opportunistic process of changing players sometimes aligning with each other and sometimes competing. As elsewhere in Africa, class formation was dynamic and fluctuating and much more closely linked to state-formation than in the West. As Young has described for Africa in general,

the state bourgeoisie has little autonomy relative to the state; its standing in society is not rooted in control of property, wealth, or productive facilities. An individual's class membership is contingent upon remaining within the orbit of established political authority; a fall from political grace can be exceedingly costly. . . . Because the state bourgeoisie is the internally dominant class, and because powerful state formations autonomous from the state are relatively lacking, the link between state and class in Africa is quite different from that which has evolved in the Western state. (Young 1982:82)

In Somalia, class formation linked to state control of resources increasingly differentiated urban merchants, businessmen, civil servants, and politicians from rural producers, educated from uneducated, politically connected from politically marginalized, and bilis from jareer as distinct classes in the national arena.

Just as private appropriation of state resources expanded during the 1980s, so did state appropriation of private resources. One of the few available areas for expanded state control over productive factors was agriculture. During the 1970s and 1980s the government introduced dozens of laws which extended state control over agriculture. Examining these laws and their effects reveals how they precipitated a decline in agricultural productivity while facilitating the continuing consolidation of a state-linked class.

The State Interest in Agriculture

In the face of economic collapse and political instability brought on by the loss of the Ogaadeen war and the influx of a massive refugee population in the late 1970s, and following an unsuccessful coup attempt and growing rebelliousness against his policies by many northerners, Barre had become increasingly desperate to regain control over his country, its people, and its resources. Unable to claim migrant workers' remittances, and unsuccessful in his attempts gain control over the northern economy by taxing livestock exports, limiting export licenses, or suppressing the lucrative qat trade,[28] Barre attempted to consolidate state control in other areas.[29] On the political front, he armed groups supporting his government against insurgent northerners, used the NSS to imprison his enemies in growing numbers, and increased his adroit use of favoritism to win supporters. On the economic front, he successfully sought financial support from the United States—which arrived in massive amounts during the 1980s—and continued to expand state control over agriculture.[30]

The need to resettle huge numbers of refugee nomads—perhaps then the largest refugee population in Africa—dovetailed with both Barre's interest in agriculture as a means toward national self-sufficiency and the widespread perspective that one way to "develop" nomads is to turn them into farmers. Agriculture emerged as a primary target of development interest by the Somali government and, in the 1980s, by foreign donors as a way to help get Somalia's economy back on track. Whereas control over livestock and livestock exports remained in private hands throughout the 1970s and 1980s (due in part to the powerful interest groups which controlled the livestock trade, and in part to Barre's reluctance to meddle in the sole remaining source of foreign currency besides donor funds),[31] Barre's attempts to develop agriculture were based on numerous laws and policies designed to extend state control over agriculture and agricultural production. Before the 1975 drought redirected state funds, 30 percent of the five-year plan budget for 1974–78 was earmarked for agricultural development[32]—which amounted to over seven times more than the plan included for the pastoral sector.[33] The funds were not directed at smallholders, but rather supported large-scale projects in keeping with Barre's vision of state-controlled agricultural development through "scientific socialism." Barre allocated agricultural development funds to expand and develop state farms in the river valleys, which were worked primarily by resettled refugee nomads (such as the 120,000 refugee nomads who were resettled onto state farms in the south following the 1974–75 drought),[34] to expand state agricultural industries such as the sugar processing plant on the lower Shabeelle and the new sugar project on the lower Jubba, and to resettle unemployed urban youths as farmers on state land through the Agricultural Crash Program.[35] Socialist policies encouraged farmers to pool their land into cooperatives by offering a promise of loans and inputs to participants. In addition to developing state-owned farms and agricultural industries, and offering incentives for cooperative farming, new laws mandated state control over private production as well. Until its repeal in 1984, Law No. 51 required private farmers to sell all their grain—beyond what they needed for domestic consumption—to the national marketing board, the Agricultural Development Corporation (ADC), which paid a lower than market price that did not keep up with inflation. By 1984, for example, the ADC purchase price for maize was 55 percent of the 1971 level in real terms.[36]

Far from boosting agricultural productivity, the effect of these new policies and laws was a decline in agricultural production, the development of parallel markets for grain, a growing national dependence on imported food, and rising landlessness and tensions in the river valleys. The three state farms developed in the lower Jubba valley in the late 1970s to produce rice and sugar for urban markets claimed 31,000 hectares of the best agricultural land in the area, alienating nearly 17,000 hectares of this claimed area by 1988, but were unable to meet even domestic demand for rice and sugar.[37] The projects uprooted dozens of lower Gosha villages and affected dozens more, but only provided jobs and resettlement opportunities on project lands for thousands of refugee nomads and Somalis from *outside* the area ("the soft-hairs," in the words of one villager). The thousands of Gosha villagers who lost some or all of their land to the state farms (without compensation) became landless laborers working for pitiful wages (or unripe bananas), sharecroppers, illegal squatters on land they had previously owned, or poverty-stricken immigrants to Modagishu. The fantastic total cost of the three projects—about U.S. $360 million paid for by Abu Dhabi, Saudi Arabia, OPEC, Kuwait, West Germany, and China in addition to Somalia—resulted in shockingly low production figures. But it provided large- and small-scale opportunities for private accumulation at all levels of the domestic management and operations hierarchy—through pilfering the operating budgets (in Somali shillings as well as in foreign currency) and the project inputs, from privately selling state farm production on the parallel market at inflated prices, and from petty graft and bribes solicited in return for the chance of a job or resettlement opportunity. The amount of money siphoned into private hands from the lower Jubba state farms amounted to tens of millions of dollars, although the Gosha villagers who lost their lands to the state farms received not a shilling.

The consequences of the laws encouraging cooperatives and requiring farmers to sell their surplus to the national marketing board (ADC) were not as dramatic, although they affected the entire valley. Middle valley villagers recalled to me how they would try to hide some portion of their surplus grain from marketing board buyers in order to sell it illicitly on the parallel market, a practice which certainly carried some risk. Villagers held bitter memories of ADC operations, recalling how after the farmers received the low state rates for their grain, which barely covered their production costs, the ADC employees would sell the grain from ADC stores on the parallel market for substantial private gain; or worse yet, they would horde it until there were local shortages, and then sell it back to the farmers at illegally inflated rates while pocketing the difference.

In contrast to their views of the ADC policy, villagers had initially supported the idea of cooperatives, although their enthusiasm eventually waned when they failed to receive promised state-supplied inputs.[38] In response to Barre's pronouncements about the benefits of cooperative farming and his promise of state assistance, twenty-one men in Loc formed a cooperative in the early 1980s to continue farming their extensive lands in Bancarab, which they had abandoned after the 1977 village consolidation. One man oversaw the labor rotation on the five-hectare farm. Each member was required to contribute two days of work a week. The farmers all started at one end of the farm and worked to the other end as a group. At harvest time, the cooperative members hired a truck to bring the production to Loc's central grassy plain, where it was stored in an underground storage pit to be divided evenly when the members' private grain stores were depleted. The cooperative fined members sixty Somali shillings for missing a day of work, or locked them in the village jail hut if they refused to complete their portion. After successfully farming the cooperative for three years, the members eventually abandoned the project in order to spend more time on their individual farms when the expected inputs from the government failed to materialize.[39] The story of this cooperative did not end here; we will return to its unjust conclusion below.

The largely donor-funded state farms on which resettled nomads were to work cooperatively also failed. The vast majority of resettled nomads abandoned the farms within a few years—55,000 abandoned the middle valley state farm at Dujuuma alone—to move into cities, emigrate to the Gulf states as migrant laborers, or return to pastoralism.

The effects in the Jubba valley of the state farms, the marketing requirements, and the support for cooperatives, while significant and reflective of the aura of private plundering of state resources, paled in comparison to the effects of the sweeping land law of 1975. The 1975 land law and its accompanying amendments introduced over the next decade set the terms of state domination over land tenure and land use, ushering in a new era of dramatic, far-reaching, and irreversible changes in the Jubba valley. The law and its amendments represented the culmination of Barre's attempts to extend state control over agricultural production, it transformed land use and land tenure practices, it amplified the negative effects of promised development projects in the valley, it facilitated the appropriation of Gosha land by people from outside the valley, and it claimed the racialized space of the Jubba valley for the benefit of the national elite. In short, it heralded the end of Gosha villagers' autonomy, self-sufficiency, and productivity and the beginning of unbridled and unproductive expropriation of Jubba valley land. The remainder of the chapter analyzes this law and its effects, demonstrating through the lens of land tenure the linked processes of class formation and state consolidation of power.

The Land Law

Originally introduced as part of Barre's socialist vision to eradicate the clan basis of authority over resources, the 1975 land law nationalized all land, made the state the sole legal authority over land acquisition and use, required individuals to obtain land titles through the government, and set up a national land registration system. The political agenda behind the law was to destroy clan control over land, "to integrate society and . . . [set up the state to] act as the central agent of social and economic progress" (Selassie 1986:11), and to "modernize" agricultural production and what was seen as an "archaic" tenure system (Gunn 1987:110). Allan Hoben explains, "Both the liberal democratic regime of the 1960s and the military socialist regime that followed were committed to the expansion of the modern sector and viewed the indigenous production systems of the traditional sector as inherently stagnant" (1988:205; see also Abdi Samatar 1989:97–98).

Government publicity accompanying the announcement of land reform emphasized "working the land together" through cooperatives, state farms and noncapitalist forms of development (SDR 1975). The failure of these agricultural schemes to boost production, coupled with the shift in patronage from the Soviets to the Americans, who lauded the benefits of privatization, resulted in a growing emphasis on individualized holdings during the 1980s.[40]

Donor support for the registration system had its roots in colonial attitudes and Western notions of private property. Based on the experience of Europe and America, many development planners have argued that title registration is an essential precondition for agricultural development because holding a title to a specific piece of land will give a farmer greater incentive to develop that land to its maximum potential.[41] For decades, planners have claimed that African customary tenure—which usually includes some form of community involvement in or control over allocating land—inhibits agricultural development because people remain uncertain about their long-term connection to specific plots of land. Furthermore, this "development wisdom" holds that customary tenure is static, rigid, and restrictive and results in low investment and poor farming techniques. Giving a farmer title to a specific plot of land, the argument goes, will raise tenure security, encourage investment, and facilitate loans, credit, and, in some cases, conveyancing. Furthermore, the creation of a national registry will facilitate national planning and tax collection. In keeping with this perspective, many African governments imposed title registration programs which privatized or individualized rights to land.

Somalia's law required anyone wishing to use land to apply to the Ministry of Agriculture (MOA) for usufruct rights. Following the lengthy application procedure, described below, the MOA could grant an applicant one individual leasehold title to a specific parcel of land for fifty years. The law allowed only one titleholder per household, and limited private individual leases to thirty hectares of irrigated land or sixty hectares of rainfed land. Reflecting state support for large-scale agriculture, the law allowed banana plantations of one hundred hectares, and placed no size limitations on cooperatives, state farms, private companies, or autonomous agencies. All registered land was to be developed for agricultural purposes within two years of registration, under threat of repossession by the state. The sale, lease, rental, subdivision, or mortgaging of a concession was illegal, although an heir could apply to the MOA to take up the lease following the death of the titleholder. The law required all farmers to immediately register their land, and stated that those who continued to farm without obtaining title were doing so illegally. Under the law, farmers held no legal rights whatsoever to land that they cultivated without a title.

The lengthy and complicated registration procedure required by the law (under the "Guidelines for the Giving of Farm Land" circular issued 24 May 1987) was supposed to begin with a letter of application to the district agricultural officer (DAO) of the Ministry of Agriculture. The DAO was required to post a notice of the application at the district party secretary's office, the district commissioner's office, the police station, the Ministry of Agriculture, and the village center where the requested land was located. After thirty days, a committee made up of the Department of Land and Water Resources (DLWR) (which became the Department of Irrigation and Land Use in 1988) district officer, a district policeman, the applicant, a draftsman, and the chairman of the village committee where the land was located was supposed to meet to adjudicate the claim, mark boundaries, and make a map. The DLWR officer and the policeman were to each draft a report to their superiors specifying the farm location, the area, the soil type, and its present use, and confirming that the parcel had no other claimants. The DAO then was to send a report to the party secretary for approval. Upon obtaining approval, a district registration number was to be assigned, and all previous reports, the map, and the original application were to be forwarded to the regional agricultural officer (RAO) for approval and the issuance of a regional registry number. The RAO was then responsible for taking the documents to the director of the DLWR of the MOA in Mogadishu. The director of the DLWR was supposed to check the application again for conflicting claims before sending the entire file to the Minister of Agriculture for his signature. Once signed, copies of the documents were to be returned to the new leaseholder and filed in the various DLWR or MOA offices. Alternatively, the registration process could begin with a letter of application submitted by an individual or cooperative to the district or regional agricultural officer, or to the national minister, requesting that he find unregistered land for the applicant.

As should be immediately clear, the requirements of the land law not only directly contradicted the system of land tenure and land use developed by farmers in the middle valley, but made virtually all aspects of their time-honored agricultural practices illegal. Limiting households to only one parcel of land challenged the risk-minimizing practice of land fragmentation; allowing only one titleholder per household jeopardized the rights of other household members, especially women; disallowing sales, leases, gifts, or subdivisions negated long-standing community labor-saving and risk management traditions of borrowing, selling, or gifting land, and inheritance; and requiring the development of the entire leased parcel meant practices of sustainability like land rotations and fallowing could result in repossession by the state. In short, local farmers could not abide by the law *and* continue using their successful farming strategies. Village councils no longer held local authority over adjudicating disputes, setting boundaries, or distributing land, which under the law became the purview of district, regional, and national officials. As it was designed to do, the law removed all community authority and decision-making power over land and granted the state complete control over land distribution and land use practices everywhere in the country.

Not surprisingly, few middle valley farmers registered their land, although all were familiar with the law and knew they risked losing unregistered parcels. The only local men in Loc to register were the two described above—the local party representative and the former ADC marketing representative. In most of the middle valley villages I visited, *no* local men had registered their land. The reasons for their lack of compliance were directly related to their historically marginalized political standing: to register one's land required a huge outlay of funds, government connections, a familiarity with state bureaucracy, and literacy, all of which were in very short supply in mid-valley villages.

First of all, despite the fact that according to the law the land registration process was to be free, virtually no state funds were made available to facilitate registrations, and civil servants, who received paltry salaries, were forced to depend on unofficial gratuities. The entire agricultural budget for the Middle Jubba Region in 1988 provided the regional agricultural officer (who also served as the district agricultural officer) with some paper every six months, one telegram or phone call to Modagishu every three months, and two liters of gasoline per day for travel throughout the region, but provided nothing for anything else—no pens, typewriter materials, photocopying, car maintenance, draftsmen's fees, and so on. His salary amounted to about U.S. $20 per month. Thus applicants had to assume the expense of everything from the physical materials required for the application, to the draftsman's fee, to transportation and gratuities for all involved officials, to the trip to Mogadishu to present the application materials to the Ministry of Agriculture. Loc farmers were told they would have to pay around 3,000–5,000 Somali shillings (U.S. $300–500 at official exchange rates) to complete the application process, far more than most farmers earned in a year. One Loc man summarized the collective village frustration at their situation when he asked me, "So is it fair that a poor man loses his land because he can't afford to register it?" In an attempt to comply with the law, the Middle Jubba RAO had held a registration drive where he personally went from village to village to assist farmers with initiating the process. Over half the men in Loc signed up to register a parcel, but when I came to live in Loc in 1987 the applications had been sitting in the RAO's office for two years awaiting further action because no one could pay to complete the processing.

Given their history of dealings with state officials, mid-valley villagers knew they could not count on government assistance in completing the registration process. Their illiteracy meant that state officials would have to be willing to help them in filling out and reading the forms throughout the entire process, which they recognized was unlikely. If maneuvering through the regional bureaucracy was daunting to some, the idea of traveling to Mogadishu to see the process through the national ministry was ludicrous to many. Many farmers also had a well-founded fear that if they identified their land to officials while trying to register it, the officials would simply register it for themselves, their relatives, or their friends. Loc farmers knew that revealing their wealth—their livelihood—to someone perfectly positioned to take it was foolhardy.

Beyond these very practical and logistical dilemmas impeding their ability to register their land, many Loc farmers rejected the idea of registration as an unacceptable form of government meddling in their affairs. The idea of allowing the state to assume complete control over land allocation and use, dictating where local farmers could hold land and how they could use it, appalled many villagers. Cabdi Nur, whose holdings I described above, presented a simple but elegant defense of his unwillingness to follow the law and register his land: "My history speaks for me. My father farmed this land and now I do. The land itself and its history is my piece of paper [title]."

Obviously, this state of affairs resulted in two mutually exclusive and directly contradictory systems of land tenure and use: one legal but locally ignored and one illegal but universally utilized by local farmers. Middle valley farmers were placed in a position of extreme—actually, complete—tenure insecurity which they were unable to resolve for political, economic, and social reasons.

Despite the fact that locals were not registering their land, regional registry records showed that approximately 300 titles were registered in Bu'aale District and 779 titles had been issued in the Middle Jubba Region by April 1988.[42] These titles were disproportionately held by nonlocals. Far from serving to raise the tenure security of Somalia's farmers, to improve agricultural productivity, or to "modernize" agriculture, the land law opened the door for land speculators, prestige-seekers, and land-bankers to grab up valley land for largely nonagricultural purposes.

But why was anyone other than Jubba valley farmers interested in

Jubba valley land? As we have seen, throughout most of the twentieth century, Somalis had not expressed much interest in acquiring agricultural land due to an unwillingness to farm and to a greater interest in livestock for both its prestige value and its higher investment value. Farming remained an occupation for lower-status Somalis and Somali jareer, considered demeaning or dishonorable by pastoralists and city dwellers alike. Why were people from outside the valley previously uninterested in farming suddenly motivated to obtain farmland?

The Desirability of Farmland

Several trends in the early 1980s altered the traditional attitude toward farmland by increasing its perceived value.[43] First, Somalia's emerging wealthier classes needed someplace to invest their wealth. Those enriched by the boom years of refugee relief in the late 1970s and development aid in the 1980s, and those with wealth from remittances, from qat sales, from the livestock export trade (prior to 1983), or from black market activities were looking for investment opportunities. Second, skyrocketing inflation rates—from 46 percent inflation per annum between 1980 and 1985[44] to over 300 percent per annum in the late 1980s[45]—made durable assets such as land a much better investment than bank accounts. Even before the banks' collapse in 1987, Michael Roth (1988:5) calculated that financial assets in the form of bank deposits would have yielded a 31 percent negative annual return in 1985. Third, the shocking 1983 ban on Somalia's livestock imports due to unfounded fears of rinderpest by Saudi Arabia, virtually the sole importer of Somali livestock, led to "catastrophic" (Little 1996:97) disruptions in the Somali economy and set off a scramble for other investment opportunities. Fourth, the Somali government liberalized grain prices and marketing in 1984 in response to donor pressure, making agriculture appear potentially lucrative as farmers were no longer required to sell any of their grain to the national marketing board. Fifth, high donor interest in developing agricultural projects led to the perception of secure donor funding for agricultural pursuits in an era of extreme overall economic insecurity. Sixth, Mogadishu's explosive growth after independence (which Cassanelli [1996:22] notes was "one of the most rapid processes of urbanization in Africa") produced a burgeoning demand for vegetables and grains. Finally, Barre's advocacy of agriculture as a nationalist obligation, as a route to wealth and prestige, and as a resource to be distributed by (and to) state officials encouraged state employees to show their nationalist spirit by obtaining farms. In short, people with access to opportunities for accumulating wealth turned to land, which had been nationalized under state control and promoted as the promise of the future, as a relatively sound investment in the midst of widespread economic collapse, especially in national financial institutions and livestock export markets.

These trends converged by the 1980s to increase the value of agricultural land as a durable asset, as an investment, and as an object of prestige. Growing class stratification as a result of opportunities for wealth accumulation through draining foreign aid, growing rural-urban divisions as the urban population grew and wealth became concentrated in urban hands, and the increasing marginalization of southern farmers in a nationalized political and economic arena ensured that competition for land claims played out in a highly unequal context of wealthy, politically connected businessmen and government employees seeking farmland previously claimed only by politically underrepresented, subsistence-oriented, low-status farmers. Investors quickly registered land along the lower Shabeelle and lower Jubba, many becoming absentee landlords; these areas were easily accessible to Mogadishu by paved roads, had a history of export-oriented agriculture, and, along the lower Shabeelle, had a partly functioning irrigation system left from the Italian years of colonial rule.

But what about the *middle* Jubba valley? Why was this remote area—which had remained geographically, politically, and economically isolated throughout the 1980s, which had little access to markets, no banks, and no all-weather roads, which was shunned even by the government officials posted there—also a target of expropriation, with almost eight hundred titles issued by 1988?

The most significant factor fueling land claims in the middle valley was the prospect of donor-funded development of this remote and previously undesirable area. In the 1970s and 1980s, the Somali government identified the Jubba valley as Somalia's "highest development priority" (ARD 1985:1). The World Bank chose the middle Jubba valley as the future location of Africa's second largest dam—after the Aswan Dam—to provide electricity for urban centers and to control flooding on the river. The U.S. Agency for International Development (USAID) and the German development agency, as well as other donor governments spent millions of dollars during the 1980s researching ways to develop irrigation schemes along the river following the completion of the dam, placing much emphasis on the irrigable potential of the mid-valley dhasheegs. The European Economic Community (EEC) developed plans to build an all-weather road through the middle valley between Jilib and Baardheere to facilitate transport of agricultural products to urban centers and ports outside the valley. Concentrating national and international attention on the agricultural potential of the Jubba valley, the government created a separate Ministry of Juba Valley Development in

1982 specifically to help plan and oversee the ecological transformation of the valley. For those in the know, these international plans identified the middle Jubba valley as a site of assured donor investment and stimulated interest in land acquisition by investors from outside the valley.

The Inequity of Titling

Outsiders—as locals called them—obtained titles to mid-valley land through various channels. Some simply went to the office of the registry in Mogadishu and asked for a chunk of land in the Jubba valley, which they were granted, sight unseen. Others registered parcels, also sight unseen, in the regional registry offices. In both cases, the outsiders were usually obtaining legal title to land already cultivated by local farmers under customary tenure arrangements, leaving the local farmers with no legal recourse when titleholders showed up—if they ever did—to claim the land.

In the area around Loc, I witnessed another more frequent method of gaining titled rights to land. Civil servants and businessmen would invoke "kinship" or "friendship" to be granted village land. A version of the following scenario played out in numerous villages in the mid-valley area: A wealthy businessman or government official from the city who shared a clan affiliation with people in a particular Jubba valley village would go to the village council, requesting to buy—for a nominal fee—or be granted a small portion of riverbank land. Having thus obtained a small piece of land "legitimately" in local eyes, the outsider then registered a much larger area of land—often up to one hundred hectares by calling himself a private company—than that which he was granted. The applicant managed to bypass the extended registration process outlined in the law, hastily sketching out a rough map himself, before seeing the process through in Mogadishu. When district, regional, or national government officials claiming "friendship" approached Loc's village council to request a "small riverbank farm," Loc's representatives were not in a position to say no. The language of friendship and kinship used by elites to obtain Loc land mirrored the attempts by pastoralists to avoid paying compensation to villagers for the damages caused by grazing their livestock on villagers' farms.

During my stay in the middle valley, Loc villagers were just beginning to discover that most of their land base had been registered by men in this way from Bu'aale and Mogadishu who initially had only been granted or sold small parcels of land by the village council. By 1988, outsiders had registered seven private farms in Loc, which, together with the two farms registered by village men, accounted for over 60 percent of Loc's land base. As I will recount below, the Bancarab cooperative had also been registered as a two-hundred-hectare cooperative. Two more farms of one hundred hectares each were pending registration during my stay. All of these titleholders, including the two resident men, were government officials when they acquired title. Altogether, these registered areas encompassed the entirety of Loc's farmland. Every single cultivated or bush farm used by every single family in Loc was thus legally held by someone else. Furthermore, the regional registry listed twelve other farms, ranging in size from two to two hundred hectares, as registered on Loc land. Officials and locals identified nine of these farms as actually located elsewhere, but could not identify the specific locations or owners of the remaining three farms. Therefore it is possible that some of Loc's land base was registered by *two* overlapping legal claims on top of the previous smallholders' (illegal) claims.

By 1988, none of the registered titleholders to Loc land had exercised their legal rights to their entire holdings, although small areas on most of the registered farms were under cultivation. In activating their legal rights to even these tiny portions, however, registered titleholders dispossessed about 20 percent of the households in Loc of some of their land, although every single family in Loc could have been legally dispossessed of its land if the titleholders had wished to take full possession. As they watched this process of physical expropriation begin to unfold during 1987–88, Loc villagers began to realize the potential extent of their losses. Uncertainly, and sometimes at odds with each other, they began contesting the rights of titleholders to their land.

The first family to protest the loss of its land during my stay consisted of eight orphaned siblings who had lost two farms to two different registered titleholders. The oldest child, a son, was away serving time in the military, after having been kidnapped by the army in one of its periodic raids on Gosha villages. The next three children were daughters, all married. The remaining four children were boys under the age of fourteen. The eldest daughter retained control over the six farms left by their deceased father, which had not yet been divided pending the eldest brother's return and the youngest brothers' coming of age. Because the daughters committed their labor to their husbands' farms, the siblings let most of the inherited six farms return to bush.

The local party representative, Ibrahim, included their riverbank farm in Jeerey as part of his titled holding when he registered his farm, reclearing it in 1987. The oldest daughter summoned the soldier brother, who returned to Loc to confront Ibrahim. When Ibrahim offered to give the brother some money to compensate for the loss of their land to his registered holding, the brother refused on the grounds that his younger brothers needed the farm for the future. The soldier offered to pay Ibrahim the cost of clearing the farm and to let Ibrahim continue to farm it until the brothers came of age if Ibrahim changed the title to exclude the siblings' farm. Ibrahim verbally agreed to this counteroffer, although the land remained legally registered as his (because, despite his promise, he never altered the title).

The oldest daughter then discovered that one of the family's cleared farms had been registered by the former marketing representative. Outraged, this time she went directly to the regional Ministry of Agriculture, which refused to hear her case. A male representative from the village council then went on her behalf, and ministry officials told him that although the former owners retained no legal rights to the newly registered land, perhaps the new registered owner could continue to allow the siblings to farm it. The registered farmer agreed to let the siblings farm the land during the remainder of his lifetime, but only on the understanding that the agreement would cease with his death. The siblings were unhappy with this unfavorable resolution, arguing that the "five boys without a father" must have something to inherit.

Shortly after this family's discoveries, two village men were working in their adjoining fields when the regional head of the Somali national militia showed up (fully armed, of course) on their farms to inform them that they were cultivating land that was now his. He told the men to take their harvests, and then abandon the land. The villagers were shocked to discover that the militia head had registered parts of Jereey, Erabley, and the Siimow, and all of Calibulahaan. Several farmers holding land in these areas tried to protest to the ministry authorities, and some tried to register their cleared farms which fell within the huge area claimed by the militia head, but they were turned away on the premise that the militia head's application had priority. Because the militia head's claim encompassed the land of so many more Loc households than had the claims of either Ibrahim or the former marketing representative, and perhaps because some village council members were among those to be dispossessed, the village response was more decisive and collective than it had been to the siblings' situation a few months earlier. Nevertheless, officials still rejected the claims of the untitled villagers (and villagers themselves saw the wisdom of dropping their case against a prominent military official with the full support of the state behind him).

Just a few months later, tensions over stolen land continued to rise as villagers made further discoveries of land expropriation. Three local men had sold small adjoining Jeerey riverbank farms to the regional ADC director during the height of the 1987 flood when they were in need of cash. The ADC director complained that the resulting parcel wasn't big enough, so the village council gave him another adjoining portion of unclaimed doonk land, which did not include any other claimed parcels. One day, he appeared at the Erabley farm of two village youths—a considerable distance inland from the parcel he had purchased and had been granted by the village council—and informed them that since he was claiming their farm as part of his registered area, they had to leave their land. Not trusting the village council to represent them forcefully enough, the two youths went straight to the Ministry of Agriculture to protest, whereupon they discovered that he was attempting to register a huge area of land one thousand paces back from the river which would encompass the land of many Loc families in the Jeerey, Siimow, Erabley, Shanley, and Dhasheeg Gora areas. After arguing among themselves over the proper course of action, the village council agreed to meet with regional authorities to settle the matter of the Loc youths' rights. The regional agricultural officer held a meeting with the village council, the ADC director (accompanied by an armed policeman), the district commissioner, and several interested village men to discuss the case. The regional agricultural officer decided that although the young farmers had no legal claim to the land, they should be compensated for their labor of clearing the land which they had been farming. He told the two village youths that "it's not good to have fights. This old man [a term of respect] bought this land and wants to register it, so let him pay you the cost of clearing the land. I request that you accept this resolution." The RAO valued the expense of clearing at a total of 10,400 Somali shillings which the youths accepted but which the ADC director rejected unless he was granted more cleared land to include in his registered farm. Fearing trickery, the youths and the village council refused this condition, leaving the matter unresolved by the conclusion of the meeting. To my knowledge, the youths were never paid for their labor, although a one hundred-hectare farm was registered in Loc to the ADC director when I inspected the registry records upon my departure from the region in May.

The fate of the Bancarab cooperative illustrates several aspects of the dynamics of title registration in the middle valley. After the villagers had been successfully farming the cooperative for about three years, four Ajuraan men from Mogadishu (three government officials and a pharmacist) showed up one day to see the cooperative. They said that they had heard about what the villagers—"their fellow clan members"—were doing and wished to help. The men explained that they were educated, that they were more involved with the government and understood the workings of bureaucracy, and that they could register the cooperative and help the members acquire a pump and inputs to increase their production and diversify the farm. In return for registering the cooperative, the four men wanted their names included as cooperative members, and they requested a "fee" of twenty-five kintals of the four hundred-kintal maize harvest. The villagers agreed, the men left with their payment (no doubt sold for profit), and the villagers heard nothing more for several years.

One day in late February 1988, some unknown men showed up in Loc asking to see the cooperative. The men were bank representatives from Jilib sent to investigate a request for a substantial loan in the name of the cooperative. The four men in Mogadishu had registered a cooperative of two hundred hectares, and with the title in their possession had applied for a loan using the cooperative land as collateral. Since the villagers' names were, in fact, included on the list of cooperative members (along with the mayor of the regional capital and the state-recognized regional mediator), they would be liable for the loan as well. Nervous about the situation, and believing that the men had not requested the loan with the intention of using it for capital improvements on the cooperative, the villagers told the bank representatives that they could not see the cooperative land because it was too far away and too overgrown. Loc villagers had, in effect, been tricked into placing their faith in their "clansmen" and allowing the cooperative to be registered. The four men from Mogadishu got their names on a title to land—as did a few regional elites with no prior claim to the land—which they retained in their possession; they stood a chance to acquire loans for private purposes for which nonbeneficiaries (Loc villagers) would also be legally responsible; and they received a substantial payment for their efforts to register.

Nevertheless, Loc villagers still made out better than their neighbors and kin in Maddow village across the river. On the same day that Loc's cooperative was registered, another two-hundred-hectare cooperative was registered in Maddow, which listed the names of the mayor, the regional mediator, and several other regional officials, but which did not include any names of Maddow villagers. When Maddow villagers discovered that practically all their farmland had been claimed by nonvillagers in a cooperative without their knowledge or consent, they made a written request to the Ministry of Agriculture to have their names added to the title. Ministry officials told them that titles could not be altered. As they were dispossessing Maddow villagers of their farms, the local officials who held title told me that they had registered the land as a cooperative in order to keep it from being claimed by people from Mogadishu.

Thus the registration law was not only bringing national elites into the valley to claim land, but it was also facilitating the emergence of increasingly powerful regional "big men" who followed the example of national elites in laying claim to the land of the people whom they were entrusted to protect and represent.

Imagined Landholdings . . . and Real Results

Clearly, the land rush of the 1970s and 1980s represented a devastating culmination of economic trends colliding with sociopolitical configurations. A racialized space for a distinct population became redefined as a place of ecological wealth claimed by the state as part of the national patrimony and made available to national elites through an inequitable legal system. In an economic environment conducive to investment in land, elites reconfigured the Jubba valley as a national resource to which they were entitled. The environmental, economic, and social ramifications of this land rush were extraordinary.

By the end of my visit in 1988, great stretches of riverbank land were being deforested and bulldozed as locals and titleholders alike were frenetically clearing their land in an attempt to establish a firmer claim to it. Titleholders were attempting to minimally comply with the land law requirement of "developing" their holdings within two years, and locals—reacting to the outcomes of negotiations between Ibrahim and the siblings and the regional ADC director and the Loc youths—were clearing land to ensure at least some small payment for their labor if their land did get registered by an outsider. Once bulldozed, many titleholders left their land bare, contributing to land degradation and soil erosion, a state of affairs observed by researchers and locals throughout the valley.[46] In this way, land once productively farmed was actually being taken out of production and degraded through the land law.

In direct contradiction to predictive theories, registration also resulted in a significant drop in agricultural productivity because registered titleholders were so much less productive than unregistered farmers due to a lack of labor, lack of interest, and lack of farming expertise. None of the registered farms in Loc were cultivated entirely; some were not being farmed at all. With the exception of the two resident men, none of the registered farmers were actually farming their land themselves and several did not even live in the valley. Some had posted impoverished relatives from other parts of the country on their land, some required their employees to cultivate their farms for them (the militia head, for example, sent his soldiers to cultivate a portion of his land), and some hired local labor or made sharecropping arrangements to cultivate small portions of their land. The productivity of registered farms was very low: during 1987–88 registered farms produced about *half* as much maize and sesame per cultivated area as unregistered Loc farmers produced on their farms.[47] Their lack of prior experience as farmers (most of the men holding title to land in Loc had never farmed before in their lives), the low productivity of their farms, and their almost complete lack of personal interest in farming reflected their attitude about acquiring middle valley land. With the exception of the two resident Loc men, none of the titleholders had acquired Loc land in order to remake themselves as farmers. Rather, their occasional efforts to use their land to produce food crops were more opportunistic than indicative of a long-term farming interest: some of those living locally hired labor to produce subsistence crops in order to feed their families, and some who had been transferred to other parts of the country allowed their relatives to use their land for subsistence.

Of the one hundred or so registered titleholders in the Bu'aale-Loc area, I was able to locate fifteen who lived locally while serving out their appointments as regional, district, or city government officials. All were clear about their intentions: they saw middle valley land as a potentially profitable investment available to them as government officials. As one man who held title to a large parcel of Loc land explained to me: "I had never thought of farming before, but when I got here, I saw that all government officials had land, so I got a farm too." This man completed the registration process himself which cost him nothing due to his official position, but a trip to Mogadishu to finish the process cost him ten thousand Somali shillings. He hired laborers to cultivate a small portion of his farm to provide food for his family, but he had no interest in investing in agriculture to further develop his farm. Another registered titleholder, who obtained his twenty-hectare holding for free and registered it through his government connections, told me he expected its value would reach two to three million shillings within a few years because of development plans for the middle valley. Clearly, land speculation rather than a burning desire to take up agriculture fueled the interest of government officials in claiming mid-valley farmland.[48] As a result of these factors, by the end of my visit in 1988 land degradation and a decline in agricultural productivity were two obvious effects of the mid-valley land rush.

Similarly, the economic consequences of the land law contradicted policy intentions and predictions. Despite the fact that the land law was intended to stimulate investment and thus productivity, the law forbade economic values being assigned to land by making it explicitly illegal to buy and sell land. The result was not that land remained an item defined by its use value. To the contrary: land was becoming highly commodified in anticipation of irrigation schemes, donor projects, and developed transportation networks. However, it was not being commodified in any uniform way. The registered titleholders I interviewed had paid wildly varying prices for land, dependent more upon who they were and from whom they were buying it than upon any objective standard of land quality. While people in mid-valley villages had bought and sold land among themselves for decades, land speculation was introducing competing perceptions of what land, especially cleared land, might be worth on the national market—and neither the buyers nor the sellers had standardized ideas of prices or value.

The commodification of land was, in this sense, imaginary, as well as chaotic: people from outside the valley with no previous experience in farming were buying and claiming land of unknown quality and quantity—but what they were really buying/claiming was the *idea* of land ownership. Outsiders were willing to pay farmers, village council members, or regional or national registry officials varying sums of money for parcels of land that they had never seen. In many cases, the titles that people held—and for which some of them had paid money—did not actually correspond to anything specific on the ground. In scrutinizing the registry, it became apparent that several people could file rough maps, which they themselves drew, delineating overlapping areas of land to which each claimed, under the law, sole title. Many individuals holding title to land in the mid-valley actually had no idea where the boundaries of their registered parcels were. In Loc, for example, when a dispute broke out over boundaries between two seasonal farms in the Siimow, the titleholder who claimed to hold all the land in the Siimow proclaimed that both disputants would have to abandon their farms if they were cultivating within his titled holding. No one, including the titleholder, was able to ascertain whether the disputants' farms actually fell within the titleholder's registered farm, so he removed himself from the debate and allowed the Loc village council to mediate the boundary dispute. Similarly, the several government officials who, according to the registry, had registered land in Loc "1000 paces back from the riverbank" had no idea where their actual farm boundaries lay. What titleholders were acquiring, in effect, was not necessarily the land itself, but the right to claim land in that area in the future if it became lucrative.

This flurry of registration took place in the absence of any certainty that any development plans would be carried out. People were investing in an imagined development package to take place sometime in the indeterminate future. What most registered titleholders ended up with were papers that said they had rights to some imagined chunk of forest or bush or already cultivated farmland, inaccessible most of the year, lacking any technology or irrigation. Because investing in possibility—rather than certainty—characterizes the nature of speculation, this may be unsurprising until we realize that speculation on the promise or hope of development marked the history of the Jubba valley for the last hundred years. During the colonial period, Italians speculated in the hope that Somalia would become a great agricultural empire, which was the Italian government's intention. Their dreams collapsed due to lack of labor, poor Italian farming expertise, and World War II. During the period of Soviet influence, talk of a dam and roads—neither of which materialized—encouraged incipient land acquisition in the lower valley. The 1980s, which we might characterize as the U.S.-Barre alliance period, produced the greatest land rush the valley had seen to date. Nothing ever materialized from any of these phases of planned development, but people nevertheless continued to speculate that something would.[49]

The story of land reform in the Jubba valley is thus a story of detrimental and unanticipated(?) consequences of an attempt simultaneously to bring ecological resources under the control of the state and to develop agriculture under the joint guidance of the state and international donor agencies. Previous chapters described how the occupation by ex-slaves of the Jubba environment rendered it marginal in every way: geographically within state borders, socially in the world of pastoralists, economically as agriculture was looked down upon and export markets existed only for bananas, racially because of the history of the inhabitants, and politically because the inhabitants had low status and few legal rights. When the valley underwent a qualitative transformation in the context of state-building and international development efforts, the environment of the valley was revalued as more central geographically, economically, and even socially. The inhabitants, however, were not included in the valley's revaluation, but remained without rights or options, almost as "nonpeople," with results that became genocidal in the 1990s.

Conclusions

Symbolic subordination, which gave perpetual meaning to racial status, set the terms of material appropriation in the postcolonial state. State policies and donor objectives/funds made such appropriation possible. Foucault's suggestion that "mechanisms of power, at a given moment, in a precise conjuncture and by means of a certain number of transformations . . . become economically advantageous and politically useful" (1980:101) provides an apt image for the plight of farmers in the Jubba valley. For particular reasons in particular cases, he suggests, the mechanisms of power at the smallest levels become useful, are "colonised and maintained by global mechanisms and the entire State system" (1980: 101). In his words, the tactics for a technology of power "were invented and organised from the starting points of local conditions and particular needs. They took shape in piecemeal fashion, prior to any class strategy designed to weld them into vast, coherent ensembles" (1980:159). This chapter has described how the state and national elites utilized particular mechanisms of power, supported by foreign donors and facilitated by state laws, to transform local fields of power defined by symbolic subordination in the Jubba valley into economic benefits for themselves.

While the Somali government may not have conceived of land reform as a way to consolidate a class effort of domination and appropriation, claiming state control of land was clearly a way to enhance state power, and thus the power of state functionaries. Taking a broad view, John Bruce argues: "Tenure reform models [in Africa] are chosen as much to maintain and enhance power as to realize more lofty objectives. The extent of experimentation with tenure reform in the post-independence period is probably explicable by the fact that the elites achieving power at independence had little vested interest in indigenous tenure systems and have been seeking ways to use tenure reforms to create new constituencies and enhance their power bases" (1988:38).

In Somalia, land reform became a new mechanism of class formation by establishing clear boundaries between those able to appropriate land and those forced to surrender their land.[50] The basis of distinguishing appropriators from the dispossessed in the river valleys was primarily racialized status. The creation of races nurtured during the process of nation-building thus served as one basis of class formation during the process of state-making. In building state and consolidating nation, race served to define a critical facet of class formation, ensuring that Jubba valley farmers remained doubly subjugated, by race-based status and by class. Tenure reform in Somalia brought an unequivocally clear political economic dimension to symbolic subordination, powerfully demonstrating H. W. O. Okoth-Ogendo's observation that "A tenure system summarizes the set of relations which emerge through the power processes of a society" (1976:152). Enormous injections of donor funds and donor promises of substantial agricultural development in the valley fueled this process to an extent unimaginable under different circumstances. In this way, development aid as an arm of Cold War geopolitics, the arrogance of development wisdom, state agendas for maximizing control, and elite efforts to accumulate wealth converged to radically transform the Jubba valley.

As I argued above, land expropriation in the Jubba valley was not a premeditated effort at class domination, but was rather an atomistic, frenzied, and chaotic undertaking by individuals using their social connections and political knowledge (and for some their access to weaponry) for private gain. Those obtaining title did not always claim control over the factors of production and did not always sell their produce in the marketplace. Most registered titleholders were not farming all their land, although some were farming some of it; only some of those were hiring labor and even fewer were producing cash crops. The laborers were local farmers—legally a proletariat (because their land was all claimed by others) but still farmers in actual practice. The nascent class structure was built on the basis of legal control over an imagined area of land and potential control over a local (landless) labor force. Class relations were thus not (yet) based on unequal control over the means of production, but rather on unequal access to the organs of the state; or on what Young called "power relations rather than relations of production" (1982:81). In other words, class formation was based on the power to *claim* control over the means of production (land), but not yet on the *actual* control over the means of production. By the late 1980s, the growing incidences of outsider appropriation of mid-valley land and expropriation of mid-valley farmers heralded an emerging regional hierarchy of exclusion, economic domination, and political polarization based on preexisting statuses of racialized ethnicity and historical experience.

A class of appropriators was thus forming on the basis of race/history which crosscut clan, region, and, within the Gosha, ancestry. To speculate, we can imagine that had this process continued—had it not been halted by the northern insurrection and brutal government retaliation which precipitated the civil war—it would have culminated in a highly stratified regional society of wealthy landowners benefiting from development largesse and impoverished landless laborers earning wages for cultivating land which had previously been theirs. (We might also speculate about a decline in agricultural productivity, a rise in urban poverty, and a feminized underclass resulting from these processes as well.) In fact, this was exactly the image of the future many Loc men and women shared among themselves in their conversations about what the loss of their land would mean to them and their children. They repeatedly talked about how they envisioned themselves as laborers for the "soft-hairs," the "slender-fingered ones," or on state farms once development projects got underway. No matter how depressing (and realistic) an image this may have been at the time, it turned out to have been optimistic. No one foresaw what was going to happen to these farmers following the collapse of the Somali state.

Chapter 9
Conclusion

A new historical nightmare invaded the valley following Siyad Barre's flight from Mogadishu in 1991 in the form of highly armed militias, "liberators," and bandits who represented the violent culmination of two decades of national claims to valley land.[1] Unarmed Jubba villagers starved, died, and fled by the hundreds of thousands as warring factions repeatedly swept across the valley, claiming food stores, material goods, and land as their right. Somalia's river valleys became war zones, as resident farmers, registered titleholders, and a new group of self-proclaimed "liberators" all claimed the right to control farmland and its accompanying development benefits that many believed would return to Somalia. Writing about the state of southern farmers three years after Barre's fall, one witness (from the nonprofit Center of Concern) observed, "Massive asset transfer has occurred in the last three years. Larger groups with military power looted the resources of many smaller, weaker communities, whom increasing banditry further decapitalized . . . many families were forced to leave their land" (Prendergast 1994b:17; see also Prendergast 1994a). Another observer wrote: "As the militias struggled for control of neighborhoods and districts, farmland was occupied and claimed by the 'liberators.' The property which the state had claimed as its own and which the rulers had exploited now became fair game for the new power brokers. Somalia's productive resources became the battleground" (Cassanelli 1996:23). The newest arrivals to the valley, the "liberators," argued that restoring the land to the titleholders would be tantamount to returning things to the way they were under Barre, which is what the "liberators" fought against and defeated.[2] The land rights of the preexisting Gosha farmers, made illegal under Barre, had become thoroughly incidental in the postcollapse period of "liberation." In addition to Mogadishu's ports, the agricultural margins have become the most highly contested areas because most Somalis realize the critical importance of Somalia's agricultural land to the economic security of a future state.

Donor agencies working in the valley following the collapse of the

Somali state took note of the increasingly virulent controversy and competition over land rights; many nongovernmental organization representatives wrote ominously about the prospects for peace in light of competing claims to land. The negotiated Jubba valley cease-fire of August 1993—which included no local Gosha farmer representation—specifically made no mention of land rights or land tenure issues, because of their "sensitivity" (Prendergast 1994b:23). Fearing the ramifications of continuing land tenure controversy, African Rights observers argued that "[d]isputes over land ownership were a central factor in the outbreak of war and the creation of famine in Somalia" (Omaar and de Waal 1993b:1), and that by ignoring the question of land rights, the UN and other international agencies could prompt "a future war directly over land rights [and consign] the minority farmers to the state of a perpetual underclass on the verge of famine" (1993b:16). John Prendergast quoted a Somali aid official who told him that competing land tenure claims in the Jubba valley were "a ticking time bomb" (Prendergast 1994b:27).

Following a fact-finding mission through the valley in 1993, an African Rights report described the atmosphere of tension, fear, terror, and threats surrounding their attempts to investigate land tenure questions. One "liberator" interrupted their meeting with a "Bantu village headman" by forcefully grabbing the headman while yelling at him, "I am your master now. I will come back and kill you if you do this [talk to outsiders about land tenure] again" (Omaar and de Waal 1993b:4). The route to autonomy pursued by ex-slaves a century ago has now become an avenue to re-enslavement, as a new form of labor bondage through violence and military control replaces their independent access to land. For those who have survived the postcollapse warfare, the weight of the historical nightmare of slavery could not be more apparent.

Land tenure questions in the valley remain as unresolved as the future political configuration of a new Somalia. The historical evidence about the trajectory of Jubba valley land tenure, however, is clear. The transformation of Jubba valley space in the context of state-making, nation-building, and donor-financed "economic development" directly contributed to murderous militia activity, environmental destruction, and the virtual annihilation of agricultural productivity in the very area targeted to provide for Somalia's future.

* * *

I went to the middle Jubba valley to avoid the state, only to find that mid-valley contemporary and historical experience—in this outpost of empire, frontier of state, backwater of nation—contained and magnified some fundmental processes of postcolonial state formation. In the remainder of this chapter I address the question of what the Jubba valley experience contributes to an understanding of different facets of state formation—and disintegration.

State-Making and the Environment

In tracing the history of a marginalized and denigrated "group" who controlled a resource increasingly perceived as valuable we see several dimensions of state, nation, and violence in Somalia. We see, most overtly perhaps, the spatial/environmental dimensions of state-making, the effects of the state consolidation of power through political transformations of space as they are experienced at the local level and the role of foreign aid in defining environments over which states receive funding to extend technologies of control.

In the 1980s "development boom" manifestation of Cold War geopolitics in Somalia, international capital, foreign aid, and superpower politics shaped the domestic economy and state power in ways inconceivable under different circumstances. Many who have provided commentary on Somalia's collapse see the vicious struggle for control of state resources—including, in particular, foreign aid—as a central factor in destroying the state (such as in Adam's [1995] charge that Somalia received too much aid), but in their analyses, *foreign aid* remained the focus. But much foreign aid targeted *land*: specifically, Jubba valley land, making it also an object of frenetic appropriation. The combination of new land tenure laws, new development plans and promises, and imported theories of agrarian productivity produced the transformations of space which were, in the 1980s, central components of the state's consolidation of power.

Our focus on land tenure has demonstrated how struggles for control over a productive environment can play a critical role in state formation, power consolidation, and class formation. This focus takes us into the often overlooked *environmental* component of state-building and state collapse. We see, in the historical trajectory of the Jubba valley, that the environment—the cultural configuring of space and the ecological attributes of that space—can be an important focus in our ongoing analyses of nation-states and the constitution of groups within and between them. Struggles over defining, controlling, using, and benefiting from the environment are as central to the projects of state-building and nation-making as are the many other processes celebrated in the anthropological literature: processes through which communities imagine themselves as nations, through which technologies of power create a civic body of disciplined bodies, through which the global political economy transforms local relations of production and produces power hierarchies, and through which races are made and ethnicities are conjured. Environments are continually evolving social as well as ecological spaces, which are constituted out of local practice, regional dynamics, state policy, and international intervention. As such, a focus on the historical environment can tell us much about the trajectories of peoples, regions, states, and nations. Whereas archaeologists continue to acknowledge the role of the environment in their analyses of state development and collapse, cultural anthropologists have become unaccustomed to considering the environment as a central component of the modern (and postmodern) people, communities, nations, and states that we seek to describe. I hope that my discussion of the how the Jubba valley has been imaginatively and practically constituted as a cultural landscape, an ecological resource, and an environment of promise contributes to stimulating interest in reintegrating the physical landscape and human agency in our understandings of state-making and state-disintegration processes.

The historical trajectory of the Jubba valley suggests a nuanced view of the role of the spatial environment—as a continually and dialectically constructed cultural and ecological landscape—in constituting identities, producing life-sustaining resources, constructing societies, supporting states, and fostering political disintegrations. We can see, in Somalia's last century, the critically close links among state-building, race-making, international intervention, and environmental degradation. The recent culmination of this history in ecological destruction and violence in the Jubba valley attests to the central importance of how environments are made, defined, utilized, and contested in our contemporary world of nation-states and their dissolutions. Communities and regions recovering from violence (along with their ethnographers) struggle to make sense of the enduring cultural scars of warfare, but the ecological scars—poisoned water sources, hidden land mines, swaths of scorched and toxic earth—are equally enduring and difficult to overcome.

Contestations over the environment reveal more than just the spatial dimension of state power. State-backed or state-directed practices of *racializing* environments have produced devastating effects throughout the world, such as the horrors of environmental racism, the devastations of inner-city transformations, and the destruction brought about by forced population relocations into state-designated reserves, homelands, and so on. The power of international capital to support state claims to the fruits of productive environments within its territory at the expense of local communities has produced ecological disasters, civil wars, and genocidal campaigns. All of this is not to say that states do not have a legitimate right to define, control, and utilize their environments; rather, it is to say that such definitions, modes of control, and uses are usually highly politicized and conducted through relations of force and inequality built on national hierarchies of race, class, region, language, religion, and even gender.[3]

State-Making, Race-Making, Class-Making, and Violence

While struggles for control of Jubba valley land did not in and of themselves bring down the Somali state, they do provide a picture of some of the processes that did: the processes of private appropriation of state resources, processes of militarization, processes of autocratic and tyrannical uses of power. Land expropriation in the Jubba valley also brings into relief another significant but overlooked dimension of Somalia's political economy: the role of racialized status in structuring private appropriation.

The historical experience of Jubba valley peoples demonstrates how race-making can become part of the nation-building and state-making effort, and how processes of class formation are tied to the politics of identity and the politics of state.[4] From the viewpoint of Jubba valley farmers, material appropriation took a very specific form, class formation had a specific basis, and state collapse brought on a specific result. Looking at these processes from the point of view of these farmers provides a clear and detailed picture of one critical facet of state formation and collapse in Somalia: how racialized status determined the losers in the battle for private appropration of state resources and the victims in the militia wars to claim poststate ascendancy.

While other authors have written about the role of stratification, private accumulation, and class formation in destroying the Somali state, the thorny issue of regional identities constructed on the basis of racial perceptions has gone largely unremarked. In the literature analyzing Somalia's collapse, "traditionalists" use the benefit of hindsight to talk about the inevitability of collapse due to the centrifugal forces of tribalism inherent in Somalia's "egalitarian" segmentary lineage structure. Materialists, rejecting this use of an enduring portrait of Somali clans and lineages, point to the role of class formation in the form of private accumulation which eviscerated the state and transformed traditional kinship practices into a highly destructive ("poisoned") form of competitive clanism. But these analyses leave race-based statuses out of the picture, ignoring the role of "race" both in structuring hierarchy within clans and between clans, and in structuring class formation.

While analysts of the Somali state and its collapse have thus focused much of their attention on clan dynamics—either conceived as traditional, unchanging social groupings or as poisonously transformed social categories—to Jubba valley farmers clan was much less important than race/status in structuring the process of private accumulation and class formation. Their "clan brethren" offered no protection from land expropriation or from violence, and even within their clans, race overrode the support system of clan affiliation, such as when "fellow clan members" used kinship to appropriate farmers' land, to charge usurious rates on loans, or to offer "assistance" with land registration. To Jubba valley farmers, clan became the least important factor in the midst of state collapse; race/status and access to weapons became the most important factors. The terrors of racial stratification maintained ideologically and economically within the context of the Somali state continued to operate, with far more lethal consequences, following the fall of the state.

The inability of Gosha farmers to acquire state resources for private gain, to use private connections to obtain windfalls or benefits, and to protect themselves in the midst of warfare thus resulted not because they were members of the wrong *clans*, but rather resulted from their history of racialized identity within the Somali nation-state. Transformed or "poisoned" clanism was undoubtedly critically important in the political jockeying for survival, profit, and ascendancy in Mogadishu (as argued by Samatar and Samatar [1987] and attested to in Simons's [1995] observations of Mogadishu's final days under Barre), but it carried considerably less significance in rural areas, where regional caricatures (as farmers, agropastoralists, Bantus, client-cultivators, ex-slaves) and village ties were more immediate and salient aspects of identity in the national and local arenas, respectively.

Looking from the agricultural margins toward the urban center thus illuminates some otherwise obscured truths about Somali state-building and the violence of disintegration: that part of the state-building effort utilized a vision of internal racialized others created by religiously justified slavery, colonial labor control practices, and state perceptions of homogenous national blood; and that such ideological visions of racial stratification provided the tragic cultural logic which patterned much of the violence during the collapse of the state.

While I am not arguing that race was the *only* factor in the collapse of the Somali state, or that it was the most important factor, I am suggesting that it was a critical factor and one that illuminates several facets of collapse and violence. These observations about the entanglements of race-making, class formation, nation-building, and state-building suggest that although clan identities became for many Somalis extremely important in the context of conflict, they did not *generate* conflict. Segmentary lineages operate as flexible systems for *managing* conflict (as well as for apprehending conflict), not for *producing* conflict. The kinds of tensions building in the Jubba valley during the 1980s and the post-collapse patterns of violence across southern Somalia suggest that tensions based in class formation, racial status, and regional competition generated conflict in a highly militarized national atmosphere of mistrust, suspicion, terror, and state abuse. While such conflict found popular expression in the Somali idiom of clan, to say that kinship, or segmentary opposition, underlay the breakdown of the Somali state into genocidal violence is a nonexplanation that ignores both the domestic repercussions of Somalia's geopolitical status during the 1980s and its internal hierarchies. In particular, the hierarchies of race-based status inherent in the Somali nation-state must be acknowledged both as a dimension of collapse and as a fundamental and undeniable component of rebirth.

Race and Class Convergences

Tracing the trajectory of race-making and class formation in the Jubba valley shows the mutually constituting nature of these two categories. The relationship between these two facets of social identity and social positioning has been much discussed in the literature: Are they identical? Which comes first? Do racial differences underwrite class formation or does class formation create races? In Somalia, does the fact that ideas about racial difference took shape in the era of slavery—an era of clearly defined "classes"—and were enhanced during the colonial era around issues of labor control suggest that class is prior to race in shaping relations of inequality? What about the significance of Islamic ideology in defining those enslaveable and the role of the postcolonial state uses of "blood" in defining internal others? In pondering these complicated connections among race, class, nation, and state, I have come to agree with Paul Gilroy that we need to make "a finer discrimination [of the differences between race and class] which appreciates the complex interplay between struggles based around different forms of social subordination. . . . The processes of 'race' and class formation are not identical. The former is not reducible to the latter even where they become mutually entangled" (1991:28, 40).

At the same time, while class and race are not identical and one cannot be reduced to the other, they are *always* related. The specific task of anthropologists is to figure out exactly how they are and have become related in any particular place: to determine how, historically, fields of power have developed that simultaneously affect peoples' categorical conceptions of themselves and others and allow for one group's ability to appropriate the material products or wealth of another. For Jubba valley farmers, I have tried to show that race, class, nation, and state are distinct but mutually constituting concepts/categories. Race does not equal class, nation does not equal state; rather cultural work has to be done to conflate race with class, nation with state. It is through analyzing the struggles and gaps inherent in such cultural work—work that attempts to naturalize and equate both race/class categories and nation/state conceptions—that we can best apprehend the relations among and between them.

The Marginal View

While anthropology has built itself into a discipline by studying the marginal members of societies and states, only recently have we begun to relate the lives of people on the margins to the central features of the states in which they reside. Anthropologists increasingly recognize that the marginalized (whether women, minority groups, children, rebels, or others)—those whose voices were long ignored or silenced in anthropology as illegitimate, unknowledgeable, or irrelevant—can offer brutally perceptive and insightful views of the societies, nations, and states in which they live. Several recent studies demonstrate the centrality of marginal groups in defining a nexus of nation, purity, race, and statehood, including Charles Carnegie's (1996) Jamaican albino, the absent Jew in Poland,[5] blacks in England,[6] Gypsies in Romania,[7] or extremist right-wing Parliamentarians in Europe.[8] From the vantage point of Gosha farmers, it is exactly their marginalized position on the political and cultural edges of the Somali nation-state that makes them such astute observers of the regime, of hegemonic Somali cultural practices, of political domination, and of economic stratification.

It is exactly in the ambiguous, fractured, and unpredictable spaces following disastrous events that discourses of marginality become powerfully apparent as they are reconfigured, recontested, renegotiated, represented, and remade. Thus we should take particular account of such discourses rather than silence them or dismiss them as simply "marginal" to the "real" projects of state and nation. Discourses of race, inequality, exclusion, and marginality are the very stuff of state and nation, of civility and citizenship, of power, of dialogue, of rebirth—and of violence. The farmers of the Gosha speak from the point of view of racialized statuses, political injustice, economic marginalization, subjugation, and racism, and not in the language of clan or segmentary lineage. Their commentary offers some new insights into Somali society and contributes to imagining a new future for Somalia.

The Contradictions of Hegemony

Above all else, looking at the Somali nation-state from its agricultural margins in the Jubba valley has demonstrated the essentially contradictory nature of hegemony. Seeking hegemony's contradictions speaks to the (by now) well-worn but ever-interesting questions about what it is that allows states to state, nations to nationalize, and the (materially and symbolically) subaltern to submit. These questions become all the more crucial and poignant when we look backward at states that have violently collapsed—at states which have lost their ability to state, at nations which failed to nationalize, and at the deteriorated position of subaltern groups in the midst of collapse.

Knowing the waves of abuse to which Jubba valley dwellers were subjected after 1991 begs the question of why these people—so obviously marginalized and subordinate prior to state disintegration—had submitted to the denigrating ideologies and practices of Somali society. Why hadn't they formed a resistance group? Why hadn't they sought political participation as a separate group, as *jareer*? Why hadn't they left Somalia much earlier? The answers to these questions have two dimensions: one speaks to the pragmatics of possibility, the other to cultural ideologies.

Pragmatically speaking, we have to wonder about the possibility that Jubba valley dwellers could have formed an opposition group in the face of extreme state repression, militarization, and surveillance. Such groups in Somalia tended to be formed outside of the territorial confines of the nation state—in Ethiopia, Rome, London. Jubba valley dwellers had no such connections, nor did they have the capital (from commercial enterprises, remittances, or expatriate communities) to invest in weapons or military technology.

The ideological reasons—the realm of hegemonic processes—are more complex, more subtle, and, certainly, more ambiguous. Looking at their history, at their view of their history, and at what they valued from that history helped to show how Jubba valley villagers *did* resist while submitting, how they recognized their subordination while claiming equality. Such conclusions are certainly not momentous in this era of finding resistances across the landscape, but I have tried to show another element of the experience of hegemony; namely, how life is thoroughly wrought with ambiguity, of the simultaneity of collusion and resistance, and of the various ways in which people creatively work out (and struggle with) living with the tensions of submission, resistance, and accommodation.

Hegemony emerges here as a process of contradictions; not as ideological glue, as false consciousness, as docile compliance. Hegemony takes form in the process of coming to agreements about what to contest, what to struggle over. As I argued in Chapter 7, although hegemony may capture the common ground, it also contains the struggles over that common ground—such as, in Somalia, how to understand the nature of nation-state citizenship or the significance of clan membership. The existence of citizenship in the Somali nation-state and the existence of clans were not themselves contested; the subaltern peoples of the Jubba valley believed in the legitimacy of nation-state citizenship and clans. Rather, they debated the substance of these categories—they waged their ideological battles in the symbolic spaces which defined the meaning of citizenship and the significance of clan membership. The power of the state at the local level lies in its ability to determine the common-ground understandings shared and debated by its citizens and to control the force and direction of the debates. As Siyad Barre lost state control over hegemonically defining the nation and the nature of citizenship, over directing class formation through overseeing processes of private appropriation of state resources, and over mediating the role of international capital, alternative discourses of community, politics, and history proliferated.

Focusing on the *ambiguities* and *contradictions* rather than the technologies of hegemonic processes is, I think, much more productive for seeking to understand the ideological power of states and nations, and the conditions of marginalization and subjugation among the peoples within those states whom we come to know. Such a perspective allows us to glimpse and honor the incredible cultural creativity of how the peoples we study work out the complex business of daily life.

Ethnicity, Identity, and the State

The historical identity politics of Jubba valley farmers demonstrate some interesting things about the slippery concepts of ethnicity and identity and their relationship to the state. While it is common in the literature to find examples of "ethnic identity" emerging in the context of nation-building and state formation as groups utilize such conceptions in their struggles for ascendancy and power, among Jubba valley farmers we may be seeing such a self-conscious identity emerging in the context of nation-state fragmentation. As I discuss in the epilogue, the same peoples who resisted group identification and ethnic labels may now be asserting their differentiation as a self-identified group in the post-nation-state rubble. Their historical trajectory as "ethnic peoples" demonstrates very clearly the ambiguous position of the state in relation to ethnic group formation. The Somali nation-state treated the Jubba valley peoples as ethnically and racially distinct while simultaneously providing the rhetoric that mid-valley farmers used to contest their ethnicization.

While Somali nation-state policies (and colonial policies) provided the grounds for constructing understandings of difference, we cannot accurately argue that such policies *created* these people as an ethnic group—a status they collectively denied until the 1990s—or even provided the political context for them to create an ethnic identity for themselves. Rather, their ethnic status was always ambiguous, undefined, and contested, a status Jubba valley peoples sought to maintain and turn to their advantage.

Indeed, the position of the peoples of the Jubba valley—as not a clearly delimited "ethnic group," nor an easily defined "race," nor a "class" within a particular hierarchy of labor relations, nor a "lineage," nor, certainly, a "tribe"—belies the facile simplicity of these terms for explaining political realities in contemporary Africa. Such narrow academic labels, whether or not heuristically useful, undermine the fantastic and diverse cultural creativities of people working through the tensions of domination and collusion, resistance and conformity, autonomy and membership, individuality and community. Although these concepts are widely employed in interpreting conflict and violence throughout the continent—and although I have made use of some of these terms in my own analysis—the historical and contemporary struggles over identity in which Gosha people have been engaged reveal their inadequacy for situating groups of people and explaining the politics of group mobilization, the patterning of banditry, and genocide within fracturing states. In analyzing the historical identity politics of Jubba valley farmers, each of these terms captures some aspect of their experience but none are themselves sufficient for describing Gosha historical experience, the status of Gosha farmers within Somali society, or the relationship between Gosha farmers and the Somali nation-state. Only by investigating the intersections of these varying categories in lived historical experience has a picture emerged of the changing nature of Gosha identity over the past century.

Carol Nagengast has called for a contemporary anthropology in which these kinds of connections assume central stage in our ethnographic analyses:

> An anthropological task for the 1990s and beyond is to continue to uncover the ways in which identities that entail inequalities are historically constructed, ascertain how those identities become deployed in time and space, determine under what circumstances people do or do not internalize and subjectify them, and how they are dismantled, disorganized, and redefined through the redistribution of people in different spaces at other times. In other words, what are the circumstances and the means through which people create identities and have them created for them? How are these identities then normalized so that resistance is domesticated, or, failing that, crushed by violent means that meet with

general social approval? Finally, how do people generate oppositional identities, a sense of self that rejects subordination and repression, how do they achieve autonomy? (1994:124)

Her final question, "how do they achieve autonomy?" is the most difficult and the most optimistically revelatory part of the task she outlines; I am, as yet, unable to imagine an answer.

* * *

Statements of a concluding nature can be spurious. Southern Somalia in the 1990s has been a bewildering place which stretches our ethnographic and theoretical abilities of understanding. How do we begin to understand a place where Foucault's disciplinary technologies of control (the army, national security service, schools, prisons, ritualized public displays of state support, state laws governing bodies) gave way to criminal terror, where Raymond Williams's hegemony (with all its inherent contradictions) was completely replaced by contradictory and alternative hegemonies, where Benedict Anderson's imagined nation gave way to antagonistic localized identities, where Marx's classes (still unconsolidated at the time of collapse) disintegrated into patronage through military might, where Weber's territorial sovereignty was replaced by millions of transnationally mobile refugees and expatriates spread throughout the globe? Is this bleak "place" an example of the fragmented nature of existence heralded by postmodernists? Maybe, but probably not.

While Somalia's collapse certainly demonstrated the failings of modernism and the crisis of the contemporary nation-state, I do not think Somalia's future will be as a model of postmodern political and civil pastiche—a pastiche currently upheld, to some extent, by the power of the gun.[9] Rather, Somalis will rebuild a state, or states, and maybe even a nation, or nations. But perhaps they will do so in novel ways; perhaps they will demonstrate new political possibilities for African states. Perhaps they will demonstrate to a world in need of new political models how the nightmare of collapse can produce new dreams—as yet unimagined in many academic and political circles—for the future.

Epilogue

At the 1993 International Congress of Somali Studies, a Somali man named Omar Eno presented a paper as part of a panel on "The Invention of Somalia." His powerful words shocked the audience, who responded with a mixture of embarrassment, silence, uncomfortable laughter, awe, and pain. Never before had a self-identified Somali "Bantu/jareer" attended an international congress of Somalist scholars to speak about the plight of Somali jareer. In English, Eno told his audience:

> I appeal to every civilized person to join me in the struggle to end the long existed and still on-going racism and discrimination which have caused untold sufferings to Bantu/Jareer people since Somalia was founded. . . . We have been and still are being discriminated against in Somalia publicly and privately. We have been systematically alienated by every Somali regime on academics, politics and economics, and often exploited as the cheapest labor force. We have been denied our Somali identities and human respect; we have been prejudged and categorized as ADOON (SLAVE)[1] and low class humans who lack the capability of normal thinking and reasoning, which undermines our general competence and dignity.
>
> The Bantu [in Somalia] have suffered right from the beginning. We have been suppressed and oppressed, robbed, raped, and killed. We have been deprived of our civil rights as Somali citizens, from independence by every Somali regime until the present. We have been stigmatized and undermined as inferior to other Somalis; yet we are never given any eligibility for opportunities in the Somali society. . . . My experience in Somalia has been [this]: we [Jareer] did not need to commit a crime of any kind, because being a Jareer itself is a crime. (Eno 1993)

His startlingly direct and groundbreaking address helped to open the floodgate of revisionist studies challenging the long-cherished image of Somali nationalist unity. Somalis, including jareer Somalis, have begun speaking in new voices about new understandings of Somali nationalism, culture, history, state structures, and the future. The next chapter in Somali cultural production and political history is, of course, unfolding as I write. It is unfolding not only in the former territory of Somalia, but also in refugee camps in Kenya, in Zegua villages in Tanzania, in factories and households in the Arabic peninsula, in Somali expatriate communities in London, Rome, Washington, D.C., Toronto, and elsewhere, in the headquarters and missions of donor agencies, refugee relief organizations, and international monitoring institutions, and, finally, in the chain of scholarly meetings of Somalia's academic elite in North America and Europe.

Where Somalia was once portrayed as a nation bound by primordial ties, now writers assert the primacy of historical regional distinctions;[2] where it was once described as one of Africa's only true nation-states because of its ethnic homogeneity, writers now highlight ethnic differences, such as in Eno's (1993) appeal to end racism or Kassim's (1993) focus on the Somali coastal descendants of Arabs and Persians; groups in exile from the latter populations have invited the historian Lee Cassanelli (1993b) to record for posterity their family—and heretofore very privately guarded—histories; national cultural heroes are being replaced with regional heroes; the claim of linguistic homogeneity has been undermined by charges of linguistic chauvinism against "non-standard" dialects; and one Somalist scholar highlights the mythical homogeneity of the imagined Somali nation in his edited volume entitled—after his conference panels of the same name—*The Invention of Somalia*.[3] This postcollapse proliferation of interest in Somalia's diversity, its heterogeneity, and the differential historical experiences of its population, when combined with the precollapse studies of Somalia's forms of class stratification, has irrevocably dismantled the image of Somali homogeneity.

Following the devastation visited on their communities, members of Somalia's Bantu/jareer population have chosen to pursue different courses in reconstructing their lives and charting their future social identities, cultural practices, and political struggles. Some are forming activist organizations for political recognition, such as the Somali African Muki Organization (SAMO), which organized a street demonstration of eight thousand supporters to protest its exclusion from the UN-sponsored March 1993 peace talks in Addis Ababa; SAMO finally received international recognition when it was included for the first time in internationally mediated peace talks later that year.[4] Some expatriate jareer, such as Eno, have formed nongovernmental organizations in order to funnel donor funds directly to Bantu communities still suffering from famine and warfare. Thousands of former Gosha villagers from the lower Jubba, mostly of Zegua descent, have "returned" to their ancestral homeland in Tanzania seeking repatriation.[5] Tens of thousands of Gosha villagers are returning to their Jubba valley villages to reassert their presence, to reclear their farmland, and to rebuild their families and communities. My former neighbors from Loc, too, have begun to return to the middle valley to renew their community and reclaim their farmland. Optimism requires one to believe that a new dream of the future can emerge from the nightmares of the past.

Glossary

addoon. A derogatory term meaning slave.

baydiya. Bush; home to pastoralists.

bilis. A term used in contrast to *jareer* to designate people considered to be ethnically "pure" Somalis; sometimes glossed as "noble."

dayr. The less predictable rainy season lasting from mid-September to mid-December.

dhasheeg. A low-lying inland area of rich soils which captures and retains water from river overflow and rains. The Gosha area of the Jubba valley is characterized by the presence of dhasheegs, which are cultivated from the edges toward the center as the water evaporates.

diya. The compensation payments paid and received by groups of Somalis tied together by political contracts on the basis of lineage and/or village networks.

doonk. Dryland areas of rainfed agriculture.

goleed. Forest; home to farmers.

gu. The main rainy season lasting from mid-March to mid-June.

jareer. A racial term that literally means "hard hair." It is used to designate people considered to be descendants from "Bantu" ancestors.

jilaal. The hot, dry season lasting from mid-December to mid-March.

jileec (tiin jileec). "Soft hair," used in contrast to *jareer* to designate people considered to be ethnically Somali.

kolonya. The Somali term for the Italian colonial practice of forcing Gosha villagers to work as laborers on Italian-owned plantations in Somalia.

ku tirsan. Literally means "leaning on"; often used to describe the informal affiliations of Gosha farmers with Somali clans.

nabadoon. A title authorized by Siyad Barre's government for local authorities who adjudicate disputes and oversee land tenure matters.

qat. A mildly narcotic plant chewed as a stimulant.

reer. Signifies a group that recognizes a group status, unified by an element of kinship. The smallest unit could be a nuclear or extended family. Thus children and grandchildren of a man called Maxamed could call themselves reer Maxamed. The largest unit would be a group like reer Shabeelle.

saab. Occupational castes of low status.

sheegad. The formal practice of affiliating with a clan other than that into which one was born.

xagaa. The season of intermittent rainfall lasting from mid-June to mid-September.

Notes

Chapter 1. Somalia from the Margins

1. I have analyzed the media coverage in greater detail in Besteman (1996a).

2. At a later date, Watts chided a roomful of anthropologists for our tendency to claim that the localities we study represent "microcosms of the world" (1996). The laughter which followed his remark showed recognition of the truth in his statement, but also our intransigence; the things we learn about in the local arena are *always* related to or are part of (in a variety of ways) the extralocal. Such has been the premise, of course, of anthropologists influenced by Marx, Weber, Gramsci, and Foucault, among others.

3. Numerous Somali and Somalist writers including Ahmed (1995), Besteman and Cassanelli (1996), Cassanelli (1996), Iyop (1994), Omaar and de Waal (1993b), and Abdi Samatar (1992), have also questioned the clan emphasis found in many media and academic analyses.

4. See also Robben and Nordstrom's (1995:3) argument that violence is a cultural construct, not something precultural, antihuman, or "outside" of culture. "As with all cultural products," they argue, "it is in essence only a potential—one that gives shape and content to specific people within the context of particular histories."

5. Barth (1969); A. Cohen (1974); van den Berghe (1973); R. Cohen (1978); du Toit (1978); Turton (1979); Kenny (1981); Galaty (1982).

6. Cf. Williams (1989); Alonso (1994).

7. Young (1982); Ranger (1983); Vail (1989); Iliffe (1979); Wilmsen (1989).

8. Colson (1968); A. Richards (1969); Asad (1970).

9. Ferguson (1990b); Ferguson and Whitehead (1992); Whitehead (1990).

10. Balibar and Wallerstein (1991); O'Brien (1986).

11. Cf. Tambiah (1989).

12. Beck (1989); Denich (1994); Foster (1991); Lingle (1992); van den Berghe (1990).

13. Lemarchand (1994); Lonsdale (1981); A. Marx (1993); Young (1982).

14. Cf. John Comaroff (1987); Cohn and Dirks (1988); Warren (1993a).

15. In 1983 Edmund Leach observed that "the word 'race' has acquired the obscene connotations which surrounded the word 'sex'" in the Victorian era (quoted in Wilmsen [1996:4]).

16. See in particular Gregory and Sanjek (1994); Rigby (1996); Vincent (1974); Williams (1989); see also Gilroy (1991); Appiah (1992).

17. The quotation from Marx reads: "Men make their own history, but not of

their own free will; not under circumstances they themselves have chosen but under the given and inherited circumstances with which they are directly confronted. The tradition of the dead generations weighs like a nightmare on the minds of the living. And, just when they appear to be engaged in the revolutionary transformations of themselves and their material surroundings, in the creation of something which does not yet exist, precisely in such epochs of revolutionary crisis they timidly conjure up the spirits of the past to help them; they borrow their names, slogans and costumes so as to stage the new world-historical scene in this venerable disguise and borrowed language" (Marx [1852] 1973:146). I am borrowing the imagery contained in the second sentence of this provocative passage, but developing it in a different direction.

18. Recent work in anthropology has demonstrated how "cultural" practices like ritual, healing, or gender dynamics in local settings develop in dialogue with the exercise and imagining of state power and authority. For two very different recent examples, see Tsing's (1993) description of shamanic songs in the "out-of-the-way" mountains of southeast Kalimantan, Indonesia, and Goheen's (1996) analysis of the relationship between localized gender dynamics in rural grassfield farming villages and state authority in Cameroon.

19. Readers interested in a more detailed overview of Somali political history should consult the most thorough work on the subject, I. M. Lewis (1988). Other books which cover more specific periods or regions of Somali political history during the twentieth century include Laitin and Samatar (1987), Markakis (1987), Abdi Samatar (1989), Ahmed Samatar (1988).

20. Laitin (1979:206).

21. See especially I. M. Lewis (1988, 1994); Laitin and Samatar (1987); Ahmed Samatar (1988).

22. Laitin (1982).

23. Amnesty International (1990:8–10). The proliferation and pervasiveness of domestic security during the 1970s prompted Laitin to write: "The greatest achievement in institution-building in the SDR [Somali Democratic Republic] has undoubtedly been that of the security services" (1982:62).

24. I. M. Lewis (1988:239).

25. I. M. Lewis (1988); Cassanelli (1993a).

26. Henze (1991); Lefebvre (1991). Menkhaus (1997) and Rawson (1994) discuss U.S. support for Somalia.

27. Rawson (1994).

28. Rawson (1994). American interest in Somalia is evidenced by the fact that in 1987, even though signs of breakdown were imminent and human rights abuses were widespread, the United States began building one of its biggest embassy compounds in the world in Mogadishu, at a cost of $35 million (which included beachfront property, two swimming pools, tennis courts, and a golf course).

29. Lefebvre (1991:14).

30. Lefebvre (1991:33).

31. I. M. Lewis (1994:179).

32. See I. M. Lewis (1994:177–219).

33. Chewing qat, a mildly narcotic plant grown in Kenya and Ethiopia, has grown in popularity in Somalia over the past few decades. Regional trade in qat generates significant revenue (Cassanelli 1986).

34. Schraeder (1993).

35. Cassanelli (1993a:14–15).

36. Gersony (1989); Human Rights Watch (1989); I. M. Lewis (1994:226).
37. See I. M. Lewis (1994); Compagnon (1990).
38. Human Rights Watch (1989).
39. This assessment was forcefully restated again two years later (Amnesty International 1990), and two years after that (Amnesty International 1992).
40. I. M. Lewis (1994).
41. Menkhaus (1991); Prendergast (1994b).
42. Shields (1993).
43. Declich (forthcoming).
44. Pawlick (1993); Menkhaus (1991); Prendergast (1994a, 1994b); Shields (1993); Africa Watch (1993).
45. Menkhaus (1991); Shields (1993); Michaelson (1993).
46. Shields (1993); Pawlick (1993); Prendergast (1994a, 1994b).
47. Shields (1993); Menkhaus (personal communication).
48. Adam (1992); see also Omaar (1992).
49. Ferguson (1990a, 1990b); Ferguson and Whitehead (1992); Lemarchand (1994); Newbury (1997); Reyna (1994); P. Richards (1996); Wolf (1982).
50. Along these lines, see also P. Richards's (1996) critique of the "New Barbarism" thesis that claims warfare in Africa (and elsewhere) is the result of primordial identities defining the lines of conflict as people fight over resources made scarce by population pressure.

Chapter 2. Fieldwork, Surprises, and Historical Anthropology

1. A pseudonym, pronounced Lo'.
2. Loc also appealed to me because I was anxious to get very far away from the effects of the Somali state's unpredictable politics and policies. The further away I was from government centers, the less subject I was to official scrutiny.
3. I defined a household as people who farmed together, whether or not they occupied the same dwelling. In almost half of the polygynous households, for example, the wives lived in separate compounds, maintained separate food reserves, ate separately, and farmed separate plots of land, but the separate families and the land they farmed were managed as part of one unit by the husband. There were other examples of individuals who lived and ate with a relative (such as an unmarried man in his early twenties who ate at his married sister's house) while maintaining separate ownership of land. I counted such cases as two households. A problem with this definition arose in the few cases where a woman held land independently of her husband from which her co-wife did not benefit and over which her husband had no control.
4. See, for example, Lan (1985) and Kuklick (1991).
5. For example, villagers teased him about having to leave the village to find a wife, due to cultural barriers against someone like him marrying a local girl, and they joked that since all the other "slender-fingered" Somalis ("ethnic" Somalis) were stealing their land, he should jump on the bandwagon and grab a piece for himself. Despite his different background, he made close friendships with several villagers, attached himself as a student to a village Quran teacher, supported villagers against outsiders in matters of land claims, and (unsuccessfully) tried to return to Loc from Mogadishu during the civil war. He was shot in the mouth on the Baydhabo-Baardheere road in 1991, and we believe he died while trying to get to a refugee camp from where he was to be evacuated by the

Swedish Church Relief. He never arrived at the camp, and we have not been able to locate him or his brother since.

6. Malkki (1995).

7. Mintz (1979a) stresses the importance of conducting the most sensitive interviews at the end of one's field research, when the anthropologist can draw upon his or her accumulated ethnographic knowledge to recognize what is meaningful, to know how to interpret the significance of what is being said, and, quite simply, to know how to engage in conversation.

8. In addition to specific interviews with mid-valley village men, village groups, and pastoralists, I also consulted British and Italian colonial archives and ethnographic accounts for historical information about slavery, land tenure, population, valley settlement, colonial agricultural policy, and whatever other tidbits I could find. Not surprisingly, the colonial views of historical events sometimes differed from local memories and sometimes differed from each other, and certain things seared into local visions of history failed to appear in colonial documents. For example, while villagers vividly recalled and British colonial reports made note of the colonial Italian forced labor policy, Italian colonial records contain no mention of this brutal chapter of colonial history. Accounts of valley history written on the basis of Italian colonial documents alone, such as Robert Hess's encompassingly titled book *Italian Colonialism in Somalia* (1966), thus ignore this highly significant practice and its effects on valley agriculture, population movements, and anticolonial sentiment.

9. See also Simons (1995) on this point.

Chapter 3. Slavery and the Jubba Valley Frontier

1. Miers and Kopytoff (1977); cf. Klein (1978), Roberts and Miers (1988).

2. Meillassoux attributes the divergent viewpoints to an overgeneralized use of the term "slave" to include serfs and other forms of servitude. In his opinion, the term "slavery" should properly be applied "to one form of servitude where the reproduction of subservience relies on capture and purchase (therefore on war and trade) and where the slave is bound to be considered a perpetual alien (i.e. the opposite of a kinsperson)." Under this definition, he argues, "slaves are not kin" (1995:410).

3. This choice of a "beginning" is not entirely arbitrary—we could also begin with the capture and transport of slaves for Somalia or with the cultural practices and political economies of the natal societies of the slaves brought to Somalia—but is determined by the focus of this book and by the evidence available.

4. Cassanelli (1993b).

5. Lee Cassanelli's masterful history of southern Somalia, *The Shaping of Somali Society: Reconstructing the History of a Pastoral People, 1600–1900* (1982), provides a superb understanding of the dynamics of southern Somali society in the precolonial period.

6. Freeman-Grenville (1962:150).

7. Geshekter (1985:6) defines Abyssinia as "a physical entity in the normally well-watered northern and central highlands [of Ethiopia], dominated culturally and politically by the orthodox Christians, Semitic-speaking Amhara and Tigre and ruled nominally by an aristocratic and ecclesiastical hierarchy based at Gondar after the seventeenth century."

8. Christopher (1844), Burton ([1894] 1987).
9. Cassanelli (1982).
10. I. M. Lewis (1988).
11. See also Abir (1968).
12. Alpers (1983).
13. Cassanelli (1982:149–60) and Abir (1968) examine in detail the caravan routes, methods of trade, and political aspects of caravan trade among Somalis in the nineteenth century. In particular they discuss the primary routes from Boran country through Lugh and Baardheere to the Benaadir in southern Somalia. Pankhurst (1965) discusses northern trade routes, linking Harar with the Benaadir.
14. Alpers (1983).
15. In 1839, Sayyid Said, the sultan of Oman, who the next year moved his court to Zanzibar, signed additions to the Moresby treaty saying that Somalis, being Muslims, were "free men" and were not to be sold as slaves. The agreement stated that any of the sultan's subjects caught selling Somalis would be punished as pirates (Nwulia 1975:54).
16. Cassanelli (1982:161).
17. Cassanelli (1982), Luling (1971).
18. Cassanelli (1982). The expansion of the utilization of slave labor in Somalia was part of a larger transformation that occurred throughout Africa. According to Manning (1983:853), by the mid-nineteenth century there was a glut on the slave market caused by the decline in demand for slaves in the New World. Prices for slaves on the African coast fell by about one-half in the latter eighteenth and early nineteenth century. Africans became able to purchase slaves in larger numbers, causing a widespread growth in the scope of slavery in Africa in the nineteenth century.
19. ASMAI 1910, ASMAI 1916, Zoli (1927:149).
20. Luling (1971), Cassanelli (1982).
21. Cassanelli (1982).
22. Cassanelli (1982).
23. Cassanelli (1982:178).
24. Luling (1971:47), Cerulli (1957:54).
25. The importance of physical features in constructing identity will be discussed in Chapter 5.
26. The best known of these groups today are the Shidle of the middle Shabeelle and the Eyle of Bur Heybe (Luling 1971:96). Cassanelli's use of the term "client" seems to be based on the juridical as opposed to economic relationship between Somali pastoralists and Shabeelle valley cultivators, as it is unclear whether the cultivators paid tribute as a function of their client status.

My discussion of Shabeelle valley "client-cultivator" groups is based upon the observations of Luling (1971) in her study of the Geledi clan and Cerulli (1957, 1959). Unfortunately, Luling reports that the "habash" of the Geledi were "uncommunicative" to her (1971:48). Cerulli's 1934 plea for ethnographic fieldwork among the populations of the river valleys (1959:121), echoed by Luling in 1983, has still not been answered to any satisfactory degree for the Shabeelle valley.

27. Alpers (1983:445).
28. Cassanelli (1989).
29. Cassanelli (1982:169).
30. Cassanelli (1982:169).

31. The letters can be found in: Anti-Slavery Society, East African Slave Trade Committee, *East African Slave Trade*, vol. 2 (London 1874), 32–34. I am indebted to Professor Kenneth Menkhaus for providing me with copies of these letters.

32. ASMAI 1865; see also Menkhaus (1989:111).

33. Hess (1966:78).

34. Luling (1971:120).

35. Hess (1966:78).

36. Many documents pertaining to this scandal are contained in the Archivio Storico del Ministero degli Affari Esteri, Rome, Italy, under "Administrazione Civile 1901–1913," position 75/6. Hess (1966) provides an excellent overview of the political history of anticolonialism and antislavery in Italy.

37. Hess (1966), Cassanelli (1988).

38. Robecchi-Brichetti (1904), cited in Cassanelli (1988:312) and in Alpers (1983:451–52).

39. Hess (1966:88).

40. Cassanelli (1988:312).

41. ASMAI 1909, ASMAI 1910.

42. Cassanelli (1988), Hess (1966).

43. ASMAI 1910.

44. ASMAI 1902a, ASMAI 1910, Hess (1966:99), Cassanelli (1988:317), Menkhaus (1989).

45. Hess (1966:100).

46. Hess (1966:100).

47. He bases his estimate on data collected by Luling (1971) in the Afgoye area.

48. The average household size where I worked was 5.9 for full-time agriculturalists. Nyhus and Massey (1986) report the average household size in the Baay Region among agropastoralists is 6.1. A 1988 survey of the Jubba valley found an average household size of 6.1 for Jubba valley agricultural households and pastoral households alike (Craven, Merryman, and Merryman 1989).

49. There are other reasons for assuming the estimates made by Cassanelli and Italian authorities did not take into account nonplantation slavery in the interior. Cassanelli is specifically discussing plantation slavery along the Shabeelle when he offers his estimates. The Italians remained confined to the coast until 1908, with the exception of the Italian outpost at the trading crossroads of Lugh on the upper Jubba. While Italian reports are clear that Lugh was a slave-trading emporium, it is doubtful the Italians knew (or cared) that slaves in significant numbers were obtained by inland Somalis for purely pastoral purposes. Hess (1966), who reviewed much of the Italian colonial material, does make mention of slaveholding by nomadic tribes, stating that nomadic tribes beyond the Shabeelle held "but few slaves" (p. 100). He does not provide reference or support for this statement, and I believe he is mistaken, for reasons that will be made clear.

50. The reasons for these migrations may never be known, but scholars have speculated that they resulted from a complex combination of factors, including drought (Cassanelli 1982:53), population pressure, Islamic militancy (I. M. Lewis 1988:23), and forced displacement as a result of chronic warfare or raiding in Somali territory further east (Cassanelli 1982:80). Although the impetus for these great migrations remains unclear, their patterns have been carefully reconstructed (I. M. Lewis 1988, Cassanelli 1982, Cerulli 1957, Turton 1975).

51. I. M. Lewis (1988:31), Kelly (1983:15).

52. Kersten (1871).
53. I. M. Lewis (1988:30).
54. *Warday* may be derived from the Arabic word *wird* (watering place). *Wirdiy* would be someone from a watering place. Alternatively, *warday* may come from the Arabic *warid* (newcomer) or *waridat* (imports) (*A Dictionary of Modern Written Arabic*, 1980, Librarie du Liban, J. Milton Cowan, ed., Wiesbaden: Otto Harrassowitz). I am grateful to Professor Thomas K. Park for providing me with this information.
55. I. M. Lewis (1988:31).
56. Cf. KNA (1931a), (1931b), (1932a).
57. I. M. Lewis (1988:31).
58. Kelly (1983:29).
59. Cassanelli (1988:324).
60. This point has been the subject of some debate in the literature between scholars who argue that the state of Shungwaya included Bantu speakers living in Somalia's southern river valleys by the tenth century (Cerulli 1957, 1959; Allan 1983; Pouwels 1987) and those who argue that no Bantu speakers inhabited the Horn prior to the arrival of Somali pastoralists (Heine 1978) and that no Shungwaya state existed (H. Lewis 1966, Turton 1975). See also de Carolis (1980).
61. Heine (1978); Kersten (1871); Dundas (1893); ASMAI (1896). In the 1980s, the Boni were a small, marginalized population (de Carolis 1980).
62. Cassanelli (1988, 1989), de Carolis (1980), Declich (1987), Menkhaus (1989).
63. Menkhaus (1989).
64. Kersten (1871).
65. Declich (1987).
66. Declich (1987), de Carolis (1980).
67. Menkhaus (1989:111); Cassanelli (1989).
68. Colucci (1924:148), de Carolis (1980:26), Menkhaus (1989).
69. Kersten (1871), Dundas (1893), ASMAI (1896), Zoli (1927).
70. Menkhaus (1989) has recorded these traditions and from them has developed a coherent and detailed account of the earliest years of valley settlement. See also Declich (1987).
71. The following reconstruction of lower Jubba history is taken largely from Menkhaus's (1989) superb study of the lower Jubba.
72. The sultan of Zanzibar could profit not only from the ivory hunted by Gosha villagers with weapons he supplied, but also through the trade generated by the Jubba farmers' agricultural surplus. Menkhaus (1989:173) further speculates that the sultan may have armed Gosha villagers in the hope that they would rout the troublesome Ogaadeeni pastoralists who occasionally raided the coastal trading towns in which the sultan held business interests.
73. In the middle Jubba the most remembered aspect of this battle is how Somalis begged not to be exterminated: "Bantu, leave us some descendants!" Menkhaus (1989:177) reports a similar memory held by villagers in the lower Gosha.
74. Menkhaus (1989), Little (1996).
75. Menkhaus (1989).
76. Menkhaus's (1989) dissertation on the historic political economy of the lower Jubba region convincingly argues that the early Gosha villages produced enough surplus agricultural products to capture the interest of Arab traders, the sultan of Zanzibar, and, eventually, Italian colonists.

77. I will discuss this issue further in Chapter 7.

78. Sullivan (1968), Miers (1974), Beachey (1976), Alpers (1975), Menkhaus (1989).

79. Menkhaus (1989:229). A historical study of the spread of Islam throughout the valley and the efforts of Sheikh Murjan, Sheikh Osman, Sheikh Cabdow Kheyr, and others would be a great contribution to our growing recognition of regional Somali historical figures.

Chapter 4. Settlement of the Upper Gosha

1. This chapter is fairly detailed because it represents the first coherent account of the settlement of the middle Jubba. Some readers may wish to skim the later sections.

2. Anon. (1906).

3. ASMAI (1916).

4. Ministero delle Colonie (1923).

5. I compared population estimates from the following documents: KNA (1902), (1914), (1915–16), and (1920–21), and GBCO (1910–18).

6. E.g., Cerulli (1959), Chiesi and Travelli (1904).

7. Chiesi and Travelli (1904:351), cited in Cassanelli (1988:317); see also ASMAI (1910).

8. Unattributed quotes are from oral histories I recorded in Somalia.

9. Somalis are called *bilis,* which Luling (1971) glosses as "noble." It is used to denote lineally "pure" Somalis, as opposed to slaves or ex-slaves. Another term used to describe Somalis is *jileec* which means "soft hair" (or *tiin jileec*). This term is used in opposition to *jareer,* which means "hard hair," and refers to people of East African descent or ex-slaves, whose hair is considered kinkier and rougher than that of ethnic Somalis. The significance of these terms will be discussed in Chapter 5.

10. The Italian observers Zoli (1927) and Stefanini (1924) similarly comment on the formation of Gosha villages along Somali clan lines.

11. I have come across the use of terms meaning "leaning on" to describe relations of clients or inferiors to social superiors from groups as diverse as the Kabyles of Algeria (Bourdieu 1977) and the Efe of central Africa (Grinker 1990).

12. These dance forms are discussed in Cerulli (1957) and are analyzed in depth in Declich (1992, 1995).

13. Lovejoy's (1983) observation that the dichotomy between plantation slavery and other forms of slavery was not always sharp pertains to the plantation-agropastoral-pastoral continuum that characterized Somali production.

14. Cerulli (1959).

15. Meillassoux's categories should not be taken as clear-cut markers, however, as evidenced by the remarkable life histories of enslaved central East African women contained in Wright (1993). These women each experienced varying kinds of enslavement and freedom in different contexts over the course of their lives, suggesting that perhaps all three of Meillassoux's categories might be present in the same society, and that an enslaved woman might experience all three types during her lifetime.

16. The term *reer* contains several meanings that cannot be translated into a correspondingly succinct term in English (see Glossary).

17. This quote is Lewis's translation of Cerulli (1934:3).
18. Cerulli (1957:64).
19. Collected from several Ajuraan sheikhs and leaders in Bu'aale in 1988.
20. This language resembled the pig Latin of English.
21. ASMAI (1902b).
22. See Menkhaus (1989) for a complete history of Italian plantations in the lower Jubba.
23. Cassanelli (1988) reviews the problem of the labor shortage for the Italians.
24. Recounting this period, one middle valley elder defined *duq-taraf* as "an elder who had separated himself from the village."
25. British colonial documents from Wajir District report that Gosha farmers ran away as far as Wajir to escape the Italian plantations "where they said life was not worth living" (KNA 1938).
26. Floods and rains occur in a bimodal pattern, but are highly unpredictable. For example, rainfall records from the early 1980s for Jilib show a range in annual rainfall from 472 millimeters (1980) to 925 millimeters (1983) (FEWS records).
27. Cf. Conforti (1954). Indeed, dhasheegs have consistently assumed central importance in development plans drawn up for the valley by foreign donors since the 1920s. In the multimillion dollar flurry of impact assessment and planning studies carried out in anticipation of the World Bank–financed dam at Baardheere, dhasheegs received top billing as the best sites for planned irrigation projects.
28. Farmers have constructed earthen levees and retaining walls, built by hand or (more recently) with a rented tractor, in order to manipulate the channels which connect dhasheegs with the river. Technological control over water entering and leaving dhasheegs through these channels remained crude, and occasionally farmers could not keep rising river water from flooding a dhasheeg already planted or with maturing crops. Such instances were disastrous for farmers, who experienced devastating losses as well as time delays before they could replant their flooded farms. Such a flood occurred in May 1987, just prior to my arrival in the valley.
29. I will be using the terms "farm" and "parcel" interchangeably to mean a unit of landholding that was noncontinguous with any other land held by the household. A household could have one or more farms/parcels.
30. In 1988, Loc villagers used the term *nabadoon* to refer to village leaders from several decades ago, although Cassanelli (1982) notes that *nabadoon* was a term authorized by the government to replace local titles after the 1969 revolution.
31. After resettlement, Maddow villagers successfully petitioned for permission to move back, arguing that by living in Loc they were at least an hour's walk from their farms, which, combined with the danger of having to cross the crocodile-filled river to reach their farms, was causing them great hardship.
32. Collecting this information required much diplomacy, as to be of slave heritage is to be inferior and discussing this issue was illegal. I did not wish to offend the sheikh, who claimed to be Quraysh (of the Prophet's tribe) by inquiring further about his ancestry.
33. The head of the barbaar explained to me that the barbaar used to consist of all the village men, boys, and unmarried girls until the local sheikh forbade

the participation of girls. He also forbade the barbaar from dancing, which he considered immoral, but they continued to dance when he was out of town.

34. Comparatively, the political scientist David Laitin (1977) recalled how surprised he was when he attended a meeting of teachers and administrators to discuss educational policy at the Somali school where he was teaching as a Peace Corps volunteer and found that the school's chauffeur participated in the meeting on equal footing with the teachers.

Chapter 5. Hard Hair

1. See I. M. Lewis (1988), Nelson (1982).

2. He changed his mind, however, after unsuccessfully trying to persuade me not to attend, having deciding that if a foreigner felt safe attending then he may as well go too. He was very surprised at what he found (as was I, given all the warnings I had received)—a highly enjoyable and festive evening—and he (and I) attended every dance thereafter.

3. Francesca Declich (1995) has studied the dance forms of the lower Jubba, which she analyzes together with the Somali attitude toward them. Somewhat ironically, she notes, "Following Independence, the dances were included as part of Somalia's artistic patrimony; many have been reconstructed and reelaborated in an artistic form by the National Theatre in Mogadishu dance company. Dances from the riverine areas . . . were often used in theatre to connote peasant agriculturalists as opposed to urban people" (1995:212 n. 6). Although ironic, such a reelaboration is not surprising given the propensity of states around the world for claiming cultural "folk" forms as part of the national heritage, while simultaneously denigrating or exterminating the cultures which produced these forms.

4. See Williams (1989), Alonso (1994).

5. See Gregory and Sanjek (1994).

6. Watts (1992:118).

7. Alonso (1994:394).

8. An initial discussion of the following points appeared in Besteman (1995a).

9. The *jareer* distinction is also used for the farmers of the Shabeelle valley whose history is unclear, but who, like the farmers of the Jubba valley, have "Bantu" physical characteristics.

10. Miers and Kopytoff (1977:47) recognized the potential importance of physical distinctions in postslavery Africa in saying: "The use of differences in ethnicity and physique as criteria for status discrimination in African societies requires more study."

11. Willis (1985c), Cooper (1981), Fisher and Fisher (1970).

12. Willis (1985a).

13. Willis (1985a). Akbar Muhammad (1985) and B. Lewis (1971) explore possible roots of the "unfavorable attitude" (Muhammad 1985:47) Arabs historically held toward blacks.

14. While Sanjek (1994) argues that such antecedents were different in meaning and effect from the post-1400s western European racial orders that define contemporary racial constructions on a global scale, these antecedents were the basis for local articulation with European racial conceptions during the imperial, colonial, and postcolonial periods.

15. It is interesting that Patterson (1982:7) notes a similar transformation

took place in the American South, where the basis of the "we-they" distinction changed from religious (Christians versus heathens) to racial (white versus black).

16. Fisher and Fisher (1970:22).

17. While I believe the data support the argument for a religious justification of slavery, the writings of nineteenth-century Europeans should not be treated uncritically, as Europeans were partly using the Indian Ocean slave trade as a basis for invading East Africa.

18. Somalis in the Jubba River valley frequently referred to the raiding of Oromo camps for slaves as jihad.

19. Kapteijns and Spaulding (1989).

20. My argument demonstrating the connection between slavery and physical characterizations is also obviously relevant for people who would be identified as jareer but who do not live in the Gosha. The client-cultivator villages of the Shabeelle valley are identified as jareer, and urban Somalis note that jareer individuals in Mogadishu often hold the most menial jobs, such as street-sweeping.

21. KNA (1922b).

22. Some early British writers refer to "the degraded state" of the WaGosha people (KNA 1917a), charging that they "are lazy and unwilling workers" (KNA 1917b) who would benefit from "an influx of Arabs or Somalis [who bring] a civilization higher than that of the [Gosha]" (ASMAI 1896:3). The Italian agronomist Tozzi echoed these sentiments forty years later, when suggesting that "the Goscia should follow the example of the Arabs, but since they are less intelligent and active, they have to be helped" (1941:34).

23. Menkhaus (1989).

24. Citations in Menkhaus are from: Alessandro Beltramini, "Mano d'opera ed economia indigena in Somalia," 1933, page 3, located in fascicolo 1602 in the Centro di Documentazione, Istituto Agronomico del'Oltremare di Firenze, in Florence, Italy; "Appunti sull'avvaloramento agrario dell'Impero," 1938, located in fascicolo 1926 in the Centro di Documentazione, Istituto Agronomico del'Oltremare di Firenze, in Florence, Italy; and Magnanensi, "L'Arachide sul lungo Giuba" page 377, no location provided.

25. Colucci (1924); Puccioni (1936).

26. Colson (1968), A. Richards (1969), Asad (1970), and Mafeje (1971) are early examples of the growing self-awareness of the colonial and anthropological role in the creation of African "tribes." More recent discussions include Young (1982), Vail (1989), Ranger (1983), Iliffe (1979), Wilmsen (1989), Adas (1995).

27. I recognize the importance of Stoler's (1989) point that colonial authorities and settlers were never monolithic groups sharing identical views and interests. Here I have attempted to sketch the broad outlines of how similar official British and Italian colonial policies influenced racial conceptions in the valley. There were undoubtedly dissenting colonial voices, which I have not attempted to recover. Menkhaus (1989) provides a thorough overview of colonial debates over labor and agricultural policies and their effects in the lower Jubba.

28. I do not know how many Boran descendants may be living in central or northern Somalia, nor do I know to what extent they may have successfully redefined themselves as Somali.

29. Helander (1986), Luling (1983). The social organization of southern Somali clans in the interriverine area differs somewhat from clans of the north. Southern clans, in general, are characterized by greater degrees of miscegena-

tion, adoption, and heterogeneity, and by their greater involvement in cultivation, which places them in an inferior position to northern Somali clans. The latter consider themselves "purer" (cf. I. M. Lewis 1955, 1971; Helander 1988).

30. I thank Jon Haukur Ingimundarson for suggesting this line of thought to me.

31. Patterson (1982) notes that slaves were never assimilated to outcaste status groups anywhere in the world. He describes the bond between the master and the slave as one of "perverse intimacy" (p. 50) which could be undesirably weakened by an ideology of ritual avoidance and spatial segregation. Slaves could be used in any capacity, whereas contact with outcastes was limited.

32. As we had one of the only half a dozen working vehicles in the region, we were frequently called upon to transport injured, beaten, or sick people to the regional infirmary. In our capacity as chauffeurs of the infirmed we knew about almost every physical assault in the Loc area.

33. A regional agricultural official told me that there had been four murders in the previous nine months in the region resulting from pastoralist incursions into farmers' fields. If true, such an astounding statistic underlines the terror and rage that so many farmers lived with that jilaal.

34. International criticism of state kidnapping practices put a halt to involuntary conscription in the early 1980s. So many men and boys were stolen from Loc that the local sheikh complained to the state authorities in Bu'aale. He demanded an end to the kidnappings in Loc, arguing that the village comprised his disciples over whom he claimed authority.

35. See Alonso (1994:391).

36. Cf. Cohn and Dirks (1988).

37. Cf. Williams (1989), Foster (1991:245).

Chapter 6. Between Domination and Collusion

1. Abu-Lughod (1986), Ong (1987), Scott (1985); see also Jean Comaroff (1985), Nordstrom and Martin (1992), Scott (1990).

2. Stories such as this one provide a hint of what is probably the highly significant role of gender in the construction of hierarchized spaces within the Somali state. Gender was clearly an important dimension of social dynamics between slaves, masters, and clients (as well as within communities of slaves and ex-slaves), and continues to serve as a critical differentiator between *jareer* and *bilis* through sanctions on "mixed" marriages. While I will not be explicitly analyzing here the role of gender in constructing and upholding racial/ethnic categorizations, state-building, or space/place dynamics, I believe such an analysis would contribute to an understanding of ethnic constructions, Somali state formation, and the dissolution of Somalia's state.

3. On the purported magical knowledge of crocodiles held by jareer boatmen on the Shabeelle River, see Franciosi and Lombardi (1989) and Luling (1971). Similarly, ex-slaves and their descendants in Mauritania hold a reputation as sorcerers (Mercer 1982).

4. The man fled Loc on foot after learning of their decision, but quietly returned six months later to take up residence and return to his farms. Although villagers treated him guardedly after his return, he was still living in Loc—without any hint of official sanction—when I left.

5. The multiple and competing uses of history in the context of commu-

nity building, political struggle, and ethnogenesis have, of course, received a great deal of anthropological attention. Some selections include Comaroff and Comaroff (1992), O'Brien and Roseberry (1991), Brow (1990), Hobsbawm and Ranger (1983), Malkki (1995), Netting (1987), Fowler (1987), and Lederman (1986).

6. An earlier analysis of this disputed history appears in Besteman (1993), from which portions of this section are drawn.

7. These documents and others which report on raids of Gosha villages for people and produce by locally dominant Somali clans, especially by the Cawlyahan clan, include KNA (1916), (1920), and (1923). Tozzi (1934) mentions that during droughts Gosha farmers would become "servants" of Somali pastoralists. See also Menkhaus's mention of Ogaadeen Somalis raiding Gosha villages (1989:197).

8. In 1916, the murder of Lieutenant Elliott (remembered by Somalis as "Elyan") at the British military outpost of Sarinley on the upper Jubba and the sacking of the town by Cawlyahan Somalis resulted in two years of warfare between the Cawlyahan Somalis and British forces in the Jubba valley. This warfare is known as the "Elyan wars."

9. "Hada wixi waa ku baxeen dowlad Soomaaliyeed ay ku tirsanyihiin."

10. There are a number of mitigating factors which may have contributed to shaping the substance of local history-telling. One, of course, was the circumstances of presenting a "group history" to me, an outsider. All the villagers with whom I spoke knew I was writing a book about valley history, and they understood very well their agency in this endeavor. Their contemporary concerns with dignity and equality of course affected their representation of themselves in the past. Furthermore, elders were not just telling me their history: they often spoke to me in the presence of their sons and daughters, grandchildren and great-grandchildren. Finally, the fear of being accused of "disloyalty" to the Somali state pervaded life throughout the country to greater and lesser degrees. The state had mandated that everyone was equal, thus bringing under suspicion those who claimed otherwise. In this aspect of official discourse, state rhetoric supported the historic vision maintained in public settings by Gosha elders. Any reticence Gosha farmers may have had about appearing disloyal, however, was also related to their own interest: Gosha farmers were willing to discuss other officially undiscussable issues such as land grabbing (by agents of the state), the continuing salience of clan identity, and the historical reality of slavery.

11. Luling's question also mirrors contemporary and highly politicized debates in the United States about the impact of continuing to recognize race in the public realm—e.g., does racism make us talk about race, or does talk about race sustain racism? (Gordon and Newfield 1995:382).

12. Cf. Eno (1993), Cassanelli (1993b), Kassim (1993).

13. I am grateful to Lee Cassanelli for his help with articulating some of the central points in this section.

Chapter 7. Negotiating Hegemony and Producing Culture

1. See, for example, Behar (1993), Bourgois (1995), Daniel (1996), Gordon (1992), Greenberg (1989), Hutchinson (1996), Mahmood (1996), Nagengast (1994), Nordstrom and Martin (1992), Nordstrom and Robben (1995), Scheper-Hughes (1992), Warren (1993b).

2. Cf. Gaventa (1980).

3. Miers and Kopytoff (1977).

4. Comparatively, Rosaldo (1988) reminds us that popular as well as academic notions of "people without culture" have included, over time and in different places, upper- and middle-class urbanites, indigenous peoples drawn into the capitalist economy, and immigrants.

5. Some slave descendants in the New World have experienced a renaissance of interest in African material and ideological culture. These efforts to forge and reclaim a sense of Pan-African heritage may be more akin to the new notion of "heritage" as a useful replacement for what some see as the outdated concept of culture.

6. Cooper (1977), Klein (1978), Meillassoux (1975), Patterson (1982).

7. Price (1975, 1983, 1990), Mintz and Price (1976), Price and Price (1980).

8. Baier and Lovejoy (1977), Levtzion (1985).

9. Murdock's (1959) world sample lists Somalia as having a high rate of manumission.

10. About the circumstances of his father's birth, the speaker explained, "My grandfather came from Mombasa and belonged to the Manyasa tribe. My grandmother was an Arab living with Mombasa people. Blacks [*madmadow*] in Mombasa and Arabs used to fight against each other sometimes, and sometimes they lived together in peace. As you know, Arabs are 'Quraysh' people [i.e., not black]. Those who were caught by black people were killed except for the women. They chose the best women to keep as wives. My grandfather got an Arab wife in that way."

11. I constructed this narrative from two conversations I had with the speaker.

12. After the revolution, Barre banned the use of regional clan authorities and clan awarded diya payments for mediation, replacing them with government-appointed mediators and state-sanctioned fines. In most areas, including the middle Jubba, the change was in name only, and the regional mediator posts continued to be filled by the Ajuraan regional leader, the Cawlyahan regional leader, and so on.

13. Furthermore, the lack of an elite Gosha political, educated, or cosmopolitan class involved in national politics helped keep political agency limited to the local arena, characterized by personal face-to-face interaction rather than group mobilizations. Although a number of Gosha villagers had experienced life outside the valley through their conscription in World War II and into Barre's military, these experiences with national and international politics had been limited, and most of the youths kidnapped into the military had not returned to the middle Jubba from the service by the time of my visit. The localized nature of life in the Jubba valley was beginning to change during the 1980s, however, as Gosha villagers increasingly became aware of their collective political and material position in the Somali nation-state through land alienation.

Chapter 8. The Political Economy of Subordination

1. See Menkhaus (1989).

2. Menkhaus (1989), (1996).

3. During its carefully watched over tenure as southern Somalia's trustee, the Italian Trusteeship Administration (AFIS) emphasized relatively nondisruptive interventions like health care, education, and localized smallholder-oriented

projects in the Jubba valley rather than large-scale undertakings (Menkhaus 1989, Besteman and Cassanelli 1996:9). Menkhaus (1989) has characterized the 1960s as an era of "benign neglect" by the state toward the Jubba valley, due to the former's lack of interest in the valley's political, economic, or social affairs.

4. Parts of this discussion draw on my previously published analyses of Loc land tenure (Besteman 1994, 1995b, 1996b).

5. The Italian ethnographer Massimo Colucci (1924) reported of the Jubba valley that when a villager left the area, he lost any right to personal property acquired since settling in the village. According to Colucci (1924:256–57), leaving a village was seen as betraying an obligation to the community. Sale of hut or land was not allowed, and in this sense the community held the final and ultimate authority over all village territory. I found no confirmation of this old rule in middle valley oral histories, however.

6. In further contrast to the description of southern land tenure presented in Colucci (1924) and later in Guadagni (1982), unmarried men in the mid-valley could (and typically did) request land through the village council prior to their marriage, and men could dispose of land through sale or gifting even if they had heirs.

7. Berry (1989); Bruce (1988); Goody (1980); Goheen (1988); Watts (1983).

8. In Somalia the term *kintal* specified volume, not weight. A *kintal* of maize equaled a quintal. A *kintal* of sesame was measured in the same sack, but its weight was unknown.

9. Cf. Menkhaus (1989:356).

10. See Besteman (1995b).

11. While I agree with the general argument that stratification has grown throughout the twentieth century, I disagree with the assumption made in some of these studies of an egalitarian precolonial Somalia. The vast numbers of slaves imported by Somalis alone suggests a much different picture, one overlooked in many contemporary studies of twentieth-century stratification in Somalia. It is hard to find a clearer picture of stratification—of absolute inequality—than that in which one class of people controls not only the means of production and the product itself, but also the rights to the bodies of the producers.

12. Swift (1979), Geshekter (1985, 1991), Kapteijns (1991), Abdi Samatar (1988, 1989).

13. I. M. Lewis (1988:40); Abdi Samatar (1989:29).

14. Abdi Samatar (1989); see also Kapteijns (1991).

15. Hoben et al. (1983), Reusse (1982).

16. Hoben et al. (1983), I. M. Lewis (1988:258).

17. See Little (1996), Menkhaus (1989).

18. Cassanelli (1996), Menkhaus (1989), Mukhtar (1989), I. M. Lewis (1988).

19. Cassanelli (1996:17).

20. Menkhaus (1989:323).

21. Menkhaus (1989:326), Abdi Samatar (1989:92–93).

22. Menkhaus 1989.

23. Abdi Samatar (1992:635).

24. Laitin and Samatar (1984).

25. Hoben (1988:198).

26. Laitin and Samatar (1984:70).

27. See Rawson (1994), Schraeder (1993), Henze (1991), Lefebvre (1991).

28. See Abdi Samatar (1988), Cassanelli (1986).

29. Cassanelli (1996:21).

30. Those familiar with Somali political history will recognize that this description, while accurate, is a much abbreviated version of events. Those unfamiliar with this period of Somali politics may wish to consult Compagnon (1990), Laitin and Samatar (1987), I. M. Lewis (1988:226–66; 1994:177–219), Markakis (1987), Cassanelli (1996).

31. See Abdi Samatar (1989).

32. I. M. Lewis (1988:215).

33. Abdi Samatar (1988:36).

34. Hoben (1988).

35. Some funds were also earmarked to support privately owned banana plantations, in which Italian donors continued to hold an interest.

36. Holtzman (1987).

37. This assessment of state farms in the lower Jubba draws on Menkhaus and Craven's (1996) careful and detailed study.

38. See also Abdi Samatar's description of a cooperative formed by smallholders in Gabileh District of northwestern Somalia (1989:129). Unlike the Loc farmers, the Gabileh farmers did receive some state inputs and tractor time prior to the Ogaadeen war, but abandoned their cooperative efforts when the state abandoned its support.

39. Private commandeering of state-supplied inputs beleaguered cooperatives throughout the country.

40. Reyna (1987) notes a similar pattern in West Africa of agricultural state corporations formed by state governments to oversee donor-funded development in their river valleys. As in Somalia, when donor support for state corporations waned, private land accumulation by a "bureaucratic gentry" soared.

41. See Besteman (1994) for a detailed review of the literature on land registration programs in Africa.

42. The national registry in Mogadishu recorded 223 titles in Bu'aale District and 479 in the Middle Jubba Region in one document, and 512 in the Middle Jubba Region in another document. The disorganized state of record-keeping made it difficult to determine the accuracy of these figures or to explain the substantial discrepancy between the national and regional registries. The difference could reflect pending leasehold requests at the regional level which had not yet been recorded at the national level, or it could reflect two different sets of titles if leases granted regionally were not recorded in Mogadishu and leases granted directly from Mogadishu were not recorded in the regional office.

43. See Besteman and Roth (1989), Merryman (1996), Cassanelli (1996).

44. Roth (1988).

45. Little (1996).

46. Deshmuck (1987), Riddell and Samatar (1988).

47. See Besteman (1994:500–501) for detailed production figures.

48. There were exceptions to this generalization. The regional agricultural officer held title to a large parcel of land in a village to the north of Loc on which he was experimenting with different agricultural techniques and seed varieties, including spinach, watermelon, tobacco, onion, tomato, dill, papaya, mango, sesame, and maize. In addition to having a great personal interest in agriculture, he viewed his undertaking as a demonstration farm for regional villagers. His interest in and commitment to agriculture made him unique among the registered titleholders I knew in the middle valley.

49. Such speculation characterized many kinds of investments in Somalia during the 1980s. Simons (1995) describes how the generalized atmosphere of

economic uncertainty encouraged people to invest in social and political networks to enhance their chances of getting on the government payroll or gaining access—no matter how small or short-lived—to some government resource or political windfall.

50. Cf. Reyna (1987).

Chapter 9. Conclusion

1. While I have not returned to the valley since my departure in 1988 and can thus claim no firsthand knowledge of militia activity or farmers' fates, news reports and eyewitness accounts (from refugees, nongovernmental organization workers, and United Nations Operations in Somalia employees) provide some compelling evidence about the pattern of violence which I draw upon here.

2. Omaar and de Waal (1993b:9).

3. The story of the Jubba valley demonstrates some of the political effects of foreign aid and the refusal to acknowledge (or the willingness to disregard) the critical dimensions of local, regional, and national politics in areas targeted for "development." Such effects are so well documented throughout Africa that development projects and foreign supported domestic policies (such as Somalia's land registration laws) introduced with such disregard for the well-being of people to be affected constitutes, I believe, a human rights abuse at the international level. People die, are imprisoned, and are tortured as a result of such programs, which should be considered shocking by an international community that professes to be so interested in human rights. The misappropriation of aid, the callousness of its dispersal, the disregard for its politicizing effects at the local level, and the massive sums involved should be an object of international (and national) outrage.

4. See also Berreman (1977), Lonsdale (1981), Vincent (1974), Young (1982).

5. Fischer (1993).

6. Gilroy (1991).

7. Beck (1993).

8. Holmes (1993).

9. Encouraging recent reports from Somalia discuss the emerging strength of local leaders in negotiating peace and mediation (Menkhaus 1998).

Epilogue

1. These words were capitalized in the original written version of the paper.

2. Kusow (1994).

3. Ahmed (1995).

4. Omaar and de Waal (1993a).

5. Declich, personal communication (November 1996).

Bibliography

Archived British and Italian colonial documents are identified in the text by the initials of the archives in which they are located. ASMAI is the Archivo Storico del Ministero degli Affari Esteri located in Rome, Italy. ASMAI documents are referenced here by position and fascicolo numbers where relevant. KNA is the Kenya National Archives and GBCO is the Great Britain Colonial Office. I consulted these archives at Bird Library, Syracuse University. The KNA holdings at Syracuse are on microfilm; I provide the reel and roll locations for those documents cited in the text.

Abir, Mordechai. 1968. "Caravan Trade and History in the Northern Parts of East Africa." *Paideuma* 14:103–20.

Abu-Lughod, Lila. 1986. *Veiled Sentiments: Honor and Poetry in a Bedouin Society.* Berkeley: University of California Press.

———. 1990. "The Romance of Resistance: Tracing Transformations of Power Through Bedouin Women." *American Ethnologist* 17 (1): 41–55.

Adam, Hussein. 1992. "Somalia: Militarism, Warlordism, or Democracy?" *Review of African Political Economy* 54:11–26.

———. 1995. "Somalia: A Terrible Beauty Being Born." In *Collapsed States: The Disintegration and Restoration of Legitimate Authority*, ed. William I. Zartman, 69–89. Boulder: Lynne Reinner.

Adas, Michael. 1995. "The Reconstruction of 'Tradition' and the Defense of the Colonial Order: British West Africa in the Early Twentieth Century." In *Articulating Hidden Histories: Exploring the Influence of Eric R. Wolf*, ed. Jane Schneider and Reyna Rapp, 291–307. Berkeley: University of California Press.

Africa Watch. 1993. "Somalia: Beyond the Warlords: The Need for a Verdict on Human Rights Abuses." *News from Africa Watch* (Washington, D.C.; New York; London), vol. 5, issue 2, March 7.

Ahmed, Ali Jimale, ed. 1995. *The Invention of Somalia.* Lawrenceville, N.J.: Red Sea Press.

Allan, James de Vere. 1983. "Shungwaya, the Segeju and Somali History." In *Proceedings of the Second International Congress of Somali Studies*, ed. Thomas Labahn, 55–72. Hamburg: Buske.

Alonso, Ana María. 1994. "The Politics of Space, Time and Substance: State Formation, Nationalism, and Ethnicity." *Annual Review of Anthropology* 23:379–405.

Alpers, Edward. 1975. *Ivory and Slaves in East Central Africa: Changing Patterns of*

International Trade in East Central Africa to the Late Nineteenth Century. Berkeley: University of California Press.

———. 1983. "Muqdishu in the Nineteenth Century: A Regional Perspective." *Journal of African History* 24:441–59.

Amnesty International. 1988. *Somalia: A Long-Term Human Rights Crisis.* AI Index: AFR 52/26/88. London: Amnesty International.

———. 1990. *Somalia: Report on an Amnesty International Visit and Current Human Rights Concerns.* AI Index: AFR 52/01/90. London: Amnesty International.

———. 1992. *Somalia: A Human Rights Disaster.* AI Index: AFR 52/01/92. London: Amnesty International.

Anderson, Benedict. 1987. *Imagined Communities: Reflections on the Origin and Spread of Nationalisms.* London: Verso.

Anonymous. 1906. "Da Giumba a Bardera a vapore." *Revista Coloniale,* year 1, vol. 2, pp. 95–62. Located in Istituto Agronomico per L'Oltremare, Florence, Italy.

Appadurai, Arjun. 1988. "Putting Hierarchy in Its Place." *Cultural Anthropology* 3 (1): 36–49.

Appiah, Kwame Anthony. 1992. *In My Father's House: Africa in the Philosophy of Culture.* New York: Oxford University Press.

ARD (Associates in Rural Development). 1985. "Juba Development Analytical Studies Project: Environmental and Sociological Assessment (Somalia)." Burlington, Vt.: Associates in Rural Development.

Asad, Talal. 1970. *The Kababish Arabs.* London: C. Hurst.

ASMAI. 1865. *Administration Report of Zanzibar for the Year 1864–65.* By R. L. Playfair, Her Majesty's Consul and Political Agent. Dated April 15.

———. 1896. Crauford, Clifford H. "Mr. Crauford to the Marques of Salisbury." July 13, Mombasa, pos. 68/1, f. 6.

———. 1902a. "Organizzazione Militaire." In Administrazione Civile 1901–1913, pos. 75/6, f. 54.

———. 1902b. Letter from C. Eliot, Agent a Console General Britannico e Commisario dell'East Afrika Protectorate to Cav. G. Pesstaloza, console Generale d'Italia in Zanzibar, June 24, Mombasa, pos. 68/2, f. 24.

———. 1909. "Considerazioni generali relativamenta alla questione della schiavitu nel Benadir ed all/azione esplicata in riguardo ad essa dalle residenze recentemente stabilite sul fiume Uebi-Scebeli." *Bollettino della Societa Antischiavista Italiana.* No. 5, September/October Rome. In Schiavismo, pos. 74/1.

———. 1910. "Schiavitu." Written by resident of Af-goi Casali. In Territorio e populazione, 1909–1916, pos. 87/2.

———. 1916. Excerpt from G. Caniglia, "Cenni di demografia sulle populazione della somalia italiana." In Territoria e populazione, 1909–1916, pos. 87/2.

Baier, Stephen, and Paul Lovejoy. 1977. "The Tuareg of the Central Sudan: Gradations in Servility at the Desert Edge (Niger and Nigeria)." In *Slavery in Africa,* ed. Suzanne Miers and Igor Kopytoff, 391–411. Madison: University of Wisconsin Press.

Balibar, Etienne, and Immanuel Wallerstein. 1991. *Race, Nation, Class: Ambiguous Identities.* London: Verso.

Barnes, Virginia Lee. 1994. *Aman: The Story of a Somali Girl.* New York: Pantheon Books.

Barth, Frederik, ed. 1969. *Ethnic Groups and Boundaries.* Boston: Little, Brown.

Beachey, R. W. 1976. *A Collection of Documents on the Slave Trade of Eastern Africa.* New York: Barnes and Noble.

Beck, Sam. 1989. "Ethnic Identity as Contested Terrain: Introduction." *Dialectical Anthropology* 14 (1): 1–6.
———. 1993. "Racism and the Formation of a Romani Ethnic Leader." In *Perilous States*, ed. George Marcus, 165–86. Chicago: University of Chicago Press.
Behar, Ruth. 1993. *Translated Woman.* Boston: Beacon Press.
Berreman, Gerald D. 1977. "Social Barriers: Caste, Class, and Race in Cross-Cultural Perspective." *Papers in Anthropology* 18 (2): 217–42.
Berry, Sara, ed. 1989. *Africa* 59 (1), *Special Issue: Access, Control and Use of Resources in African Agriculture.*
Besteman, Catherine. 1993. "Public History and Private Knowledge: On Disputed History in Southern Somalia." *Ethnohistory* 40 (4): 563–86.
———. 1994. "Individualisation and the Assault on Customary Tenure in Africa: Title Registration Programmes and the Case of Somalia." *Africa* 64 (4): 484–515.
———. 1995a. "The Invention of Gosha: Slavery, Colonialism, and Stigma in Somali History." In *The Invention of Somalia*, ed. Ali Jimale Ahmed, 43–62. Lawrenceville, N.J.: Red Sea Press.
———. 1995b. "Polygyny, Women's Land Tenure, and the Mother-Son Partnership in Southern Somalia." *Journal of Anthropological Research* 59 (3): 193–213.
———. 1996a. "Representing Violence and 'Othering' Somalia." *Cultural Anthropology* 11 (4): 120–133.
———. 1996b. "Local Land Use Strategies and Outsider Politics: Title Registration in the Middle Jubba Valley." In *The Struggle for Land in Southern Somalia: The War Behind the War*, ed. C. Besteman and L. V. Cassanelli, 29–46. Boulder: Westview Press.
Besteman, Catherine, and Lee V. Cassanelli. 1996. "Introduction: Politics and Production in Southern Somalia." In *The Struggle for Land in Southern Somalia: The War Behind the War*, ed. C. Besteman and L. V. Cassanelli, 3–13. Boulder: Westview Press.
Besteman, Catherine, and Michael Roth. 1988. "Land Tenure in the Middle Jubba Valley: Issues and Policy Recommendations." JESS Report No. 34. Burlington, Vt.: Associates in Rural Development.
Bourdieu, Pierre. 1977. *Outline of a Theory of Practice.* Cambridge: Cambridge University Press.
Bourgois, Philippe. 1995. *In Search of Respect: Selling Crack in El Barrio.* Cambridge: Cambridge University Press.
Brow, James. 1990. "Notes on Community, Hegemony, and the Uses of the Past." *Anthropological Quarterly* 63 (1): 1–6.
Bruce, John. 1988. "A Perspective on Indigenous Land Tenure Systems and Land Concentration." In *Land and Society in Contemporary Africa*, ed. Richard Downs and Stephen Reyna, 23–52. Hanover, N.H.: University Press of New England.
Burton, Sir Richard. [1894] 1987. *First Footsteps in East Africa.* Mineola, N.Y.: Dover.
CNN (Cable News Network). 1992. "History of Somalia Prior to Present Anarchy." December 8. Atlanta: Cable News Network.
Carnegie, Charles V. 1996. "The Dundas and the Nation." *Cultural Anthropology* 11 (4): 470–509.
Cassanelli, Lee. 1982. *The Shaping of Somali Society: Reconstructing the History of a Pastoral People, 1600–1900.* Philadelphia: University of Pennsylvania Press.
———. 1986. "Qat: Changes in the Production and Consumption of a Quasilegal Commodity in Northeast Africa." In *The Social Life of Things: Commodities*

in Cultural Perspective, ed. Arjun Appadurai, 236–57. Cambridge: Cambridge University Press.

———. 1988. "The Ending of Slavery in Italian Somalia: Liberty and the Control of Labor, 1890–1935." In *The End of Slavery in Africa*, ed. Suzanne Miers and Richard Roberts, 308–31. Madison: University of Wisconsin Press.

———. 1989. "Social Construction on the Somali Frontier: Bantu Former Slave Communities in the Nineteenth Century." In *The African Frontier: The Reproduction of Traditional African Societies*, ed. Igor Kopytoff, 216–38. Bloomington: Indiana University Press.

———. 1993a. "Explaining Ethnic Conflict in Somalia." In *High Conflict/Low Conflict: Six Case Studies of Ethnic Politics*. Report of a workshop held at the Woodrow Wilson International Center for Scholars. Pp. 2–26. Washington D.C.: Woodrow Wilson International Center for Scholars.

———. 1993b. "History and Identity among Somali Refugees: A Recent Example from Coastal Kenya." Presented at the African Studies Association Meetings, Boston, December 3–6.

———. 1996. "Explaining the Somali Crisis." In *The Struggle for Land in Southern Somalia: The War behind the War*, ed. C. Besteman and L. V. Cassanelli, 13–26. Boulder: Westview Press.

Cerulli, Enrico. 1934. "Gruppi etnici negri nella Somalia." *Archivio per l'antropologia e la etnologia* 64:177–84.

———. 1957. *Somalia: Scritti vari editi ed inediti*. Vol. 1. Rome: Istituto Poligrafico dello Stato.

———. 1959. *Somalia: Scritti vari editi ed inediti*. Vol. 2. Rome: Istituto Poligrafico dello Stato.

Chiesi, Gustavo, and Ernesto Travelli. 1904. *Le Questioni del Benadir: Atti e relazione della Commissione d'inchiesta della Società del Benadir*. Milan: Bellini.

Christopher, Lieutenant W. 1844. "Extract from a Journal by Lieut. W. Christopher, Commanding the H. C. Brig of War 'Tigris' on the East Coast of Africa. Dated 8 May 1843." *Journal of the Royal Geographic Society of London* 14:76–103.

Cohen, A., ed. 1974. *Urban Ethnicity*. London: Tavistock.

Cohen, Ronald. 1978. "Ethnicity: Problem and Focus in Anthropology." *Annual Review of Anthropology* 7:379–403.

Cohn, Bernard S., and Nicholas B. Dirks. 1988. "Beyond the Fringe: The Nation State, Colonialism, and the Technologies of Power." *Journal of Historical Sociology* 1 (2): 224–29.

Colson, Elizabeth. 1968. "Contemporary Tribes and the Development of Nationalism." In *Essays on the Problem of the Tribe*, ed. June Helm, 201–6. Seattle: University of Washington Press.

Colucci, Massimo. 1924. *Princippi di diritto consuetudinario della Somalia italiana meridionale*. Florence: Editrice La Voce.

Comaroff, Jean. 1985. *Body of Power, Spirit of Resistance: The Culture and History of a South African People*. Chicago: University of Chicago Press.

Comaroff, John. 1987. "Of Totemism and Ethnicity: Consciousness, Practice, and the Signs of Inequality." *Ethnos* 52 (3–4): 301–23.

Comaroff, John, and Jean Comaroff. 1992. *Ethnography and the Historical Imagination*. Boulder: Westview Press.

Compagnon, Daniel. 1990. "The Somali Opposition Fronts: Some Comments and Questions." *Horn of Africa* 13 (1–2): 29–54.

———. 1992. "Political Decay in Somalia: From Personal Rule to Warlordism." *Refuge* 12 (5): 8–13.

Conforti, E. 1954. "Studi per opere di resanamento e valorizzazione dei descek del Giuba." Centro di Documentazione, Istituto Agronomico per L'Oltremare, Florence, Italy.

Cooper, Frederick. 1977. *Plantation Slavery on the East Coast of Africa.* New Haven: Yale University Press.

———. 1980. *From Slaves to Squatters: Plantation Labor and Agriculture in Zanzibar and Coastal Kenya, 1890–1925.* New Haven: Yale University Press.

———. 1981. "Islam and Cultural Hegemony: The Ideology of Slaveowners on the East African Coast." In *The Ideology of Slavery in Africa,* ed. Paul Lovejoy, 271-307. Beverly Hills: Sage.

Coronil, Fernanco, and Julie Skurski. 1991. "Dismembering and Remembering the Nation: The Semantics of Political Violence in Venezuela." *Comparative Studies in Society and History* 33 (2): 288–337.

Craven, Kathryn, James Merryman, and Nancy Merryman. 1989. *Jubba Environmental and Socioeconomic Studies.* Vol. 3: *Socioeconomic Studies.* Burlington, Vt.: Associates in Rural Development.

Daniel, E. Valentine. 1996. *Charred Lullabies: Chapters in an Anthropology of Violence.* Princeton: Princeton University Press.

de Carolis, Adriana Piga. 1980. "Il quadro etnico tradizionale nelle prospettive di sviluppo della valle del Giuba." *Africa* (Rome) 35:17–42.

Declich, Francesca. 1987. "I Goscia della regione del medio Giuba nella Somalia meridionale: Un gruppo etnico di origine Bantu." *Africa* (Rome) 42 (4): 570–99.

———. 1992. *Il processo di formazione della identità culturale dei Bantu della Somalia meridionale.* Ph.D. diss., Istituto Universitario Orientale, Naples, Italy.

———. 1995. "Identity, Dance and Islam among People with Bantu Origins in Riverine Areas of Somalia." In *The Invention of Somalia,* ed. Ali Jimale Ahmed, 191–222. Lawrenceville, N.J.: Red Sea Press.

———. Forthcoming. "Fostering Ethnic Reinvention: Gender Impact of Forced Migration on Bantu Somali Refugees in Kenya." *Cahiers d'Etudes Africaines.*

Denich, Bette. 1994. "Dismembering Yugoslavia: Nationalist Ideologies and the Symbolic Revival of Genocide." *American Ethnologist* 21 (2): 367–90.

Deshmuck, Ian. 1987. "Riverine Forests of the Jubba Valley: Issues and Recommendations for Conservation." JESS Report No. 17. Burlington, Vt.: Associates in Rural Development.

Doornbos, Martin, and John Markakis. 1994. "Society and State in Crisis: What Went Wrong in Somalia?" *Review of African Political Economy* 21 (59): 82–88.

Drake, St. Clair. 1990. *Black Folk Here and There: An Essay in History and Anthropology.* Vol. 2. Los Angeles: Center for Afro-American Studies, University of California at Los Angeles.

Dundas, F. G. 1893. "Expedition up the Jub River through Somali-Land, East Africa." *Geographic Journal* 1:209–23.

du Toit, Brian. 1978. Introduction. In *Ethnicity in Modern Africa,* ed. Brian du Toit. Boulder: Westview Press.

Eno, Omar A. 1993. "The Untold Apartheid in Somalia Imposed on Bantu/Jareer People." Presented at the Fifth International Congress of Somali Studies, College of the Holy Cross, Worcester, Mass., December 1–3.

Ferguson, Brian. 1990a. "Blood of the Leviathan: Western Contact and Warfare in Amazonia." *American Ethnologist* 17 (2): 237–57.

———. 1990b. "Explaining War." In *The Anthropology of War,* ed. Jonathan Haas, 26–55. Cambridge: Cambridge University Press.

Ferguson, Brian, and Neil Whitehead, eds. 1992. *War in the Tribal Zone.* Santa Fe, N.M.: School of American Research Press.

FEWS (Food Early Warning System). Records. Ministry of Agriculture, Mogadishu.

Fischer, Michael M. J. 1993. "Working through the Other: The Jewish, Spanish, Turkish, Iranian, Ukrainian, Lithuanian, and German Unconscious of Polish Culture or One Hand Clapping: Dialogue, Silences, and the Mourning of Polish Romanticism." In *Perilous States: Conversations on Culture, Politics, and Nation,* ed. George Marcus, 187–234. Chicago: University of Chicago Press.

Fisher, Allan, and Humphrey Fisher. 1970. *Slavery and Muslim Society in Africa: The Institution in Saharan and Sudanic Africa and the Trans-Saharan Trade.* London: C. Hurst.

Foster, Robert J. 1991. "Making National Cultures in the Global Ecumene." *Annual Review of Anthropology* 20:235–60.

Foucault, Michel 1980. *Power/Knowledge: Selected Interviews and Other Writings, 1972–1977,* ed. Colin Gordon. New York: Pantheon.

Fowler, Loretta. 1987. *Shared Symbols, Contested Meanings: Gros Ventre Culture and History, 1778–1984.* Ithaca, N.Y.: Cornell University Press.

Franciosi, P., and E. Lombardi. 1989. "I padroni dei coccodrilli: Note sui baxaar della Somalia." *Africa* (Rome) 19 (1): 127–32.

Freeman-Grenville, G. S. P. 1962. *The East African Coast: Select Documents from the First to the Earlier Nineteenth Century.* Oxford: Clarendon Press.

Galaty, J. 1982. "Being 'Maasai'": Being People of Cattle: Ethnic Shifters in East Africa." *American Ethnologist* 9 (1): 1–20.

Gaventa, John. 1980. *Power and Powerlessness: Quiescence and Rebellion in an Appalachian Valley.* Oxford: Clarendon Press.

GBCO. 1909–10. Great Britain Colonial Office, British East Africa Protectorate Report for 1909–10.

———. 1910–18. Annual Reports of British East Africa Protectorate.

Genovese, Eugene. 1974. *Roll, Jordan, Roll: The World the Slaves Made.* New York: Pantheon Press.

Gersony, Robert. 1989. "Why Somalis Flee: Conflict in Northern Somalia." *Cultural Survival Quarterly* 13 (4): 45–58.

Geshekter, Charles. 1985. "Anti-Colonialism and Class Formation: The Eastern Horn of Africa before 1950." *International Journal of African Historical Studies* 18 (1): 1–32.

———. 1991. "Somali Maritime History and Regional Diversity: An Introduction." Presented at the thirty-fourth Annual Meeting of the African Studies Association, St. Louis, Missouri, November 23–26.

Gilroy, Paul. 1991. *"There Ain't No Black in the Union Jack": The Cultural Politics of Race and Nation.* London: Hutchinson.

Goheen, Miriam. 1988. "Land Accumulation and Local Control: The Manipulation of Symbols and Power in Nso, Cameroon." In *Land and Society in Contemporary Africa,* ed. Richard Downs and Stephen Reyna, 280–308. Hanover, N.H.: University Press of New England.

———. 1996. *Men Own the Fields, Women Own the Crops: Gender and Power in the Cameroon Grassfields.* Madison: University of Wisconsin Press.

Goody, Jack. 1980. "Rice Burning and the Green Revolution in Northern Ghana." *Journal of Development Studies* 16 (2): 136–55.

Gordon, Avery, and Christopher Newfield. 1995. "White Philosophy." In *Identi-*

ties, ed. Kwame Anthony Appiah and Henry Louis Gates, Jr., 380–400. Chicago: University of Chicago Press.

Gordon, Robert. 1992. *The Bushman Myth: The Making of an African Underclass.* Boulder: Westview Press.

Gramsci, Antonio. 1971. *Selections from the Prison Notebooks.* Ed. and trans. Quintin Hoare and Geoffrey Nowell Smith. New York: International Publishers.

Greenberg, James. 1989. *Blood Ties: Life and Violence in Rural Mexico.* Tucson: University of Arizona Press.

Gregory, Steven, and Roger Sanjek, eds. 1994. *Race.* New Brunswick, N.J.: Rutgers University Press.

Grinker, Richard Roy. 1990. "Images of Denigration: Structuring Inequality between Foragers and Farmers in the Ituri Forest, Zaire." *American Ethnologist* 17 (1): 111–30.

Guadagni, Marco. 1982. "The Evolution of Proprietary Land Rights in Somali Customary Law." *Italian National Reports to the Eleventh International Congress of Comparative Law,* 25–63. Milano: Giuffre Editore.

Gunn, Susan. 1987. "Somalia." In *The Peasant Betrayed: Agriculture and Land Reform in the Third World,* ed. John Powelson and Richard Stock, 109–24. Boston: Oelgeschlager Gunn and Hain.

Gupta, Akhil, and James Ferguson. 1992. "Beyond 'Culture': Space, Identity, and the Politics of Difference." *Cultural Anthropology* 7 (1): 6–23.

Heine, Bernd. 1978. "The Sam Languages: A History of Somali, Rendille, and Boni." *Afroasiatic Linguistics* 9 (2): 1–93.

Helander, Bernhard. 1986. "The Social Dynamics of Southern Somali Agro-Pastoralism: A Regional Approach." In *Somalia: Agriculture in the Winds of Change,* ed. Peter Conze and Thomas Labahn, 93–114. Saarbrücken-Schafbrücke, Germany: EPI Verlag.

———. 1988. "The Slaughtered Camel: Coping with Fictitious Descent among the Hubeer of Southern Somalia." Ph.D. diss., Uppsala University.

———. 1996. "Power and Poverty in Southern Somalia." Working Papers in Cultural Anthropology, No. 5. Uppsala, Sweden: Department of Cultural Anthropology, Uppsala University.

Henze, Paul. 1991. *The Horn of Africa: From War to Peace.* New York: St. Martin's Press.

Hess, Robert. 1966. *Italian Colonialism in Somalia.* Chicago: University of Chicago Press.

Hoben, Allan. 1988. "The Political Economy of Land Tenure in Somalia." In *Land and Society in Contemporary Africa,* ed. Richard Downs and Stephen Reyna, 193–220. Hanover, N.H.: University Press of New England.

Hoben, Allan, Susan Hoben, and John Harris. 1983. *Somalia: A Social and Institutional Profile.* African Studies Center Working Paper. Boston: Boston University.

Hobsbawm, Eric, and Terence Ranger, eds. 1983. *The Invention of Tradition.* Cambridge: Cambridge University Press.

Holmes, Douglas. 1993. "Illicit Discourse." In *Perilous States: Conversations on Culture, Politics, and Nation,* ed. George Marcus, 255–81. Chicago: University of Chicago Press.

Holtzman, John. 1987. "Maize Supply and Price Situation in Somalia: An Historical Overview and Analysis of Recent Changes." Working Paper 5. Mogadishu: Ministry of Agriculture, Directorate of Planning and Statistics, Food Security Project.

Human Rights Watch. 1989. "Human Rights in Selected African Countries." Remarks prepared for the House Subcommittee on Foreign Operations by Holly Burkhalter, Africa Watch. February 7.

Hutchinson, Sharon. 1996. *Nuer Dilemmas: Coping with Money, War, and the State.* Berkeley: University of California Press.

Iliffe, John. 1979. *A Modern History of Tanganyika.* Cambridge: Cambridge University Press.

Iyop, Ruth. 1994. "The Somali Crisis." *Ufahamu: Journal of the African Activist Association* 22 (1–2): 3–10.

Kapteijns, Lidwien. 1991. "Women and the Somali Pastoral Tradition: Corporate Kinship and Capitalist Transformation in Northern Somalia." Working Papers in African Studies, no. 153. Boston: African Studies Center, Boston University.

Kapteijns, Lidwien, and Jay Spaulding. 1989. "Class Formation and Gender in Precolonial Somali Society: A Research Agenda." *Northeast African Studies* (East Lansing: African Studies Center, Michigan State University) 9 (1): 19–38.

Karp, Mark. 1960. *The Economics of Trusteeship in Somalia.* Boston: Boston University Press.

Kassim, M. 1993. "Aspects of the Banadir Cultural History: The Case of the Bravan Ulama." Presented at the Fifth International Congress of Somali Studies, College of the Holy Cross, Worcester, Mass., December 1–3.

Kelly, Hilarie. 1983. "Orma and Somali Culture Sharing in the Juba-Tana Region." In *Proceedings of the Second International Congress of Somali Studies,* ed. Thomas Labahn, 13–38. Hamburg: Buske.

Kenny, M. G. 1981. "Mirror in the Forest: The Dorobo Hunter-Gatherers as an Image of the Other." *Africa* 51 (1): 477–95.

Kersten, Otto, ed. 1871. *Baron Carl Claus von der Decken's Reisen in Ost Afrika in den Jahren 1862 bis 1865.* Vol. 2. Leipzig and Heidelberg: C. F. Winter.

Klein, Martin. 1978. "The Study of Slavery in Africa." *Journal of African History* 19 (4): 599–609.

———. 1989. "Studying the History of Those Who Would Rather Forget: Oral History and the Experience of Slavery." *History in Africa* 16:209–17.

KNA. n.d. Extract from the notes on the Abd Wak and their country by Lt. Col. Llewellyn, Commanding 5th King's African Rifles. Miscellaneous correspondence, reel 2804, roll 8.

———. 1902. Letter from Major Harrison, Officer Commanding Jubaland, on April 22 to Kismayu, to Subcommissioner of Mombasa. Miscellaneous correspondence, reel 2804, roll 9.

———. 1914. "The Juba River." Correspondence from W. McGregor Ross, Div (or Dir) PWD to E. P. Evans, Ag Chf Secty to R. S. Selkeld, AgPC, June 9. Miscellaneous correspondence, reel 2804, roll 8.

———. 1915–16. Jubaland Province Annual Report. Miscellaneous correspondence, reel 2804, roll 8.

———. 1916. The Administration of Jubaland. Coast Province. Miscellaneous correspondence, reel 2804, roll 9.

———. 1917a. Memorandum re Jubaland Somalis, WaGosha, and Bajun Tribes, by AgPC, December 20. Miscellaneous correspondence, reel 2804, roll 8.

———. 1917b. Handing Over Report, DC Office, Mfudo. Located in the Kenya National Archives in Nairobi, Kenya.

———. 1920. Correspondence from DC Serenli to PC Jubaland at Kismayo. April 30. Miscellaneous correspondence, reel 2804, roll 8.

———. 1920–21. Annual Report for Alexandria District, by AgDC R. S. Anden.

———. 1922a. Letter to the Chief Native Commissioner from Darod Somalis, August 1. Miscellaneous correspondence, reel 2804, roll 8.
———. 1922b. Letter from DC, Kismayo (Jennings) to the Ag Senior Commissioner, Kismayo, re "Racial Status of Somalis," August 8. Miscellaneous correspondence, reel 2804, roll 8.
———. 1922c. Letter from SC, Kismayo (Hastings Horne) to the Chief Native Commissioner, Nairobi, October 30. Miscellaneous correspondence, reel 2804, roll 8.
———. 1923. Serenli District, October 31. Kenya Colony Intelligence Reports. Reel 2805, roll 4.
———. 1924. Kenya Colony Intelligence Reports. March. Reel 2805, roll 4.
———. 1925. Handing Over Report, Wajir District, Capt. Mahoney to S. V. Cooke, September 1. Reel 2803, roll 12.
———. 1930. "Questionnaire" by R. G. Darroch, ADC, Garissa District, with Addendum by H. B. Sharpe, DC, Garissa District. Document signed by M. R. Mahone, District Commissioner. Reel 2802, roll 3.
———. 1931a. Kenya Colony Intelligence Report, Bura District Diary of H. B. Sharpe, DC, Tellemugger, March. Reel 2805, roll 5.
———. 1931b. Kenya Colony Intelligence Report, Tellemugger District, July. Reel 2805, roll 5.
———. 1932a. Kenya Colony Intelligence Report, Tellemugger District, March. Reel 2805, roll 5.
———. 1932b. Kenya Colony Intelligence Report, Garissa District, June. Reel 2805, roll 5.
———. 1932c. Kenya Colony Intelligence Report, Garissa District. Report on Safari in Abdulle Country, May–June. June 19. Reel 2805, roll 5.
———. 1932d. Kenya Colony Intelligence Report, Garissa District. July. Reel 2805, roll 5.
———. 1932e. Garissa District Political Record Book, July 28. Reel 69, roll 41.
———. 1938. Wajir District Annual Report. Reel 2801, roll 47.
Krech, Shepard III. 1991. "The State of Ethnohistory." *Annual Review of Anthropology* 20:345–75.
Kuklick, Henrika. 1991. "Contested Monuments: The Politics of Archeology in Southern Africa." In *Colonial Situations: Essays on the Contextualization of Ethnographic Knowledge*, ed. George Stocking, 135–69. Madison: University of Wisconsin Press.
Kuper, Adam. 1982. "Lineage Theory: A Critical Retrospect." *Annual Review of Anthropology* 11:71–95.
Kusow, Abdi Mohamed. 1994. "The Genesis of the Somali Civil War: A New Perspective." *Northeast African Studies* (East Lansing: Michigan State University), n.s., 1 (1): 31–46.
Laitin, David. 1976. "The Political Economy of Military Rule in Somalia." *Journal of Modern African Studies* 14 (3): 449–68.
———. 1977. *Politics, Language, and Thought: The Somali Experience.* Chicago: University of Chicago Press.
———. 1979. "Somalia's Military Government and Scientific Socialism." In *Socialism in Sub-Saharan Africa: A New Assessment,* ed. Carl Rosberg and Thomas Callaghy, 174–207. Institute of International Studies. Berkeley: University of California Press.
———. 1982. "The Political Crisis in Somalia." *Horn of Africa* 5 (2): 60–64.

Laitin, David, and Said S. Samatar. 1984. "Somalia and the World Economy." *Review of African Political Economy* 30:58–72.
———. 1987. *Somalia: Nation in Search of a State.* Boulder: Westview Press.
Lan, David. 1985. *Guns and Rain: Guerillas and Spirit Mediums in Zimbabwe.* Berkeley and London: University of California Press and James Currey.
Lederman, Rena. 1986. "Changing Times in Mendi: Notes towards Writing Highland New Guinea History." *Ethnohistory* 33 (1): 1–30.
Lefebvre, Jeffrey. 1991. *Arms for the Horn: U.S. Security Policy in Ethiopia and Somalia, 1953–1991.* Pittsburgh: University of Pittsburgh Press.
Lemarchand, Rene. 1994. *Burundi: Ethnocide as Discourse and Practice.* Cambridge: Cambridge University Press and Woodrow Wilson Center Press.
Levine, Lawrence. 1977. *Black Culture and Black Consciousness: Afro-American Folk Thought from Slavery to Freedom.* New York: Oxford University Press.
Levtzion, Nehemia. 1985. "Slavery and Islamization in Africa: A Comparative Study." In *Slaves and Slavery in Muslim Africa,* ed. John Ralph Willis, 182–98. London: Frank Cass.
Lewis, Bernard. 1971. *Race and Color in Islam.* New York: Harper and Row.
Lewis, Herbert S. 1966. "The Origins of the Galla and Somali." *Journal of African History* 7 (1): 27–46.
Lewis, Ioan M. 1955. *The Peoples of the Horn of Africa.* Oxford: Oxford University Press.
———. 1961. *A Pastoral Democracy.* London: Oxford University Press.
———. 1971. "From Nomadism to Cultivation: The Expansion of Political Solidarity in Southern Somalia." In *Man in Africa,* ed. Mary Douglas and Phyllis Kaberry, 61–79. London: Tavistock.
———. 1988. *A Modern History of Somalia: Nation and State in the Horn of Africa.* Boulder: Westview Press.
———. 1994. *Blood and Bone: The Call of Kinship in Somali Society.* Lawrenceville, N.J.: Red Sea Press.
Lingle, Christopher. 1992. "Collectivism and Collective Choice: Conflicts between Class Formation and Ethnic Nationalism." *Ethnic Groups* 9 (3): 191–201.
Little, Peter. 1996. "Rural Herders and Urban Merchants: The Cattle Trade of Southern Somalia." In *The Struggle for Land in Southern Somalia: The War behind the War,* ed. Catherine Besteman and Lee V. Cassanelli, 91–114. Boulder: Westview Press.
Lonsdale, John. 1981. "States and Social Processes in Africa." *African Studies Review* 24 (2/3): 139–225.
Lovejoy, Paul. 1983. *Transformations in Slavery: A History of Slavery in Africa.* Cambridge: Cambridge University Press.
Luling, Virginia. 1971. "The Social Structure of Southern Somali Tribes." Ph.D. diss., University of London.
———. 1983. "The Other Somali-Minority Groups in Traditional Somali Society." In *Proceedings of the Second International Congress of Somali Studies,* ed. Thomas Labahn, 39–55. Hamburg: Buske.
Mafeje, Archie. 1971. "The Ideology of Tribalism." *Journal of Modern African Studies* 9 (2): 253–61.
Magnino, Leo. 1933. "Aspetti e problemi della regione del Giuba, Somalia." F. 829, Centro di Documentazione, Istituto Agronomico per L'Oltremare, Florence, Italy.
Mahmood, Cynthia. 1996. *Fighting for Faith and Nation: Dialogues with Sikh Militants.* Philadelphia: University of Pennsylvania Press.

Malkki, Liisa. 1995. *Purity and Exile: Violence, Memory, and National Cosmology Among Hutu Refugees in Tanzania.* Chicago: University of Chicago Press.

Manning, P. 1983. "Contours of Slavery and Social Change in Africa." *American Historical Review* 88 (4): 835–57.

Markakis, John. 1987. *Nation and Class Conflict in the Horn of Africa.* Cambridge: Cambridge University Press.

Marx, Anthony. 1993. "Contested Images and Implications of South African Nationhood." In *The Violence Within: Cultural and Political Opposition in Divided Nations,* ed. Kay Warren, 157–79. Boulder: Westview Press.

Marx, Karl. [1852] 1973. "The Eighteenth Brumaire of Louis Bonaparte." In *Surveys from Exile,* ed. David Fernbach, 143–249. New York: Random House/ Vintage.

Meillassoux, Claude. 1975. *L'Esclavage en Afrique precoloniale.* Paris: Maspero.

———. 1983. "Female Slavery." In *Women and Slavery in Africa,* ed. Claire Robertson and Martin Klein, 49–66. Madison: University of Wisconsin Press.

———. 1995. "Slaves Are Not Kin: Reply to Kopytoff." *American Ethnologist* 22 (2): 410.

Menkhaus, Kenneth. 1989. "Rural Transformation and the Roots of Underdevelopment in Somalia's Lower Jubba Valley." Ph.D. diss., University of South Carolina.

———. 1991. *Report on an Emergency Needs Assessment of the Lower Jubba Region (Kismaayo, Jamaame, and Jilib Districts), Somalia.* July. Seattle: World Concern.

———. 1996. "From Feast to Famine: Land and the State in Somalia's Lower Jubba Valley." In *The Struggle for Land in Southern Somalia: The War Behind the War,* ed. C. Besteman and L. V. Cassanelli, 133–54. Boulder: Westview Press.

———. 1997. "U.S. Foreign Assistance to Somalia: Phoenix from the Ashes?" *Middle East Policy* 5 (1): 124–149.

———. 1998. "Somalia: Political Order in a Stateless Society." *Current History* 97 (619): 220–24.

Menkhaus, Kenneth, and Kathryn Craven. 1996. "Land Alienation and the Imposition of State Farms in the Lower Jubba Valley." In *The Struggle for Land in Southern Somalia: The War Behind the War,* ed. C. Besteman and L. V. Cassanelli, 155–77. Boulder: Westview Press.

Mercer, John. 1982. *Slavery in Mauritania Today.* Edinburgh: Human Rights Group.

Merryman, James. 1996. "The Economy of Geedo Region and the Rise of Smallholder Irrigation." In *The Struggle for Land in Southern Somalia: The War behind the War,* ed. C. Besteman and L. V. Cassanelli, 73–90. Boulder: Westview Press.

Michaelson, Mark. 1993. "Somalia: The Painful Road to Reconciliation." *Africa Today* 40 (2): 53–75.

Miers, Suzanne. 1974. *Britain and the Ending of the Slave Trade.* London: Africana Publishers.

Miers, Suzanne, and Igor Kopytoff, eds. 1977. *Slavery in Africa.* Madison: University of Wisconsin Press.

Ministero delle Colonia. 1923. Map of "Le Regione del Medio e Basso Giuba." Comp. A. Dardano. Istituto Agronomico per L'Oltremare, Florence, Italy.

Mintz, Sidney. 1979a. "The Anthropological Interview and the Life History." *Oral History Review* 7:18–26.

———. 1979b. "Slavery and the Rise of Peasantries." In *Roots and Branches: Current Directions in Slave Studies,* ed. Michael Craton, 213–74. Toronto: Pergamon Press.

Mintz, Sidney, and Richard Price. 1976. *The Birth of African-American Culture: An Anthropological Perspective.* Boston: Beacon Press.

Muhammad, Akbar. 1985. "The Image of Africans in Arabic Literature: Some Unpublished Manuscripts." In *Slaves and Slavery in Muslim Africa,* ed. John Ralph Willis, 47–74. London: Frank Cass.

Mukhtar, Mohamed H. 1989. "The Emergence and Role of Political Parties in the Inter-River Region of Somalia from 1947 to 1960 (Independence)." *Ufahamu* 16 (2): 75–95.

Murdock, George. 1959. *Outline of World Cultures.* Human Relations Area Files Manuals Series.

Nagengast, Carole. 1994. "Violence, Terror, and the Crisis of the State." *Annual Review of Anthropology* 23:109–36.

Nelson, Harold. 1982. *Somalia: A Country Study.* Area Handbook Series. Washington, D.C.: Foreign Area Studies, American University.

Netting, Robert McC. 1987. "Clashing Cultures, Clashing Symbols: Histories and Meanings of the Latok War." *Ethnohistory* 34 (3): 352–80.

Newbury, David. 1997. "Irredentist Rwanda: Ethnic and Territorial Frontiers in Central Africa." *Africa Today* 44 (2): 211–22.

New York Times. 1992. "Barrier to Somali Unity: Clan Rivalry." By Jane Perlez. August 30, A12.

Nordstrom, Carolyn, and JoAnn Martin, eds. 1992. *The Paths to Domination, Resistance, and Terror.* Berkeley: University of California Press.

Nordstrom, Carolyn, and Antonius C. G. M. Robben. 1995. *Fieldwork under Fire: Contemporary Studies of Violence and Survival.* Berkeley: University of California Press.

Nwulia, Moses. 1975. *Britain and Slavery in East Africa.* Washington, D.C.: Three Continents Press.

Nyhus, Sheila, and Garth Massey. 1986. "Female Headed Households in an Agro-Pastoral Society." Paper presented at the 1986 Conference on Gender Studies in Farming Systems Research and Extension, University of Florida, Gainesville.

O'Brien, Jay. 1986. "Toward a Reconstitution of Ethnicity: Capitalist Expansion and Cultural Dynamics." *American Anthropologist* 88 (4): 898–907.

O'Brien, Jay, and William Roseberry, eds. 1991. *Golden Ages, Dark Ages: Imagining the Past in Anthropology and History.* Berkeley: University of California Press.

Okoth-Ogendo, H. W. O. 1976. "African Land Tenure Reform." In *Agricultural Development in Kenya: An Economic Assessment,* ed. Judith Heyer, J. K. Maitha, W. M. Senga. Nairobi: Oxford University Press.

Omaar, Rakiya. 1992. "Somalia: At War with Itself." *Current History* 91 (565): 230–35.

Omaar, Rakiya, and Alex de Waal. 1993a. *Somalia: Operation Restore Hope: A Preliminary Assessment.* May. London: African Rights.

———. 1993b. "Land Tenure, the Creation of Famine, and Prospects for Peace in Somalia." October Discussion Paper No. 1. London: African Rights.

Ong, Aihwa. 1987. *Spirits of Resistance and Capitalist Discipline: Factory Women in Malaysia.* Albany: State University of New York Press.

Pankhurst, Richard. 1965. "The Trade of Southern and Western Ethiopia and the Indian Ocean Ports in the Nineteenth and Early Twentieth Centuries." *Journal of Ethiopian Studies* 3 (2): 37–74.

Patterson, Orlando. 1982. *Slavery and Social Death: A Comparative Study.* Cambridge, Mass.: Harvard University Press.

Pawlick, Thomas. 1993. "Grim Sower, Grim Harvest." *Ceres* (Rome: UN Food and Agriculture Organization) 25 (1): 31–38.
Pigg, Stacey Leigh. 1992. "Inventing Social Categories through Place: Social Representations and Development in Nepal." *Comparative Studies in Society and History* 34 (1): 491–513.
Pouwels, Randall. 1987. *Horn and Crescent: Cultural Change and Traditional Islam on the East African Coast, 800–1900.* Cambridge: Cambridge University Press.
Prendergast, John. 1994a. "The Bones of Our Children Are Not Yet Buried: The Looming Spectre of Famine and Massive Human Rights Abuse in Somalia." January. Washington D.C.: Center of Concern.
———. 1994b. "The Gun Talks Louder than the Voice: Somalia's Continuing Cycles of Violence." July. Washington D.C.: Center of Concern.
Price, Richard. 1983. *First Time: The Historical Vision of an Afro-American People.* Baltimore: Johns Hopkins University Press.
———. 1990. *Alabi's World.* Baltimore: Johns Hopkins University Press.
———, ed. 1975. *Maroon Societies: Rebel Slave Communities in the Americas.* Garden City, N.Y.: Anchor Books.
Price, Richard, and Sally Price. 1980. *Afro-American Arts of the Suriname Rain Forest.* Berkeley: University of California Press.
Puccioni, Nello. 1936. "Caratteristiche Antropologiche ed etnografiche delle popolazioni della Somalia." *Bolletino della Reale Societa Geografica Italiana* 1:209–25.
Ranger, Terence. 1983. "The Invention of Tradition in Colonial Africa." In *The Invention of Tradition,* ed. Eric Hobsbawm and Terence Ranger, 211–262. Cambridge: Cambridge University Press.
Rawson, David. 1994. "Dealing with Disintegration: U.S. Assistance and the Somali State." In *The Somali Challenge: From Catastrophe to Renewal?* ed. Ahmed I. Samatar, 147–87. Boulder: Lynne Reinner.
Rebel, Hermann. 1989. "Cultural Hegemony and Class Experience: A Critical Reading of Recent Ethnological-Historical Approaches." *American Ethnologist* 16 (2): 117–36.
Reusse, E. 1982. "Somalia's Nomadic Livestock Economy." *World Animal Review* 43:2–11.
Reyna, Stephen. 1987. "The Emergence of Land Concentration in the West African Savanna." *American Ethnologist* 14 (3): 523–41.
———. 1994. "A Mode of Domination Approach to Organized Violence." In *Studying War: Anthropological Perspectives,* ed. Steve Reyna and Richard E. Downs, 29–65. Langhorne, Pa.: Gordon and Breach.
Richards, Audrey. 1969. *The Multicultural States of East Africa.* Montreal: McGill-Queen's University Press.
Richards, Paul. 1996. *Fighting for the Rain Forest: War, Youth, and Resources in Sierra Leone.* Oxford: James Currey.
Riddell, James C., and Mohamed Said Samatar. 1988. "JESS Report on Land Tenure Dynamics in the Jubba Valley." JESS Publication No. 31. Burlington, Vt.: Associates in Rural Development.
Rigby, Peter. 1996. *African Images: Racism and the End of Anthropology.* Oxford and Washington, D.C.: Berg.
Robben, Antonius C. G. M., and Carolyn Nordstrom. 1995. "The Anthropology and Ethnography of Violence and Sociopolitical Conflict." In *Fieldwork Under Fire: Contemporary Studies of Violence and Survival,* ed. Carolyn Nordstrom and Antonius C. G. M. Robben, 1–23. Berkeley: University of California Press.

Roberts, Richard, and Suzanne Miers. 1988. "The End of Slavery in Africa." In *The End of Slavery in Africa,* ed. Suzanne Miers and Richard Roberts, 3–70. Madison: University of Wisconsin Press.

Rosaldo, Renato. 1988. "Ideology, Place, and People Without Culture." *Cultural Anthropology* 3 (1): 77–87.

Roseberry, William. 1989. *Anthropologies and Histories: Essays in Culture, History, and Political Economy.* New Brunswick, N.J.: Rutgers University Press.

Roseberry, William, and Jay O'Brien. 1991. "Introduction." In *Golden Ages, Dark Ages: Imagining the Past in Anthropology and History,* ed. Jay O'Brien and William Roseberry, 1–18. Berkeley: University of California Press.

Roth, Michael. 1988. "Somali Land Policies and Agrarian Performance: The Case of the Lower Shebelli." Paper presented at the Fifteenth Annual Symposium on African Agrarian Systems, April 10–12.

SDR (Somali Democratic Republic). 1975. "Why We Chose Scientific Socialism." Mogadishu: Ministry of Information and National Guidance.

Samatar, Abdi I. 1988. "The State, Agrarian Change, and Crisis of Hegemony in Somalia." *Review of African Political Economy* 43:26–41.

———. 1989. *The State and Rural Transformation in Northern Somalia, 1884–1986.* Madison: University of Wisconsin Press.

———. 1992. "Destruction of State and Society in Somalia: Beyond the Tribal Convention." *Journal of Modern African Studies* 30 (4): 625–41.

Samatar, Abdi, and A. I. Samatar. 1987. "The Material Roots of the Suspended African State: Arguments from Somalia." *Journal of Modern African Studies* 25 (4): 669–90.

Samatar, Ahmed. 1988. *Socialist Somalia: Rhetoric and Reality.* London: Zed Books.

Sanjek, Roger. 1994. "The Enduring Inequalities of Race." In *Race,* ed. Steven Gregory and Roger Sanjek, 1–17. New Brunswick, N.J.: Rutgers University Press.

Scheper-Hughes, Nancy. 1992. *Death Without Weeping: The Violence of Everyday Life in Brazil.* Berkeley: University of California Press.

Schraeder, Peter. 1993. "U.S. Intervention in the Horn of Africa Amidst the End of the Cold War." *Africa Today* 40 (2): 7–28.

Scott, James. 1985. *Weapons of the Weak: Everyday Forms of Peasant Resistance.* New Haven: Yale University Press.

———. 1990. *Domination and the Arts of Resistance: Hidden Transcripts.* New Haven: Yale University Press.

Selassie, Bereket. 1986. "The Bardera Dam Project and the Development of the Juba Valley: Legal and Institutional Questions." Unpublished report for the Juba Valley Advisory Panel, December.

Shields, Todd. 1993. "Biting the Hand that Feeds." *Ceres* (Rome: UN Food and Agriculture Organization) 25 (2): 38–40.

Sider, Gerald. 1986. *Culture and Class in Anthropology and History: A Newfoundland Illustration.* Cambridge: Cambridge University Press.

———. 1987. "When Parrots Learn to Talk, and Why They Can't: Domination, Deception, and Self-Deception in Indian-White Relations." *Comparative Studies in Society and History* 29 (1): 3–23.

Simons, Anna. 1994. "Somalia and the Dissolution of the Nation-State." *American Anthropologist* 96 (4): 818–24.

———. 1995. *Networks of Dissolution: Somalia Undone.* Boulder: Westview Press.

Southall, Aidan. 1986. "The Illusion of Nath Agnation." *Ethnology* 25 (1): 1–20.

Stefanini. 1924. "Tribu e villaggi in Somalia—IV." *Rivista geografica italiana* 31:73–76. Istituto Agronomico per L'Oltremare. Florence, Italy.

Stoler, Ann Laura. 1989. "Rethinking Colonial Categories: European Communities and the Boundaries of Rule." *Comparative Studies in Society and History* 31 (1): 134–61.

Sullivan, G. L. 1968. *Dhow-Chasing in Zanzibar Waters and on the Eastern Coast of Africa.* London: Frank Cass.

Swift, Jeremy. 1979. "The Development of Livestock Trading in a Nomad Pastoral Economy: The Somali Case." In *Pastoral Production and Society,* ed. L'Équipe écologie et anthropologie des sociétés pastorales, 447–66. Cambridge: Cambridge University Press.

Tambiah, Stanley. 1989. "Ethnic Conflict in the World Today." *American Ethnologist* 16 (2): 335–49.

Time magazine. 1992. "How Somalia Crumbled: Clan Warfare and a Glut of Weapons Have Plunged the Country into Anarchy." By Sophronia Scott Gregory. December 14:34.

Tozzi, Ruggero. 1934. "Popolazioni delle Somalia (Giubaland)." Centro di Documentazione, Istituto Agronomico per L'Oltremare, Florence, Italy.

———. 1941. "Cenni sull'agricoltura e l'economia degli indigeni del Basso Giuba." Regio Istituto Agronomico per L'Africa Italiana. Centro di Documentazione, Istituto per L'Oltremare, Florence, Italy.

Tsing, Anna Lowenhaupt. 1993. *In the Realm of the Diamond Queen.* Princeton: Princeton University Press.

Turton, E. R. 1975. "Bantu, Galla, and Somali Migrations in the Horn of Africa: A Reassessment of the Juba/Tana Area." *Journal of African History* 16 (4): 519–37.

———. 1979. "A Journey Made Them." In *Segmentary Lineage Systems Reconsidered,* ed. Holy Queens University. Papers in Social Anthropology 4:119–43.

Vail, Leroy, ed. 1989. *The Creation of Tribalism in Southern Africa.* London: James Currey; and Berkeley: University of California Press.

Van den Berghe, Pierre. 1973. "Pluralism." In *Handbook of Social and Cultural Anthropology,* ed. J. J. Honigmann, 959–78. Chicago: Rand McNally.

———, ed. 1990. *State Violence and Ethnicity.* Niwot: University Press of Colorado.

Verdon, Michael. 1982. "Where Have All Their Lineages Gone? Cattle and Descent Among the Nuer." *American Anthropologist* 84 (3): 566–79.

Vincent, Joan. 1974. "The Structuring of Ethnicity." *Human Organization* 33 (4): 375–79.

Warren, Kay. 1993a. "Introduction: Revealing Conflicts Across Cultures and Disciplines." In *The Violence Within: Cultural and Political Opposition in Divided Nations,* ed. Kay Warren, 1–23. Boulder: Westview Press.

———, ed. 1993b. *The Violence Within: Cultural and Political Opposition in Divided Nations.* Boulder: Westview Press.

Washington Post. 1993. "Courting Somalia's Clan Elders: System Represents Sole Government." By John Burgess. March 28, A30.

Watts, Michael J. 1983. "Good Try Mr. Paul: Populism and the Politics of African Land Use." *African Studies Review* 26 (2): 73–83.

———. 1992. "Space for Everything (A Commentary)." *Cultural Anthropology* 7 (1): 115–29.

———. 1996. Commentary on the panel "Critiquing the New World Order II: The Shifting Terms of Global Capitalism." Ninety-fifth meeting of the American Anthropological Association, San Francisco, November 20–24.

Webb, James. 1995. *Desert Frontier: Ecological and Economic Change Along the Western Sahel, 1600–1850.* Madison: University of Wisconsin Press.

Whitehead, Neil. 1990. "Carib Ethnic Soldiering in Venezuela, the Guianas, and the Antilles, 1492–1820." *Ethnohistory* 37 (4): 357–85.

Williams, Brackette. 1989. "A Class Act: Anthropology and the Race to Nation Across Ethnic Terrain." *Annual Review of Anthropology* 18:401–44.

Williams, Raymond. 1977. *Marxism and Literature.* New York: Oxford University Press.

Willis, John Ralph. 1985a. "The Ideology of Enslavement in Islam." In *Slaves and Slavery in Muslim Africa,* ed. John Ralph Willis, 1–15. London: Frank Cass.

———. 1985b. "Jihad and the Ideology of Enslavement." In *Slaves and Slavery in Muslim Africa,* ed. John Ralph Willis, 16–26. London: Frank Cass.

———, ed. 1985c. *Slaves and Slavery in Muslim Africa.* London: Frank Cass.

Wilmsen, Edwin. 1989. *Land Filled with Flies: A Political Economy of the Kalahari.* Chicago: Chicago University Press.

———. 1996. "Introduction: Premises of Power in Ethnic Politics." In *The Politics of Difference: Ethnic Premises in a World of Power,* ed. Edwin Wilmsen and Patrick McAllister, 1–24. Chicago: University of Chicago Press.

Wolf, Eric. 1982. *Europe and the People Without History.* Berkeley: University of California Press.

Wright, Marcia. 1993. *Strategies of Slaves and Women: Life Stories from East/Central Africa.* New York: Lilian Barber Press; and London: James Currey.

Young, Crawford. 1982. "Patterns of Social Conflict: State, Class, and Ethnicity." *Daedalus* 3:71–97.

Zoli, Corrado. 1927. *Oltre-Giuba.* Rome: Sindicato Italiano Arti Grafiche.

Index

Page numbers in italics refer to illustrations.